NIGHT HAWK

NIGHT HAWK

*The biography of Flight Lieutenant
Karel Kuttelwascher, DFC and Bar,
the RAF's greatest night intruder ace*

ROGER DARLINGTON

WILLIAM KIMBER · LONDON

First published in 1985 by
WILLIAM KIMBER & CO. LIMITED
100 Jermyn Street, London, SW1Y 6EE

© Roger Darlington, 1985

ISBN 0-7183-0574-4

Typeset by Spire Print Services Ltd.,
Salisbury Wilts
and printed in Great Britain by
The Garden City Press Limited,
Letchworth, Hertfordshire, SG6 1TS

Dedicated to all the Czechoslovak airmen
who flew with the RAF in World War II

*Věnováno všem Československým letcům
kteří létali u RAF ve druhé světové válce*

Contents

List of Illustrations

*Photographs are from the author's collection
unless otherwise credited.*

Introduction

It was an autumn evening in West Sussex more than forty years after the Battle of Britain was fought in the blue skies above that part of the country. We had finished some Sunday afternoon tea and conversation turned to the war-time exploits of the Czech night intruder ace Flight Lieutenant Karel Kuttelwascher, or 'Kut' as he was usually known to his Royal Air Force colleagues.

Suddenly Kut's former wife, Ruby, amazed us all by pulling out from under an antique sideboard a large red trunk from which she withdrew Kut's leather-bound RAF flight log containing a brief note on every one of his sorties. Tucked in the back of the log were thrilling combat reports for a number of his most successful operations. Also in the trunk were a whole collection of photographs and a substantial batch of cuttings from British and American newspapers for the war period, while later we found over 100 items of correspondence.

No one in the room had ever studied these absolutely fascinating records. From that evening, 29 November 1981, I was consumed by a relentless desire to research and record the life of a man who had been dead over twenty years before I met and subsequently married one of his daughters. Ruby died of cancer shortly afterwards but, using all this material, I started to write about Kut with an article in the monthly journal of the trade union for which I work as a National Official. The October 1982 issue carried a piece of just under 1,000 words – but that started the endeavour.

A matter of days after publication of the article, a member of the union called Stan Greenwood telephoned me to say that he had read the article with great interest because he had actually served with Kut in No 1 Squadron in 1942. I now blame him for this book because he named other contacts for me who in turn named others; each made valuable suggestions for further sources of information; and so it went on. Eventually my researches brought me into contact with over 150 individuals and organisations in twelve countries. I visited places like the former airfield of Tangmere

11

where all No 1 Squadron's intruder operations were flown. I was pleased to be allowed to visit the present home of No 1 Squadron at RAF Wittering and honoured to be permitted to attend a squadron reunion at the RAF Club in London.

Karel Kuttelwascher was one of the RAF's greatest fighter aces and arguably its most brilliant night fighter pilot. During the war, he was a well-known hero but his name has subsequently been almost forgotten. Now, for the first time, this is his full story.

So many biographies of World War II fighter pilots are written like novels, full of conversations that could not possibly have been recorded, still less remembered. It might enliven the narrative, but it makes it difficult to know what is verifiable fact and what is essentially fiction. *Night Hawk* eschews such a style. Kut's story is sufficiently exciting not to require artificial embellishment, so everything in this book – to the best of my efforts as a researcher – is fact and every quote is authentic. I have chosen not to quote combat reports since the texts are stylised and dated, but the reader can be assured that every date and time, every reference to the weather, every burst of fire has a documentary source.

Essentially, *Night Hawk* is a biography of one extraordinary man. However, it outlines as well the tremendous contribution to the war effort made by Czech airmen as a whole, a story not yet fully told anywhere in the English language. Also it describes an aspect of the last war – night intruder operations – which has previously received too little examination and appreciation.

It is a story that needs to be told. Even those who knew Kut and are interested in aviation history have not appreciated the full nature of his exploits. For instance, Wing Commander Pat Hancock, who knew Kut briefly at No 1 Squadron and is now Honorary Secretary and Treasurer of The Battle of Britain Fighter Association, wrote to me: 'In truth I had not realised just how famous Kut had become.' Also, it is a story which really had to be written in the 1980's before too much source material was lost, too many memories had irretrievably faded, and too many of those personally involved reach the end of their fascinating lives. As one of Kut's wartime colleagues put it, many of his contemporaries are now 'flying with angels'.

It is clear from a letter quoted in the text that Kut had thought of writing a book about the exploits of himself and his fellow Czechs in the RAF. Indeed his wife Ruby helped him to prepare a lengthy article which was published in 1943, but their subsequent divorce precluded any further such efforts. Now, more than 40 years later, Kut's dream of a permanent record has come true.

As with Kut, the background of my parents involves a mid-European upbringing and service in the RAF. My mother is Italian and lived in Italy until 1947 before her marriage to my father who was there with the RAF. Trained as a fighter pilot, after the war he continued to fly – mainly at weekends – with the RAFVR. His regular usage of the call 'Roger and out' led him to the selection of my christian name and his time with the RAFVR provided me with my first opportunity to sit in an aircraft cockpit. This family background created in me a tremendous interest in aircraft in general and fighter aces of the last war in particular. In 1981, this long established interest of mine came together with the personal records of Karel Kuttelwascher. Out of that combination has come *Night Hawk*.

ROGER DARLINGTON
London
March 1985

CHAPTER ONE

The Czech Odyssey

Earlier on that spring day in 1942, the young pilots of the famed No 1 Squadron had celebrated the official birthday of the Royal Air Force. Now the cold white light of a full moon bathed a camouflaged Hawker Hurricane night fighter in an ethereal glow as it squatted on the field at Tangmere ready for take-off. A lone pilot who would later be dubbed the 'Czech Night Hawk' strode out to the aircraft with a mixture of apprehension and excitement. He settled himself into the ample cockpit and quickly brought to life the controls and the machine. Tonight was the first occasion of night intrusion for No 1 Squadron. Yet for this particular pilot it was to be a baptism of cannon fire and, by the end of the squadron's three months on night intrusion, he would have turned it into almost an art form.

The Hurricane accelerated down the runway and – ponderous with the extra fuel in drop tanks – clawed its way up and into the blackness of the night. The pilot handled the controls with a deftness which came from years of the best of training, followed by more years of tough combat experience, all combined with an inborn instinct for flying and fighting. Leaving behind the tranquillity and safety of the Sussex countryside, the Czech ventured out across the English coast and over the Channel. Above him, a brilliant moon hung suspended in a jewelled sky, while below the reflection of a million stars shimmered on the calm sea.

Once over France, he penetrated deep into the enemy's lair, constantly scanning the sky and searching the ground for evidence of the Luftwaffe. At last he came across an enemy base but there were no bombers to break the stillness. Resolutely he pressed further into the slight haze and eventually found that for which he had come so far. There beneath him the flarepath of a German airfield exhibited a bright collection of colours which could not fail to attract his ever-roaming vision. A new kind of tension crept over him, but it was controlled: he was trained, he was ready, he knew what to do.

As he swung his Hurricane round over the inviting target, he saw a Luftwaffe aircraft climbing heavily from the runway and heading into the protection of the night before it set course for England where it would rain its bombload on families asleep in some English town. He opened the throttle and boosted the power from his Merlin engine to bring him closer to the enemy craft and positioned his Hurricane snugly behind the bomber. As he pulled still nearer to the German, his right thumb found the red button at the top of the control column and gently he started to squeeze the device that would unleash an explosive hail of blazing cannon fire. It was as if all his life had been but a prelude and a preparation for just this moment.

*

Karel Miloslav Kuttelwascher – or Kut as he was later known to his RAF comrades – was born on 23 September 1916. His actual place of birth was a hamlet in the heart of the collapsing Austro-Hungarian Empire. Svatý Kříž – which in English means Holy Cross – is not on most maps. Therefore his birthplace is usually given as Německý Brod, a town in Bohemia about 70 miles south-east of Prague. In 1945, the town lost its pre-war name and became known as Havlíčkův Brod. The area is rough but very beautiful – pinewood hills, lots of lakes, and the river Sázava.

Two years after Kut's birth, the conclusion of the First World War brought about the break-up of the old Austro-Hungarian Empire and he became by citizenship what he had always been by birth, a Czech. The modern state of Czechoslovakia came into existence on 28 October 1918, this land-locked nation being surrounded by a variety of other countries: Germany, Poland, Rumania, Hungary and Austria. Therefore, from the start, Czechoslovakia's geographical position in Europe was central and twenty years later its political situation in world politics became similarly so.

The Kuttelwascher family (the 'w' is pronounced as a 'v') had for generations been in the brewing industry in Bavaria before migrating to Bohemia. This is doubly ironic: first because Kut himself drank alcohol so rarely that most regarded him as teetotal and second, of course, because his German antecedents were certainly no obstacle to his later conflicts with the Luftwaffe.

Kut's father, Josef, was trained as a carpenter but employed as a

Karel Kuttelwascher (back row, extreme left) together with fellow trainees of Room No. 75 at the Prostějov Flying Training School in pre-war Czechoslovakia. Note that the trainees have one bar on their shoulders while those who have received their wings bear two bars on their shoulders plus the pilots badge on the right breast pockets. 22 February 1936

A Šmolik 118 of the type on which Karel Kuttelwascher received his early flying training in the pre-war Czech Air Force at Prostějov.

A Praga E.39 powered by a Walter engine. This bi-plane was used as a training aircraft by the Czech Air Force at Prostějov before the war. Karel Kuttelwascher was one of many Czech pilots to receive early flying experience in an aircraft of this type.

An Avia B-534 of the pre-war Czech Air Force's 32 letka photographed just before mobilisation in Summer 1938 at the airfield of Hradec Králové. The code letter of 32 letka was letter L and this photograph shows the aircraft 10 L in the foreground and the one 15 L in the background. Both these aircraft are samples of the early types of B-534 with an open cockpit. It was with these two aircraft that 32 letka took part in the mobilisation of September 1938 when they were stationed in East Slovakia.

railway inspector with the Czechoslovak state railways, Československé statní dráhy. His mother, Kristina, was a housewife and mother who helped out in the fields. Over a 25-year period, they had six children: older than Kut were sister Anna (born 1904) and brother Jan (1912), while younger than him were sister Františka (1919) and brothers Miroslav (1925) and Josef (1929). At first, the family lived in a rented place at Svatý Kříž, but in 1934 they managed to build their own little house in the nearby hamlet of Herlify, Kut helping to construct the new home. Of the six children, only two – Miroslav and Josef – are still living, both in Czechoslovakia.

Miroslav Kutlvašr (the family now spell the surname the Czech way) explains – in translation as he knows no English – that the future fighter ace had an early yearning for the air:

> Even as a small boy, Karel was interested in aircraft. He cut out from wood small models of aircraft and propellers which he fixed with a nail and then in the wind, or while he was running, the propeller turned round which gave him great pleasure and by making the sound vr ... vr ... vr ... he imitated the engine.

After a conventional education at local primary and secondary schools, Kut went on to three years at a commercial school in Německý Brod. At the age of seventeen, he left home for his first job as a clerk with a company called Duda which operated flour mills near Kladno, not far from Prague. However, as he himself put it in a post-war interview: 'It was not much fun.' His brother explains:

> Karel did not like work in an office. One day he came home and asked father and mother to sign his application form to join the air force as a volunteer at the age of eighteen. His parents were against it but my brother eventually succeeded in persuading them.

Kut's enlistment in the Czech Air Force was on 1 October 1934, just one week after his eighteenth birthday. It was his good fortune that new recruits to the Air Force were taken in on 1 October each year, so that he had to wait no time at all.

In fact, the Air Force was a branch of the Army like the infantry, artillery and cavalry, but it had a special pride in its competence and professionalism. Since it was a country with no access to the sea, Czechoslovakia had always looked to the air and indeed the Czechs had a saying '*Vzduch je naše moře*' which means 'The air is our sea'. However, in 1918 the new state found itself with a few primitive aircraft and only a handful of pilots. It had merely three aerodromes and no domestic aircraft production facilities. By the time Kut joined it, that position was immensely improved and changing fast. The previous year Hitler had come to power in next-door Germany and the Czech armed forces were being strengthened all the time.

After basic infantry training, Kut went to the principal flying school at Prostějov in Moravia, the Czech equivalent of the RAF's Cranwell. After the war, he characterised his first year's training as 'solid engineering, scrubbing, cleaning and oiling'. During this, he first went into the air, initial training being in the Šmolik 118, a two-seater biplane powered by a Walter engine and not unlike the RAF's de Havilland Tiger Moth. Later he went onto the Praga E-39, another biplane powered by a Walter engine. Years later, he described his first flight:

> I was eighteen. I was a little bit frightened. You know my teacher he tried to frighten me. But I came down all right, thanks very much. I knew he must kill himself first before he could kill me, you see.

His brother insists: 'He finished the school at Prostějov with excellent results and he received his wings as a fighter pilot as one of the best students.'

At around 5 ft 8 in Kut was of shortish build with fair hair, parted almost centrally, and penetrating blue eyes. Except for some small facial moles, he had unexceptional – if rather sharp – features, but he was blessed with exceptional eyesight. Perhaps because of this, he liked all sports involving speed and coordination: he played football and ice hockey and shot pigeons and partridge. He always dressed neatly, behaved properly and brought a disciplined approach to all he did. Like most Czechs he was brought up a Roman Catholic. However, the Czechs – unlike the Poles – have never been especially ardent Catholics and certainly he himself was not particularly religious.

Nevertheless, Kut was an abstemious character, especially by the lively standards of his later RAF comrades: he never smoked and he drank little alcohol. Perhaps as a result, Kut was not universally popular with his fellow trainees. One of them – Ladislav Světlík who now lives in New Zealand – states that Kut was not an easy personality and did not mix or talk very much with people who were outside a small circle of friends: 'He wasn't a man I liked.'

As Kut neared the end of his training, war broke out on the continent of Europe after an uneasy peace of only eighteen years. This was a civil war in Spain and among the many around Europe who flocked to the International Brigade on the Republican side were nine volunteers from the Czech Air Force.

Meanwhile, his training at Prostějov now complete, in March 1937 Kut was initially allocated to 1 Flying Regiment based at Prague and later transferred to 32 stíhací letka (fighter squadron) at Hradec Králové, 70 miles east of Prague. His unit was led by Staff Captain Evžen Čížek. Like all Commanding Officers, Čížek would review his men with the greeting '*Nazdar!*' (a form of 'Hello') to which they would shout in unison '*Zdar*' ('To success!'). On less formal occasions, Kut would join in squadron renderings of a special song dedicated to the Czech Air Force, '*Vám, letci, Vám!*' ('To you, airmen, to you!').

Another pilot serving at Hradec Králové at this time (but in a different squadron) was Antonín Liška. From Czechoslovakia, he provides this illuminating pen portrait of Kut:

He was rather a small man with a slim, almost fragile, figure (at least measuring by a Czech standard) and a finely featured face. He had a quiet and kind behaviour and I never saw him get noisy or irritated. He was self-possessed, disciplined, purposeful and I guess ambitious a bit too.

Hitler had called Czechoslovakia 'the spear in my side' and the German threat grew more and more acute. On 20 May 1938, it really looked as if Czechoslovakia was to be invaded. Literally overnight the Czechs mobilised 174,000 men in an exercise of such speed and efficiency that Hitler backed off – for the time being. Then came the Munich crisis of September 1938. By contrast with the position in 1918, now the total strength of the Czech Air Force was about 1,300 aircraft, out of which some 650 were front-line machines (but mostly biplanes), and there were over 100 aerodromes ready for immediate use as operational bases. Supplying this air force, the Czechs now had six aircraft factories turning out complete machines (Aero, Avia, Beneš-Mráz, Letov, Tatra and Zlín) and three factories producing aircraft engines (Škoda, Walter and Českomoravska-Kolben-Danek).

In short, the Czech Air Force was able, ready, and indeed desperately eager to defend the integrity of Czechoslovakia against German aggrandisement and throughout the country pilots and groundcrew were put on a permanent state of maximum alert. For a period of two weeks, Kut and all the other fighter pilots would spend every daylight hour strapped into their Avia machines ready to take off at a moment's notice.

One of those moved in the massive and rapid mobilisation at the time of Munich was Jindřich Prokop, an engineering officer at a research unit who was moved to the operational airfield at Hradec Králové where he met Kut for the first time. Now living in London, his assessment of Kut is a perceptive one:

Kuttelwascher's appearance was unassuming but his eyes were very observant. He was not an extrovert and not at all a pub bloke. On the contrary, he was a studious type who was always absorbed in something. He was very keen to learn and ambitious to succeed in the air force. This made him something of a loner and some people resented this.

Of Kut's flying prowess, Prokop has no doubts:

He was a meticulous and skilled flier. In fact, he was more or less a genius at flying. Once a year every unit went to Malacky [a military airfield, north of Bratislava] where they practised firing in a dive and he was one of the best. This caused quite a bit of rivalry.

One of the other pilots involved in the mobilisation was Miroslav Jiroudek who now lives back in Czechoslovakia. He comments (in translation):

We met at Hradec Králové and I can tell you we were good friends. 32 letka used then the best Czechoslovakian fighter aircraft, the Avia B-534. With these planes, we together experienced the Czechoslovakian Mobilization and during those days we were transferred from Hradec Králové to field aerodromes in East Slovakia at Košice and Sabinov (near Prešov), where we patrolled against the Hungarians.

The B-534 single-seat biplane fighter had first flown in 1933. The version used in the mobilisation of September 1938 was an open cockpit affair, but shortly afterwards it was fitted with a canopy. Powered by an Avia-built Hispano-Suiza engine, it had a maximum speed of 245 mph and an armament of four 7.92 mm machine guns. Its most significant quality was its rate of climb – 15,000 feet in four minutes – which was essential in view of the fact that, in order to engage an enemy from an adjoining country, the Czech aircraft had to reach operational heights very quickly. One of those Czechs who flew it describes the experience as 'marvellous, something wonderful'. Some of these aircraft were later acquired by the Luftwaffe and used on the Russian front.

On 29 and 30 September 1938, the British Prime Minister, Neville Chamberlain, and the French Prime Minister, Edouard Daladier, met at Munich with the German Führer, Adolf Hitler, and the Italian Duce, Benito Mussolini. An agreement was reached on Nazi Germany's territorial claims against democratic Czechoslovakia, but no representative of Czechoslovakia was present. At the time, most of the British regarded the Munich Agreement as having brought peace; subsequently they all came to learn that it was a false peace; but what most British people to this day do not fully comprehend is the territorial price that was paid by the Czechs for that false peace.

On the western half of the country, Germany took huge chunks of Czechoslovakia all around Bohemia, Moravia and Silesia; on the south-east, Hungary acquired the most fertile land of Slovakia as well as the best part of Ruthenia; and to the north, Poland obtained another piece. In total, Czechoslovakia lost over a quarter of its entire territory and about a third of all its population. In strategic terms, the most serious loss was the German acquisition of the mountains, which provided the Czechs with a natural protective barrier, together with a line of special fortifications. The closest part of the German border to the Czech capital was now a point just outside Mělník which is less than twenty miles north of the centre of Prague. In effect, this annexation guaranteed that Czechoslovakia could not effectively defend itself against Germany.

The Munich Agreement was the beginning of the end for Czech independence and the end itself was not long in coming. Six months later, at 6 a.m. on 15 March 1939 – the fateful Ides of March – German troops marched over light snow into Czechoslovakia and the Czech armed forces were ordered to offer no resistance. That night Hitler slept in Prague. Czechoslovakia was then divided into two: the so-called Protectorate of Bohemia and Moravia which became part of Germany and Slovakia which was made 'independent'. In a post-war article written while he was in Czechoslovakia, Kut described the occupation as his country having received '*trnovou korunu své poroby*' ('the crown of thorns of our subjugation').

The second day after the Germans took over the country, the Czech Air Force was demobilised. However, by this time, Kut had already spent 4½ years in the service, clocking up a useful total of flying hours that few RAF pilots would have had at the start of the war. In all, he flew twelve different types or marks of aircraft with the Czechs. This service in the Czech Air Force gave Kut the extra age and considerable experience that must in the war years have been decisive factors leading to his success and survival.

The former Czechoslovak airmen now left their stations and airfields to disperse to their homes. In Kut's case, he returned to Herlify to rejoin the family. However, like so many Czech airmen and soldiers, he was determined to escape from Czechoslovakia in spite of the risk to his relatives of retaliation, so that he could fight the Germans on more hopeful terms than would have been the case at the time of the occupation of his homeland. His younger brother, Miroslav Kutlvašr explains:

He spent three months at home where he occupied himself with various jobs around the house in order to forget the bitterness of the occupation. From time to time, he would go to Prague where the escape of our airmen abroad was being organised.

When Kut's family knew that he was to leave the country, perhaps never to see them again, his mother gave him a special ring as a memento. And so the Czech odyssey began.

Kut – now a sergeant at 22 – made his escape, like so many others, in a small group of half a dozen or so, this being the size of unit judged by the underground to be most effective for securing a speedy and safe exit from Czechoslovakia. The other six members of his particular escape group were his brother Jan Kuttelwascher (who had been a policeman at Karlovy Vary), his 32 letka colleague Miroslav Jiroudek (who subsequently served in the RAF's 310 Squadron), plus František Baňka, Josef Janeba (who eventually joined the RAF's 312 Squadron), Ladislav Procházka, and Vladimír Vašek (who was later killed while flying with the French Air Force's I/5 Squadron).

The escape was executed on the night of 13/14 June 1939. The first part of the plan was to proceed from Prague 200 miles east to the town of Moravska Ostrava on the Czechoslovakia-Poland border. At regular intervals trains full of coal were entering Czechoslovakia and empty trains were returning to Poland, so the Czech railwaymen used this arrangement to smuggle groups of their countrymen across the border. In the case of Kut's intrepid group, the crossing was arranged for around midnight when the pitch darkness would afford them the best protection. Miroslav Jiroudek explains in a matter of fact style what happened then:

We were ferried behind the frontier by goods train from Ostrava to Bohumín which was at that time in Poland. For our escape, we were helped by a member of the railway station personnel in Ostrava. We reached Bohumín at about 1 am. From there our group was ferried by bus to Fryštát where we stayed in the Police Training School. Then after some days we were sent by train to Cracow, where we were recorded as members of the newly formed Czech military units in Poland.

A month after their bold escape, on 15 July Kut's group was sent to Malé Bronowice, a military complex which had served as a prisoner of war camp in the First World War. Hundreds of other Czech airmen and soldiers were already there and all of them were assured that arrangements were being made to take them to France as soon as possible. Soon transport became available and most of the men were able to leave the camp.

However, not all of later escapers departed the country. When the Germans did attack Poland, some Czech pilots flew with the Polish Air Force and four were killed (actually on the ground). When the Luftwaffe had taken its toll, the Czech and Polish airmen crossed into Rumania and they too began the tortuous journey to France via the Balkans, Syria, and North Africa. Meanwhile some Czechs under the command of Lieutenant-Colonel Ludvík Svoboda later fell into Russian captivity and remained prisoners of war until the German invasion of the USSR in June 1941.

In Kut's case, it was 25 July when he and others marched excitedly to the railway station at Cracow where they boarded a train which took them north to the capital city of Warsaw and then north-west through the so-called 'Polish Corridor' – which divided East Prussia from the rest of Germany – to the port of Gdynia on the Gulf of Danzig. Here a total of 90 Czech airmen – including Kut – boarded the Swedish steamship *Castelholm*; a later group of some 190 would use the crowded but more comfortable *Astrid*; while others would use various Polish ships. The *Castelholm* set sail on 26 July.

Next morning they could see Sweden to the starboard and Denmark to the port and later they stopped at the Danish port of Frederikshavn at the northernmost tip of this country. That night the ship set sail once more and the following morning the Czechs found themselves in the North Sea. During the next night, they sailed into a ferocious storm which led the captain to order a change of course into German coastal waters. However, the Czech leader was well aware that the fate awaiting any Czech military personnel found fleeing from the so-called Protectorate of Bohemia and Moravia in the Third Reich was likely to be unceremonious suspension from a butcher's hook. Kut and his colleagues never learned quite what pressures were brought to bear on that faltering Swedish captain, but next morning they found the *Castelholm* approaching the Belgian coast in a quiet sea.

On 1 August, the Czechs' vessel entered Calais Harbour and in an air of euphoria the airmen tumbled onto French soil at last. Kut had come a long way and endured much since he had first left Prague, but now the odyssey was over. At least, that is what he thought.

As soon as they had disembarked from their Swedish ship, Kut and his colleagues boarded a train which took them via Amiens to Paris. French Air Force lorries were waiting at Gard du Nord and drove them south of the Seine to their new base. They discovered later that this was the former factory of the cigarette paper company Zig-Zag, now requisitioned by the Air Ministry. Most of them must have found this tantalising since they were desperate for a cigarette but, not sharing this particular vice, Kut himself was totally unmoved by the irony of his new environs.

The huge open area outside the mess on the other side of the river was the site of daily assemblies held immediately after breakfast and addressed by the Czechs' Commanding Officer in Paris, Staff Captain Josef Duda. He explained that the French Government was studying various options for the assignment of the

Czechs pending the actual outbreak of war. The problem was that the German authorities would have protested vehemently if the French had simply drafted foreign nationals into their domestic armed forces at a time of notional peace. The option to which Duda now gave most prominence was the posting of the Czech Air Force personnel to various squadrons in the French Empire until war was formally declared. As further transports of Czechs from Poland were organised, the assemblies in Paris became larger and larger until soon Duda was addressing some 400 compatriots while standing on an old table from the mess.

The escape of hundreds of Czech airmen and soldiers to Poland and then to France led to intense diplomatic discussions in a variety of European cities. Both Poland and France – like Britain and the USA – retained the Czech diplomatic missions in their countries; only the Russians – then allied to the Germans – closed the Czech mission. So Czech diplomats had been able to negotiate the passages to France and to arrange for money earned by Czech companies around the world like Bata and Škoda to be earmarked to the Czech Embassy in France for the initial support of the exiles. Now they had to come to see some understanding for the harbouring of the Czechs until the war. The Czechoslovak Ambassador in Paris – actually a Slovak – was Štefan Osuský and he eventually concluded an agreement with the French Government which was secret at the time so as to keep the German authorities ignorant of the details. Kut was about to learn the essence of the agreement.

The first Czechs had been in Paris for three weeks, when one mild August morning the assembly was told that one group after another was to be sent to La Légion Étrangère, the French Foreign Legion. So this was the 'solution': the German authorities could not object but the Czechs were horrified at the thought of exchanging the comfort and charms of metropolitan France for the blistering barrenness of North Africa. Yet they had no choice. The names of the first group were called and Kut was among them. So was Jindřich Prokop, the groundcrew member who had been with him at Hradec Králové.

Next morning they were driven to a recruiting bureau – Place de Paris 2913 – near the Place de la Bastille where they were required to sign agreements to serve five years in the Legion. Denied their Czech ranks, they all became mere infantrymen 2nd class. Then later in the day they were marched to Gare de Lyon and put on an overnight train from Paris south to Marseille. Once at Marseille, the Czechs made an early morning march to the notorious Foreign Legion depot of Fort St Jean where their ragged civilian clothes were exchanged for the khaki uniform of a *légionnaire* complete with puttees for the legs. Three days later, on 23 August, they were marched down to the port for their journey to North Africa. By now, the Czech group was enlarged by others, including many Spaniards who had fought on the losing Republican side of the Civil War and were fleeing Franco and the Falange.

The ship which took them from France, the SS *Sidi-bel-Abbès*, carried more cargo than passengers and the newly-recruited *légionnaires* were herded on deck by armed guards who only relaxed once the vessel had passed Monte Cristo Island. Late afternoon on the next day, under a brilliant azure Mediterranean sky, the ship steamed into the Algerian port of Oran. The last stage was a train journey from Oran south to Sidi-bel-Abbès, a distance of 50 miles as a North African crow would fly, but of some three hours on the meandering railway.

The French Foreign Legion may have a romantic image but, to Kut and the other Czechs forced into it until the impending war finally arrived, it presented an experience of unrelenting heat and dust, shouted commands and continual counting, and – most punishing of all – forced marches. In his post-war article in Czechoslovakia, Kut wrote: '*Pobyt v cizinecké legii, kde jsme musili setrvati 2 měsíce, které jsme ztrávili v Severni Africe, byl pro nás dobou poníženi, nebot v ní nebylo úcty před lidskou duši a životem.*' ('Our stay in the Foreign Legion, where we had to remain for two months which we spent in North Africa, was for us a time of degradation because in it there was no feeling for the human spirit and human life.')

Jindřich Prokop recounts:

We had to make 30-mile forced marches carrying full field pack but only one bottle of water. We would start at 4 am and there was one 19-year old boy who drank all his water too soon and collapsed to the ground. The NCOs would kick the ribs of any who fell until they rejoined the march. Kuttelwascher was not a strong man physically but he had exceptional self-control and I'll swear that he brought water back.

Nevertheless, among the *légionnaires*, there was a comradeship which bound men together like brothers; indeed in Kut's case his older brother Jan was experiencing the same ordeal.

The Czechs knew – perhaps even more than most of the French – that the war could not be long in coming, so this sojourn in Northern Algeria was a time of waiting. The British ultimatum to Hitler expired at 11 am on Sunday, 3 September 1939 and the French ultimatum expired at 5 pm the same day. The Second World War had started and the Czech airmen were itching to join French squadrons.

Of course, this had always been the intention of the French Government once war was declared and those Czech airmen – perhaps 50 or so – who had been drafted into the Foreign Legion had had typed on the otherwise standard documentation the words '*au titre de l'armée de l'air*'. But they had signed five-year agreements and a measure had to be put through the French Parliament before they could be released from their obligation. Therefore, it was not until early October – two months after joining and a month after war was declared – that Kut and the others were finally discharged from the Legion.

Kut – now just turned 23 – returned to France to join the air force, the Armée de l'Air, and train as a fighter pilot. On 28 October, he started at the Centre d'Instruction de la Chasse (CIC) or fighter training school at Chartres, the cathedral city just south-west of Paris. The senior Czech instructor here was František Novák, the star of pre-war international competitions. Sadly he himself was never able to take on the Germans in combat because, just a fortnight before they attacked, he died from a stomach disease, possibly occasioned by his competitive aerobatics. One of the other Czech instructors was Bohumil Fiřt who gave Kut some aerobatics training in the Morane-Saulnier MS 230.

The 'Phoney War' provided valuable time for the Czech pilots to be trained on French machines, but they knew that it could only be a matter of time before the Germans attacked and there would then begin the Battle of France.

CHAPTER TWO

The Battle of France

Only when France entered the war was it possible for the Czechoslovak National Committee in Paris – in effect, the Government-in-exile – to renew negotiations with the French Government about the deployment of Czech exiles. Under an agreement between the Czech National Committee and the French Government formally dated 17 November 1939, the Czech 'volunteers' were allowed to cancel their obligations to the Foreign Legion and had their previous ranks restored to them. The army personnel went to the new Czech Army which was quickly being formed at Agde on the southern coast of France and the airmen were sent to the French Air Force.

The Czechs wanted to keep their pilots together as much as possible in the course of their training and allocations to squadrons but the French did not cooperate, so that Czechs were trained at a variety of different air bases and distributed eventually among seventeen different fighter squadrons. The first Czech pilots were taken into French squadrons in November 1939 and gradually the dark blue uniforms and winged-sword badge of the Czech airmen became well-known throughout France.

On 10 May 1940, the German Air Force launched a devastating blitzkrieg against airfields in Holland, Belgium and France. The total serviceable strength of French fighter squadrons that day has been established as 552. When one adds the RAF fighters in France – four squadrons of Hawker Hurricanes and two of Gloster Gladiators – and the small Dutch and Belgian Air Forces, the Allied total was only around 650 fighters. Ranged against them were the Luftwaffe's mighty Luftflotte 2 and Luftflotte 3 which between them mustered 3,902 aircraft, 1,264 of them fighters including the superb Messerschmitt Bf 109E with its top speed of 350 mph. Within hours, the Dutch and Belgian Air Forces had virtually ceased to exist. The Phoney War was over and the Battle of France had commenced.

Only after actual hostilities had started was a further agreement signed on 1 June 1940 between the French Air Minister Laurent Eynac and the Czech General Sergĕj Ingr. Effectively this implemented the initial agreement of seven months earlier. The Czech airmen were given their original ranks in the Czechoslovak Army and wore the uniform of the French Air Force with Czechoslovak badges of rank. It was intended that there would be a special Czech air base in Cognac and arrangements were being made for the establishment of eight fighter squadrons and four bomber squadrons which would have been independent Czechoslovak units within the framework of the French Air Force. However, the catastrophic collapse of the French and the rapid advance of the Germans overtook these hopes.

For some reason, Kut was not transferred to the front line until a week after the Germans launched their attack. On 18 May, he and two other Czech pilots, František Běhal and Bedřich Krátkoruký, flew from the Chartres CIC training school to join Pursuit Squadron III/3 which had moved that day to Tillé, outside Beauvais, north of Paris. III/3 was the Sixth Flight which was known as 'the Pirates' and commanded by Capitaine le Bideau. Its aircraft at this time was the Morane-Saulnier MS 406, by far the most common aircraft in the French Air Force when war broke out. It had a top speed of 300 mph – dangerously slower than the Messerschmitt – and was armed with two 7.5 mm machine guns and one 20 mm cannon.

Kut's arrival at the squadron coincided with some chilling news. That day the death of a Czech member of the squadron, Lieutenant Jindřich Beran, was confirmed: he had gone missing six days previously and it was now known that he had been killed by a bullet in the head during an aerial combat.

Kut himself experienced an immediate and unnerving baptism of fire. The very next day 'Sergent Kutelvacher' – as the French *compte-rendu détaille d'engagement* (combat report) insisted on calling him – was one of the group of three that took off at 9.50 am with orders to patrol the Beauvais area. The patrol was led by the French Adjutant-chef Leblanc and the other pilot was the Czech Caporal Václav Šlouf. The patrol sighted a cohort of six Dornier Do 17s to the east. Kut managed to engage them at long range, but had to retire after expending his ammunition. Meanwhile Šlouf was hit by several bullets during his attack and, with his aircraft on fire, he was forced to bale out. There was trouble with his parachute and he had to struggle desperately before it finally opened sufficiently far from the ground for him to land safely on the edge of the runway not far from where his MS was blazing. During the mêlée, contact had been lost with Leblanc and he did not return to the airfield. This made the squadron anxious and tense and in a mad moment, as it overflew the area, one of the French Potez 63s was fired on by the airfield ground defences. Next day, Leblanc turned up with news of his destruction of a Dornier near Estrées-St-Denis. His own aircraft had been hit mainly in the engine and so he landed alongside the enemy bomber and claimed a German cap and a watch as war booty.

One of the two Czechs to accompany Kut from Chartres to Tillé, Bedřich Krátkoruký, had an even more personally eventful arrival at the squadron. An hour after Kut's own operation he took off with two other Czechs, Lieutenant Běhal the third of the Chartres trio and Lieutenant Evžen Čížek – Kut's CO back in Czechoslovakia – who was already with III/3. In a heated dog fight with five Messerschmitts, he attacked one of the German aircraft at the same time as another MS 406 and saw it breaking up in flames as it lost height.

Next morning, all five of the squadron's available aircraft were on patrol when they encountered nine Heinkel He 111s. Kut's two Chartres colleagues were back in action. Běhal destroyed a Dornier. Krátkoruký followed another and eventually destroyed it near Rouen before he himself was shot down and reported missing. Later that day he turned up at the squadron to announce that he had had to land miles away with his radio out of action. And so it went on. When III/3 Squadron was not actually attacking enemy aircraft, it was carrying out ground strafing sorties against advancing German columns. However, the squadron was constantly hard pressed by the Luftwaffe and frequently on the move.

Only three days after arriving at Tillé – on 21 May – Kut and his French and Czech comrades moved down to Cormeilles-en-Vexin, just to the north-west of Paris. The very same day the place was plastered by 36 Dorniers and Heinkels, leaving four dead and several wounded. On 24 May, III/3 Squadron – like all the others in the French Air Force – received a General Order from the General-in-Chief Vuillemin: '*Notre ciel doit rester français*' ('Our sky must remain French'). But all too obviously this was increasingly not the case. Kut had another reminder of this on 27 May when he was one of nine members of the squadron who escorted two Potez 63s on a mission over German lines in the Douai area near the Belgian border. All the Moranes returned safely, but two Bloch 152 fighters were intercepted by Bf 109s and shot down.

According to one account, on another memorable occasion, Kut himself almost lost his life. He found himself with no ammunition and not much fuel facing no less than five Messerschmitts. He decided to duck into a cloud but, as he came out of the other side, the Germans were waiting for him. He repeated the tactic, burning much precious fuel, only to find that the Messerschmitts were still circling and waiting. Suddenly something went wrong with his engine and he fell into a screaming spin, the aircraft totally out of control. Struggling frantically with the controls, it was seemingly only feet from the ground when he regained control and pulled out of the dive. The Germans were nowhere to be seen, no doubt convinced of his demise.

In spite of the seriousness of the times, the squadron records frequently managed to strike a light-hearted note rarely observed in equivalent RAF documentation. For instance, on 31 May, they observed: *'D'après certains connaisseurs, les cuisses du poulet sont moins fermés que celles de Colette, la nouvelle serveuse de la popote'* ('According to certain experts, the chicken legs are less closed than those of Colette, the new waitress in the mess').

On 3 June, the squadron flew down via Châteauroux to the Toulouse airfield at Francazals where the following day each pilot exchanged his MS 406 for a Dewoitine D.520. The D.520 was certainly the best French fighter available at this time. It had a top speed of 335 mph and armament of four 7.5 mm machine guns and one 20 mm cannon. Kut was thrilled to have his hands on something that could begin to rival the Bf 109. But already it was too late. The German drive was so relentless that from now on the squadron was constantly on the retreat from one airfield to another. The chaos was so great that often the squadron was broken up into different groups of pilots at different fields and sometimes a group would transfer to a new base one morning only to have to move to another the same afternoon.

Not only was the squadron peripatetic; sometimes it was powerless to resist the German onslaught. For instance, on 11 June, they reached Chapelle-Vallon in the Aube district only to find a large formation of German bombers appearing out of low clouds to bomb the field and the nearby town of Troyes before returning to machine-gun everything en route, but the French could not even take off because there was no fuel. Three days later, the disorientation proved so great that at Pithiviers two of the French pilots contrived to land simultaneously and in opposite directions: the pilots were unscathed but the aircraft were wrecked.

Apparently, during this last phase of the Battle of France, the French III/3 Squadron and the British No 1 Squadron found themselves sharing the same airfield near Amiens and both retired together until they parted company near Melun. No 1 had been the first RAF fighter squadron to reach France and on 30 October 1939 one of its pilots, Pilot Officer P. W. O. 'Boy' Mould, became the first member of the RAF in the war to shoot down a German aircraft. Before it became the last but one squadron to leave (73 Squadron left fifteen minutes later), it destroyed an incredible number of German aircraft. The squadron's participation in the Battle of France was described graphically in a book called simply *Fighter Pilot* written by (then Flight Lieutenant) Paul Richey who claimed that No 1 destroyed an amazing total of 155 enemy aircraft, 114 of them in only the first ten days. It is not surprising that Kut was enormously impressed by the British squadron; what he could not know was that a few months later he would be joining it.

On 14 June, the German juggernaut reached Paris and, two days later, III/3 Squadron was ordered to retreat to La Salanque airfield at Perpignan in the southernmost corner of France. There were not enough aircraft to go round and several pilots as well as the ground crew had to take various coaches which struggled south along roads jammed with people travelling on every available form of transport. At La Salanque, hundreds of French aircraft were gathering. Then, on 17 June, Marshal Pétain asked Hitler for an Armistice.

Two days later, the pilots of III/3 Squadron left La Salanque for North Africa. The captain, le Bideau, decided to lead the Dewoitines from on board a Bloch 174 but, when it arrived at the base, it managed to spin round, run into a group of other aircraft and catch fire, leaving him seriously injured with a fractured skull. Nevertheless, 22 Dewoitines set off as planned: one pilot became bogged down, another clipped him with a wing, and a third hit a pylon. Eventually the rest reached Algiers and that evening several of the Czechs arrived, but there was still no sign of Kut.

It was two days later when Kut took off from Toulouse only to find himself in a thunderstorm. He was forced to land where he

The Czech section of the French Foreign Legion—Karel Kuttelwascher is on the back row, second from the right—at Sidi-bel-Abbès, Algeria.

Karel Kuttelwascher on board ship at the Rock of Gibraltar on his way from Casablanca to Cardiff in 1940.

(*Right*) Karel Kuttelwascher photographed in his French Air Force uniform. 25 March 1940.

(*Below*) Two of Karel Kuttelwascher's French Air Force colleagues in front of a Morane-Saulnier 406 of a type which he himself flew. Northern France—1940.

could, but fortunately this was near a farm where he was given shelter and some breakfast. Four hours after leaving Toulouse, he had covered the mere 100 miles to La Salanque. Next morning – on 22 June – at 8 am Kut and ten others took off for North Africa. Four of the pilots were from III/3 Squadron and the other Czech, Evžen Čížek, was obliged to return to La Salanque immediately because his undercarriage did not retract. Using dead reckoning, the others flew via the Balearic Islands – which Kut had last seen from the SS *Sidi-bel-Abbès* ten months previously – and landed at Algiers about two hours later. Just as Kut was reaching Algiers, the main block of III/3 Squadron was on the move again – this time west along the coast to Relizane, the Group's summer base – and he joined them later.

This was the day that the Franco-German Armistice was concluded: it was signed at Compiègne in the same railway carriage in the same forest in which the Armistice of 1918 had been signed. The official records of III/3 Squadron reflected the pervading atmosphere of gloom: *'Impression trop triste pour être définissable. La grande vie est terminée'* ('Our feelings are too sad to be able to be expressed in words. The good life is over').

The scale and speed of the French collapse – the battle had lasted a mere six weeks – can only be explained by the political and moral corruption of the Third Republic. The British pilots – and even more so the Czech airmen – could be forgiven some bitterness and cynicism over this débâcle. As Kut himself put it in a post-war article in Czech: *'Vlivem naprosté desorganisace, po níž následovala bezhlavost, skončilo to ve Francii divoce'* ('Due to complete disorganisation, followed by loss of rational thinking, the end of France was very wild indeed').

It is impossible to be sure of the scale of Kut's victories in the Battle of France. Searches by the Service Historique de l'Armée de l'Air (SHAA) in Paris have revealed no evidence of victories. However, a 1965 Czech study based on official war records attributes two (shared) victories to him. In 1942, the Royal Air Force citation for his first DFC referred to his participation in the Battle of France and stated: 'During this period he destroyed three German bombers.' In his personal records, Kut himself claimed to have shot down a total of six aircraft.

The SHAA suggests that the failure of French records to assign any victories to Kut might have been because he used a *nom de guerre* and points out that the squadron records usually only identified him as 'K ... R'. A more likely explanation is that Kut was changing bases and away from the main body of III/3 Squadron so often and the pace of events and collapse of resistance was so fast that the records fail to reflect fully all individual victories. A third possibility – which cannot be discounted – is that, in the first flush of combat, he allowed his enthusiasm to overrule his eyesight. In any event, the issue is unlikely ever to be resolved conclusively: of the dozen Czechs who served with III/3 Squadron, almost all are dead and the couple of survivors unable or unwilling to talk about their wartime experiences.

A similar problem occurs when it comes to medals. The SHAA can discover no record of any decorations awarded to Kut. However, a succession of military press releases and newspaper reports during the war refer to his receipt of the Croix de Guerre twice and wartime photographs clearly show him wearing ribbons of the Croix and Palm. Again one explanation would be the incompleteness of French war records, but others have offered less charitable accounts.

Equally, the record is somewhat blurred on the precise contribution made by Czechs overall to the Battle of France.

There is a fair degree of certainty on the number of Czechs assigned to French fighter squadrons. A list compiled by the SHAA in 1977 suggests that a total of 123 personnel – 114 pilots and 9 mechanics – served in 17 Groupes de Chasse, although it is possible that this number is a slight underestimate. Although the vast majority of Czech airmen served with fighter squadrons, six flew with battle formations and eight were with bomber units. In all, 27 Czech airmen were killed in France.

At this point, the records diverge. According to the SHAA, Czech pilots were credited with 142 confirmed victories, but a 1942 publication of the Inspectorate-General of the Czechoslovak Air Force claims that the Czechs destroyed 158 enemy aircraft 'either single-handed or in cooperation' besides achieving a number of notable successes in attacks on German tank and motor transport concentrations. Perhaps the discrepancy can be explained in part by the higher figure including shared victories. In either case, it is a most creditable record.

Certainly, the Czech stars of the Battle of France were Capitaine Alois Vašátko and Lieutenant František Peřina who both flew with I/5 Squadron, the most successful of all the French Air Force units. Official records credit Vašátko with 15 victories and the Croix de

Guerre with five Palms and Peřina with 14 victories and the Croix de Guerre with four Palms. According to many accounts, a Czech who would later distinguish himself brilliantly in the Battle of Britain, Josef František, shot down 11 aircraft during his time with the Polish and French Air Forces. However, neither Polish nor French records confirm this.

The other Czechs who did really well in the Battle of France were Sergent Václav Cukr of II/3 Squadron, Sergent-Chef Josef Stehlík of III/3 Squadron (like Kut), and Lieutenant Tomáš Vybíral of I/5 Squadron (like Vašátko and Peřina), each of whom – according to the Czech records – scored eight victories.

According to a memorandum prepared a few days after the fall of France, the overall size of the Czechoslovak Air Force in France was much larger than the 137 men who were active at the front. In all there were 724 including 208 fighter pilots, 90 bomber pilots and 45 Army cooperation pilots. All of them were determined to reach Britain but the means of doing so varied considerably as each took the chance that he could find in the cauldron that was now France. Some caught ships from Bordeaux, Port Vendres, and finally Sète. Others flew out of the country in French or sometimes British aircraft.

Kut and some other Czech pilots were still with their French squadrons. In his case, III/3 Squadron was at its summer base of Relizane in North Africa, apparently removed from the conflict. The Dewoitines were grounded and the mechanics had immobilised them by removing all fuses. At 4 am on 3 July, the armourers started to disarm the aircraft. At 9 am such activity was interrupted by a full dress inspection from Général Hébrard. Then at noon an urgent order arrived from Algiers: the aircraft were to be re-armed and the pilots were to be on constant standby.

At 5 pm the reason for the mobilisation became clear. The British Royal Navy was attacking the French fleet at Oran and Mers-el-Kébir, after the French Admiral there had refused to join with Britain. The pilots of III/3 Squadron were shocked and the hand-written records of this day exhibit a distinct change of character. Yet the British action was logical enough: those French ships were now at the disposal of the German Command and could be used against them unless they could be destroyed in a pre-emptive attack.

French air patrols were made ready to engage the British ships about 50 miles west of Relizane. The Czech pilots were astonished at the bizarre picture now unfolding before their eyes. There was no way that Kut and his compatriots were going to fly against the British: in the Battle of France, they had fought alongside RAF pilots and they earnestly hoped that before too long they would do so again. So the only III/3 pilots dispatched to Mers-el-Kébir were French. One patrol of six took off at 6.25 pm and another patrol of three took off at 7.25 pm. The naval battle took place below them as they circled impotently and all the aircraft returned shortly before nightfall.

The following day it became clear that the French had had several ships sunk or damaged and French sailors had been killed. The III/3 records noted: *'Une certaine fièvre s'est emparée de Relizane'* ('A sure fever seizes everyone at Relizane'). Several years later, Kut told an American newspaper: 'It was the biggest disappointment of my life.' Appropriately enough, that day it was agreed that Kut and nine other Czechs would leave the French Air Force. A farewell Franco-Czech dinner was held at the Hôtel de Paris and at 4 am next day the Czechs left by train heading for Casablanca. The squadron records commented: *'Nous perdons de bons camarades'* ('We are losing some fine comrades').

This time with the French Air Force provided Kut with new experiences to add to his previous flying hours with the Czech Air Force. He accumulated another couple of hundred hours flying time on another nine aircraft types. Above all, however, he had had some tough combat experience against the Luftwaffe and he had come to know well the airfields of north-west France which he would later visit to devastating effect on his night intruder operations.

Meanwhile Kut and his fellow Czechs had lived to fight another day, another battle, the Battle of Britain.

CHAPTER THREE

The Battle of Britain

Kut knew where he had to reach if he was to have another crack at
the Luftwaffe; the problem was how to get there. In accordance
with advice from British diplomatic sources, he and the nine other
Czechs made their way west by stages from Relizane in Algeria to
Casablanca in Morocco. They approached the British Consul and
found that luck was with them: they were put on one of the last
British cruisers to leave the port and taken to the Rock of Gibraltar.

From Gibraltar, Kut and the others embarked on a ship
bound – they thought – for Canada. In all there were some 50
Czech military personnel including 30 pilots and 14 mechanics.
One of the pilots was Josef Jaške who had come across Kut in the
Czech Air Force before the war:

> We were on a small ship called – I believe – the *David Livingstone*
> but it was part of a large convoy. This convoy took an erratic
> route designed to evade German submarines; one week we were
> experiencing semi-tropical heat and the next the weather was
> bitterly cold. Really we had no idea where we were going.

It was clear to Kut that, if they were heading for North America, he
was going to have to pick up some English. Always keen to learn,
he found a 'teacher' from Britain; unfortunately the
English-speaker turned out to be a working-class Scot with a
pronounced accent and the pupil learned very little indeed.

The remarkable voyage lasted for an interminable 21 days and
finally one misty morning – it was probably 5 August 1940 – they
reached their destination. To their amazement, it proved to be
Cardiff in South Wales, a town where four years later Kut would
become the father of twin girls. Following this shock came an even
greater one of the first cup of English tea. Kut told a BEA colleague
after the war: 'It was terrible. None of us could finish it!' However
bad the tea, there was no doubt about the welcome for Kut and the
other Czech exiles. As he expressed it in a postwar article in Czech:
'*Byli jsme skvěle přijati*' ('We were received magnificently').

37

In fact, the first 30 Czech pilots to reach Britain had landed in an RAF aircraft at Hendon on 17 June. Next day, the Czech President-in-exile, Dr Eduard Beneš wrote on behalf of the Czechoslovak National Committee to the British Secretary of State for Air, Sir Archibald Sinclair, pleading that a special effort be made to bring the remaining Czech airmen out of France and over to Britain in order that they could continue the fight. Then, on 2 July, he submitted to the British Government a memorandum urging that the Czech airmen be allowed to participate at once in the defence of Britain and that a formal agreement covering the status of Czech military personnel in Britain be concluded as soon as possible. The British Government acted quickly: within a month of the Beneš memorandum, a Czech fighter squadron and a Czech bomber squadron had been formed.

The Czechs were desperately eager to fight and they brought invaluable flying experience and an unquenchable hatred of the Germans who were occupying their country. For its part, the Royal Air Force needed as many trained aircrew as it could muster as what was to become known as the Battle of Britain was about to commence. However, there was no time to conclude a formal agreement on the status of the Czech airmen prior to their deployment in the RAF. Therefore, all Czech officers and airmen were immediately commissioned or enlisted in the Royal Air Force Volunteer Reserve (RAFVR).

Originally all officers, irrespective of their Czechoslovak rank, were commissioned in the rank of pilot officer, the lowest commissioned rank in the RAF. The only exceptions made were in the case of flight and squadron commanders who were necessarily granted the appropriate acting ranks. All airmen were enlisted with the lowest possible classification of aircraftmen 2nd class and awarded a higher acting rank to fill establishment posts as applicable, so that most were soon granted the temporary rank of sergeant.

In the beginning, the Czech airmen were concentrated at the Czech Air Force depot at Cosford, near Wolverhampton, through which they all passed before they joined a squadron. It has to be admitted that, at this sensitive time, relations between the Czechs and the British were not always of the best. Munich was still fresh in Czech minds and the British were seen by some to have failed to stand by Czechoslovakia. More generally, the Czech fliers had by now developed something of a detached, rather cynical, even a little superior attitude characterised by the Czech maxim '*Všecko známe – všude jsme byli*' ('We've been everywhere – we know everything'). But this feeling soon passed and any doubts about Britain's commitment to the war effort totally evaporated.

Most of the Czechs who joined the RAF trained at No 6 Operational Training Unit (OTU) at Sutton Bridge beside the Wash before going into specially formed Czech squadrons. These squadrons all had numbers in the 300 range, since RAF practice was that units of Allied personnel who had escaped from Europe should carry numbers in this series: the Czechs were allocated six (310–315) but in the event only used four.

On 10 July, the first Czech fighter squadron, 310, was quickly established at Duxford. It became operational on 17 August and its Hurricanes fought in the Battle of Britain. The squadron's English motto was 'We fight to rebuild'. Less than three weeks after the formation of 310, a second Czech squadron, 311, was formed at Honington on 29 July. This was a bomber squadron equipped with Wellingtons and commenced raids on 21 September. Its Czech motto was '*Na množství nehleďte*' ('Ignore their numbers'). According to an official minute, by 2 August there were 481 Czech airmen at Cosford, 245 at Honington and 169 at Duxford, making 895 in all. When one adds Kut's group of 50 who reached the country on 5 August, one finds that there were approaching 1,000 Czech airmen in Britain at this time.

On 29 August, a second Czech fighter squadron was able to be set up. Like 310, 312 Squadron started at Duxford with Hurricanes – it became operational on 2 October, just in time to join the Battle. Its Latin motto was '*Non multi sed multa*' ('Not many but much'). Almost a year later, the fourth and last Czech squadron within the RAF would be created – it was a third fighter squadron. 313 was set up at Catterick on 10 May 1941 flying Spitfires. For this squadron's motto, it was back to Czech: '*Jeden jestřáb mnoho vran rozhání*' ('One hawk chases away many crows'). In April 1942, 311 Squadron was transferred from Bomber Command to Coastal Command. Then, in February 1944, the three Czech fighter squadrons were assembled into a Czech Wing – No 132 Wing of the Second Tactical Air Force (2nd TAF) – and they operated together until the end of the war.

While most of the Czechs went into these special squadrons, about 100 others served in RAF and Allied units. For instance, following its reforming on 10 January 1941, No 68 Squadron –

which flew Blenheims and then Beaufighters on night fighter duties – received a particularly high proportion of Czechs throughout the war, so much so that it had a Czech flight and a Czech motto: *'Vždy připaven'* ('Always ready').

The incorporation of the Czechs in the RAFVR and the formation of the Czech squadrons was all part of a process formally recognised in an official agreement between the British Government and the provisional Czech Government concluded on 25 October 1940. It was signed by the respective Foreign Ministers, Lord Halifax and Jan Masaryk. The agreement confirmed the employment of the Czech airmen with the Royal Air Force, the personnel being members of both the RAFVR and the Czechoslovak Armed Forces, subject to the laws of both countries and disciplinary regulations of both forces. Any cost of maintaining the Czechoslovak military effort was to be refunded by the Czechoslovak Government from credits granted by the British Government.

Emotionally what mattered most to the Czechs was that, together with the RAF ensign, the Czechoslovak flag – with its blue, white and red segments – was to fly at all stations where Czechoslovak units were based; aircraft used by Czechoslovak units attached to the RAF would carry, as well as British military marks, a distinctive Czechoslovak marking – actually a lion – on the fuselage; and the normal RAF uniform was to be proudly embellished on both sleeves with a distinguishing badge bearing the word 'Czechoslovakia'.

Originally, the interests of the Czech pilots in Britain had been entrusted to the RAF commanders who were responsible for their administration. Then, with the drawing up of the agreement, an Inspectorate of the Czech Air Force was established. It was based in London and responsible to both the British Air Ministry and the Czechoslovak Ministry of National Defence. Acting Air Commodore Karel Janoušek was appointed Inspector-General and it would not be too long before another Karel became very well known to him.

Thanks to that sea journey from Gibraltar, by the time Kut managed to reach England, the historic and decisive Battle of Britain had commenced without him; officially it started on 10 July 1940. Flying from newly acquired bases in Northern France like those Kut had just left behind, the Luftwaffe aimed to destroy the RAF's fighters, so clearing the way for the invasion of Britain in the autumn of 1940. The Luftwaffe units started by bombing Britain's south coast ports and shipping in the Channel. From 8 August, the attacks became heavier and more numerous and, as far as the Germans were concerned, the real Battle of Britain began on 12 August.

It was on 14 August that Kut was enlisted in the RAFVR as No. 787696 Aircraftman 2nd Class, Aircrafthand/General Duties stationed at Cosford. Practically, if not officially, the Battle of Britain was as good as over on 15 September, so Kut missed the real action. The day before – 14 September – he was appointed sergeant pilot and sent to No 5 OTU at Aston Down in the Cotswolds. Here he came across two remarkable characters, both of whom had won DFCs for outstanding service in France with No 1 Squadron.

His flight commander in charge of D Flight was the moustached Prosser Hanks. During peace-time, Hanks had taken part in such escapades as changing seats while flying in a Hawker Hart and in the Battle of France he had shot down eight enemy aircraft. Now residing in South Africa, he still remembers the young Kut:

> He was keen to get into the air at every possible opportunity and was more amenable to flying discipline than many of his fellow countrymen and certainly the Poles. In other words, he was a professional. He had no trouble converting to the Hurricane and I remember him saying that it was by far the best aircraft that he had ever flown.

Then, in overall charge of the OTU, there was the Irish Wing Commander Patrick John Handy Halahan who commanded No 1 Squadron in France and scored three victories of his own. He was known universally as 'the Bull' for he was built like an ox with a stocky physique, broad shoulders and a square jaw. One of his pilots in France insists: 'He was a hard man'.

Kut's very first flight at the OTU came two days after arrival when he was a co-pilot in a North American Harvard with Pilot Officer Moloney at the controls. The next three flights saw the Czech flying the Miles Master, the advanced trainer which had started to be delivered to the RAF in the spring. Then, on 23 September (actually his 24th birthday), he made the first of very many trips in a Hawker Hurricane. Of all the aircraft eventually flown by Kut in his long flying career, none was more special to him than the Hurricane became: in this he scored his greatest successes and made his reputation.

The Hurricane was conceived in 1933 by Hawker's chief designer Sidney Camm. The aircraft had its first flight on 6 November 1935 and the name was sanctioned by the Air Ministry in June 1936. The first RAF squadron to be equipped with it – 111 at Northolt – received its aircraft in December 1937. It was the first RAF aircraft to exceed 300 mph and the first eight-gun monoplane to enter squadron service. The eight Browning machine guns fired 0.303 in (7.7 mm) rimmed ammunition and – at a rate of fire of 9,600 per minute – the 2,660 rounds were enough for about 15–20 seconds of firing. The Hurricane may not have had the grace or speed of the Spitfire, but it was rugged and more manoeuvrable and, in the early days of the war, it was available in greater numbers and served Britain supremely well.

Following Kut's first flight in the Hurricane, over the next few days he practised aerobatics and formation flying. After just 13 hours' flying with the RAF, he was accredited in his flight log as 'Above the Average' over the signature of Halahan – a real achievement from such a demanding character as 'the Bull'. This really means that Kut was a natural pilot, since the only higher rating was 'exceptional' which was a rarity.

There is some suggestion that Kut had come across No 1 Squadron during his time in France and so he might have expressed a wish to join it. However, he was just one of many Czechs who were posted to this particular unit at this time. Since Halahan and Hanks had so recently left No 1 Squadron, this might be why so many Czechs, once trained at No 5 OTU, were sent to this unit. A more likely explanation is offered by Hanks himself:

> After a number of us left the squadron, the new boys took a pasting. My own replacement, although an experienced pilot, was shot down within a week and spent the rest of the war as a POW. All the Czechs were experienced pilots and most had had combat experience. It was clearly more prudent to send the most experienced pilots to the front line squadrons and of course at that time these consisted almost entirely of Czechs and Poles.

In any event, on 3 October 1940, Kut joined the famous No 1 Squadron at Wittering in Lincolnshire and he eventually spent almost two years with them.

No 1 Squadron was one of the four original squadrons in existence when the Royal Flying Corps was established on 13 May 1912 and it was then equipped with airships. The RFC became the Royal Air Force on 1 April 1918 and by then the squadron was flying the SE 5A. The squadron's motto was '*In omnibus princeps*' ('In all things first'), a reference to both its long history and its splendid achievements, although No 2 Squadron was always quick to point out that it was the first to fly 'real' aeroplanes. In the early part of 1939, No 1 Squadron exchanged the Hawker Fury for the Hurricane. While Kut was flying for the French Air Force during the early months of 1940, the squadron was making its own outstanding contribution to the Battle of France. Later that summer, King George VI announced a unique block of decorations – including no less than ten DFCs – to Kut's comrades at No 1 for their gallantry in France. No doubt this excited ambitions of his own, but he would have to wait another year and a half for them to be fulfilled – however, then they were to be doubly so.

The full history of No 1 Squadron was eventually written up 30 years later by Michael Shaw in the first class book *Twice Vertical*. The title is not a reference to the sexual proficiency of the squadron's pilots but to the progression from airships in 1912 to Harrier jump jets 60 years later. In this historical account, Kut rates many honourable mentions. When he wrote the book, Shaw was a serving officer with the squadron taking a conversion course onto Harriers and the combined pressures of flying and writing were such that he achieved the dubious distinction of crashing three Harriers in as many days.

By the time Kut joined it in early October, No 1 Squadron had been in the thick of the Battle of Britain at Northolt as part of No 11 Group and it was now at Wittering as part of No 12 Group. It had been posted there on 9 September: the pilots were supposed to be having a rest and the Hurricanes a re-fit and the installation of VHF radio sets. The Commanding Officer was Squadron Leader D. A. Pemberton who had taken over in May during the squadron's superlative effort in the Battle of France and then been awarded the DFC at the start of October.

During October, many of the men who had flown with the squadron throughout the Battle of Britain were posted out, most of them to become instructors at the fighter schools. In their place, there came a large influx of Czech pilots, mostly from No 6 OTU (although Kut himself was of course from No 5), so that soon the unit was awash with a variety of tongue-twisting names. A role of the squadron was to train them all in fighter tactics but, in fact, a number had served with French squadrons and three of them – František Běhal, Evžen Čížek and Bedřich Krátkoruký – had actually been with Kut in III/3 Squadron.

The range of nationalities and the variety of personalities in No 1 Squadron at this time made it both cosmopolitan and colourful. During October, the squadron was joined not just by Czechs and Poles but by a Frenchman. Lieutenant Jean Demozay had been with the squadron during its stay in France, acting as an interpreter and liaison officer with the Armée de l'Air. A few days before the fall of France, he found a Bristol Bombay twin-engined transport and flew himself and fifteen British soldiers to England. He joined the RAF and, after training at No 5 OTU (the same as Kut), he was posted to No 1 Squadron two weeks after the Czech. He used the *nom-de-guerre*, Moses Morlaix, the surname referring to his home town in Brittany.

Over the next few months, the iron of the British and the carbon of the Czechs were forged together in the furnace of battle to produce the steel of No 1 Squadron and the sprinkling of other nationalities made it a particularly tough alloy.

Understandably, the air and ground crew of No 1 Squadron found Karel Kuttelwascher's name something of a mouthful and so he soon came to be called by a variety of affectionate abbreviations: mostly 'Kut', other times 'Kuttel', and – perhaps reflecting the fact that he was a little older than many of them – sometimes 'Old Kut' or 'Old Kuttel'. For his part, Kut – like all his Czech colleagues – was struggling to come to terms with the intricacies of the English language. Fortunately he did not need to know much to fly. The word 'bandit' in Czech means robber which was self-explanatory enough.

On the morning of 5 October, two days after joining the squadron, Kut took Hurricane V7376 out on his first flight with the unit. It was simply an hour's map-reading exercise around the local area. That afternoon, he made his second trip when, together with two other Czechs, he was led in formation practice by Flying Officer Pete Matthews, a squadron veteran of the French campaign who had taken over B Flight a few days previously and was soon promoted to flight lieutenant. He explains:

We had a great time at Wittering, but we felt left out of the Battle. We were training like mad at this time and I recall Kut very well. He was not looked on as a new boy but as an experienced pilot. He was finding English difficult and was quite quiet, but he was a great character and stood out among the flight which was all Czech apart from Pat Hancock. He was one of the best of all the Czechs I met.

The following day, 6 October, Kut was up a third time when he was one of six pilots practising formation flying. All but two of the men were Czechs, one of the exceptions being Pilot Officer Tim Elkington who was posted from Cranwell direct to No 1 Squadron in July 1940:

> I first met Kut at Wittering in October 1940 when I returned to the squadron after being shot down. It said something for all the Czechs that they would fly No 2 to those like myself who had only 150 hours on Hurricanes. And with such good grace. He was somewhat enigmatic, serious and unemotive – but I imagine there could be exceptions to this!

Kut's fifth flight with the squadron (7 October) was to practise advanced formation with Matthews and another colleague, Pilot Officer Jocelyn Millard. Although Millard left No 1 at the end of October to join Douglas Bader at the Canadian 242 Squadron, he remembers Kut but notes: 'He was a quiet chap and we were not aware of his victories in the Battle of France.' The Czech's seventh trip (8 October) was a patrol with two British pilots, Pilot Officer Pat Hancock and Sergeant Warren. Hancock recollects of Kut: 'He stood out amongst the very fine bunch of Czechoslovak pilots. He was a handsome man with a fine personality who was always very neat and presentable.' As for Sergeant Warren, the next day he took off in Hurricane V7376 (the same aircraft used on Kut's first flight with the squadron) and joined Pilot Officer Goodman and Sergeant Krátkoruký on a formation exercise off the Lincolnshire coast, but he never returned.

Although the final month of the Battle of Britain was a much quieter period for No 1 Squadron at Wittering than its earlier time at Northolt, there was still some excitement and on occasions victories.

On 8 October, Pilot Officer Goodman and Flying Officer Matthews chased an enemy aircraft over Hucknall and Goodman thought that he had killed the German rear gunner. The following day, Pilot Officer Elkington and Sergeant Davies were practising dog fighting in bad weather when they were vectored to a Junkers Ju 88 which Davies believed he shot down into the sea. Then, on 15 October, Pilot Officer Clowes was making a journey to Northolt in a Miles Magister trainer and near Hendon suddenly saw a Ju 88 coming out of the cloud. Not being armed, his natural inclination was to avoid contact but, to his amazement, the Junkers turned tail and fled!

Three No 1 pilots – Flight Lieutenant Brown, Pilot Officer Clowes and Pilot Officer Kershaw – were ordered to intercept 'Raid 10' on 24 October. They spotted a Dornier Do 17 and suffered some fire from the rear gunner, but between them sent the bomber down at St Neots, Brown firing the most rounds. Another three members of the squadron – Pilot Officers Goodman, Elkington and Robinson – were out on 27 October when they saw Feltwell ground defences engaging enemy aircraft. The Hurricanes attacked immediately and then had to break away on account of Bofors fire from the ground, but Goodman presumed that he had at least damaged a Dornier.

Two days later, Blue section of B Flight – Sergeant Page leading Pilot Officer Robinson and Sergeant Jícha – engaged the enemy and destroyed a Do 17. Next day, 30 October, Pilot Officers Goodman and Lewis with Sergeant Jícha sighted a bomber. Goodman mistook it for a Blenheim, but Lewis and Jícha recognised it as a Ju 88 and shot it down.

While the Czech Václav Jícha – an aerobatics champion before the war – was obviously having some luck, a few of his compatriots on the squadron were having a little trouble even mastering the Hurricane. On 16 October, Sergeant Josef Příhoda had to make a forced landing; then, on 29 October, Pilot Officer Evžen Čížek – Kut's CO in the Czech 32 letka – wrecked an aircraft on landing; while the very next day, Sergeant Josef Dygrýn crashed when landing and wrote off another fighter. Fortunately, Kut was proving most adept at the Hurricane's controls and a quick learner of aerial techniques. For all No 1's pilots, October was a time of very intensive training; the weather was good all month and the squadron achieved the exceptionally high total of 1,003 flying hours.

November opened tragically. In the early morning of the third day, Squadron Leader Pemberton took off from Collyweston (the satellite field to Wittering), made a slow roll at low altitude, crashed and was killed. The incident astonished his men because he had been an instructor and gave hell to any of his pilots who performed aerobatics anywhere near the ground. Since he had led the squadron through the hazards of the Battle of Britain, it seemed particularly brutal to lose him through such an accident. The command of No 1 passed to one of the squadron's flight commanders, Mark Henry 'Hilly' Brown, a Canadian with a ginger moustache who had been with the outfit since 1937. He had started as a pilot officer and this chain of promotion in the same unit may be unique in the history of the RAF. Brown was the first Canadian pilot of the war to become an ace and had been awarded a DFC for his work in France. During his stay with the squadron, he destroyed a total of at least 18 enemy aircraft.

Besides Brown and Matthews, the only remaining pilot who had been with the squadron in France was Arthur Victor 'Darkey' Clowes who now took over responsibility for A Flight. Clowes – the unofficial squadron artist – was a remarkably relaxed and warm Welshman who had zoomed from sergeant to flight lieutenant in a mere six weeks but remained respected by all. His particular aircraft JX:B P3365 carried a wasp motif on the nose and Clowes added a new stripe to the body of the wasp for each enemy aircraft he shot down. His final score at the end of the war was at least twelve. Airfix Products Ltd manufacture a 1/72 scale construction kit of the Hawker Hurricane I flown by Clowes during his time at Wittering.

Officially the Battle of Britain ended on 31 October 1940, but No 1 Squadron continued to be scrambled and engage in dog fights quite regularly during its last six weeks at Wittering. On a training flight on 8 November, Jean Demozay managed to shoot down a Ju 88 and a few days later on another training flight he destroyed a Bf 109. On the night of 14/15 November, certain members of the squadron tried unsuccessfully to engage the Luftwaffe which was carrying out the devastating blitz of Coventry. However, Kut was still not allowed to take up his Hurricane at night.

Meanwhile, the training of the new pilots continued. In Kut's case, the training included just one flight in aircraft other than the Hurricane to obtain 'experience on type'. This first experience of the Miles Magister, a basic trainer, was on 24 November and his 'teacher' was Pat Hancock who, conscious now of Kut's enormous flying experience, describes the occasion as 'a little ironic'. On 18 December, the Czech managed to spend an hour and a quarter on his first flight in the other great fighter of the Battle, the Supermarine Spitfire. In his flight log, he described it as an 'experiment' – certainly it was something he would not be able to do again for a long time.

The British cannot be reminded often enough that, in the so-called Battle of Britain, no less than one-fifth of the RAF's 3,000 pilots were not in fact British. Of 'the few', 147 were Poles and the next largest foreign contingent was 87 Czechs including Kut. These expatriates, whose countries had been invaded, flew with a special passion and fought with a deep vengeance, so it is no accident that a Czech – Josef František with his top-scoring record 17 victories – and a Pole – Flying Officer Witold Urbanowicz with 14 victories – were among the top ten fighter aces of the Battle.

Sergeant Josef František was a pre-war pilot with the Czech Air Force. Like Christ, he was the son of a carpenter but he most certainly did not have the Lord's temperament for he was regularly involved in various disciplinary proceedings resulting from absences from barracks or fights in pubs. Though ordered not to fight when the Germans marched into his country, he took off in an adapted trainer aircraft and machine-gunned the advancing troops. He then escaped to Poland where he fought against the Luftwaffe for three weeks until escaping to Rumania where he was interned. He escaped from the camp, travelled through the Balkans, and eventually reached Syria and then France.

In 1940 František flew with the French Armée de l'Air. According to some accounts, by the conclusion of the Battle of France, his total score was 11 and he had been awarded the Croix de Guerre. On reaching Britain and joining the RAF, strangely he was posted to the Polish 303 Squadron at Northolt where he was the only Czech. As the months went on, the Czech Air Force never reclaimed him – they could do without the disciplinary problems – and the Poles had come to terms with this ebullient character.

For all his skills, František lacked air discipline and more than once his conduct – chasing madly after Germans – endangered the men who flew with him and so, after repeated reprimands, he was allowed to fight his own war. The result was a staggering 17 victories in just 27 days of September 1940 – three achieved on one day – which made him the top-scoring pilot of the Battle of Britain.

Then tragically on 8 October, while landing at Northolt, he crashed and died. Aged 27 when he was killed, he was granted posthumously the rank of flying officer and awarded the Distinguished Flying Medal.

Kut could not fail to be inspired by his compatriot's success in the Battle of Britain and he was now looking for victories of his own. He appreciated that he was unlikely to find them in the relative quiet of the skies of Lincolnshire, but fortunately this problem was about to be remedied.

CHAPTER FOUR

Kisses and Kills

On 15 December 1940, No 1 Squadron moved south to Northolt on the north-west outskirts of London to rejoin No 11 Group: it was back to the front line. By the time the squadron returned to the London area, the capital was becoming used to night bombing raids by the Germans. However, without technical aids, the RAF's Hurricanes and Spitfires had little luck in shooting down the enemy bombers.

Nevertheless, on New Year's Day 1941, No 1 Squadron returned to France for its first offensive mission of the war. Three Hurricanes piloted by Flight Lieutenant Clowes, Pilot Officer Kershaw and Pilot Officer Lewis took off from Northolt, refuelled at Hawkinge, and strafed German installations inland between Calais and Dunkirk. It was a start at hitting back – and it felt good. Over the next few months, the squadron made many such 'hit and run' operations, these sorties being known as 'rhubarbs'.

After only three weeks at Northolt, on 4 January 1941, No 1 moved to Kenley, south of London in Surrey. At the new station, the squadron combined with No 615 to form a Hurricane Wing led by Wing Commander Johnnie Peel. He is credited with firing the opening shots of the Battle of Britain on 8 August 1940 when, as CO of 145 Squadron, he destroyed two aircraft in the morning and one in the afternoon, before being himself shot down and then strafed while being picked up! 9 January saw No 1 Squadron's first offensive 'sweep' over Northern France. Nine of its Hurricanes joined twelve of 615 Squadron for a tour up the French coast from Cap Gris Nez to Calais. There was no sign of the Luftwaffe, but it was grand to be over enemy territory in some strength.

It was at Kenley that Kut took upon himself the responsibility of maintaining for his B Flight colleagues a board that was as much a work of art as a state of readiness. One of the other B Flight members, Tim Elkington, has particular reason to remember the 'state board' because he adopted the style of neat capital letters with which his Czech comrade decorated it:

This state of readiness board was made up of folds of light canvas with little pockets filled with cards that showed the status of each pilot – duty, leave or sick – and the allocation and availability of each aircraft. Kut was a most meticulous person, he took the state board very seriously – as he took life in general – and it always looked so immaculate. If anyone messed about with it, they would soon hear from him!

Elkington describes himself as then being 'a very young 19'. At this time, Kut was 24 and had of course seen action in France as well as Britain, so the other pilots tended to look up to him (metaphorically rather than physically in most cases). Elkington says of the Czech sergeant: 'He soon had the respect of the other pilots and rather mothered us. He was less larky than most and, if provoked, could fly off.'

As the New Year commenced, the RAF's new Fighter Command chief, Air Marshal Sir William Sholto Douglas, instructed the Commander of 11 Group, Air Vice Marshal Trafford Leigh-Mallory, to set operational instructions for a new type of operation, the 'circus'. This was a daylight attack by heavily escorted light bombers aimed at specific targets within the operational range of the accompanying fighters. The object of the attack was to force the enemy to give battle under conditions tactically favourable to the RAF's fighters. At first the fighter accompaniment to the bombers consisted of an escort wing of three squadrons, usually with a high cover wing of two or three more squadrons and sometimes with a mopping up wing of two or three more squadrons. Then in the summer, following the German invasion of Russia and the stepping up of these sweeps, the original concept of six fighter squadrons was replaced by a minimum requirement of eighteen squadrons. In fact, the circus concept proved to be both ineffective and costly.

Kut was one of the pioneers of this new type of operation, flying on four of the first five circuses. The first circus was flown on 10 January, but winter weather prevented another one for three weeks. When Circus No 2 was held on 2 February, No 1 Squadron was there – as it was for all four circuses that month – and Kut came as near as he had yet done with the RAF to scoring a victory, but he still fell short of achieving his first earnestly-sought kill.

The circus was centred on six Bristol Blenheims of 139 Squadron whose task was to bomb the Boulogne docks. Close escort was provided by the Northolt Wing of 1, 303 (Polish) and 601 Squadrons with further cover afforded by the three Spitfire squadrons from Biggin Hill. At 1.15 pm twelve Hurricanes from No 1 Squadron – five of them with Czech pilots – took off from Kenley to rendezvous with the six Blenheim bombers and their escort of fighter squadrons from Northolt. No 1 took station at 500 feet above the bombers and to the right at a height of 5,000 feet. Having assembled over the Kenley base, the formation moved over to the Continent for the bombers to attack the port of Boulogne at 10,000 feet.

No 1 Squadron was operating in pairs and Kut was Blue 2 to Squadron Leader Brown's Blue 1. Four pairs of Messerschmitt Bf 109s – yellow-nosed with yellow wing tips – appeared from above before and after the target was attacked. They did not press their attack on the bombers but the Hurricanes engaged them. The CO and Kut sped after two of the Messerschmitts. The squadron leader let off a three-second burst but without success. For his part, Kut delivered a burst of fire for two seconds at a distance of 150 yards. Back at base, he marked it up in his log book as a probable.

Three days later, on 5 February, Hurricanes from Nos 1, 302 (Polish) and 615 Squadrons accompanied a doubled force of Blenheim bombers over to St Omer in Circus No 3. Kut had to return almost immediately with engine trouble and it was a tough mission for other pilots of No 1. Kut's flight commander Pete Matthews was hit in the starboard wing. Then Pilot Officer R. G. Lewis was lost when, with his engine on fire from a Bf 109 attack, he parachuted into the Channel and repeated efforts by Squadron Leader Brown to contact Control and guide a rescue ship resulted in no answer. Lewis – known to all as Lew – was a rather shy and retiring Canadian, but he had served with the squadron in France where he had claimed several victories and his loss was certainly felt by his colleagues.

Circus No 4 came on 10 February. Blenheims attacked Dunkirk docks with Nos 1, 605 and 615 Squadrons providing withdrawal cover, not an activity which gave Kut any particular excitement.

On the afternoon of 13 February, Kut thought that he might find his elusive first kill with the RAF when he was scrambled over Beachy Head and spotted six Messerschmitt fighters. One of his companions on this occasion, Tim Elkington – who kept a more detailed flight log than most – noted in it: 'Chased e/a in cloud. No joy. 4 bursts of flak near *us*.' On his scramble to Maidstone of 22 February, Kut was back in less than half-an-hour and had to note in his flight log: 'Returned – air pressure!' Then, after a circus (No 5) over Calais on 26 February, he noted with frustration: '3 Me 109 – too late – nil.' Finally, at the conclusion of a scramble over Dungeness on 11 March, he recorded flatly: '4 Me 109 – too far – nil.' Would he never manage that first kill? He did not know it but he had only a month to wait.

Someone who recollects clearly Kut's commitment to his flying and his eagerness to succeed is Ben Bolt. Trained as an aircraft apprentice at Halton, this particular 'Trenchard Brat' was posted to No 1 Squadron in 1937 and spent the next four years – including the assignment in France – with the unit. At this point in his service career, Bolt was working on the Czech's Hurricane and, now in his 70s, he explains: 'I can remember the man very well indeed. He made a great impression on me – so much so that, when I was commissioned, I asked to go to a Czech squadron and was sent to 313 Squadron.'

Bolt continues:

I recall KK's complete dedication to his work, his obsession to shoot down Germans, his wonderful personality and his sense of humour, his ability to overcome the 'nationality gap' and become 'one of the team' and his almost fanatical urge to 'stay in the air'. Once, when I had serviced his aircraft, I told him that the engine was 'a bit rough and needed some attention'. He 'ran it up', climbed out and said with a smile, 'I can't hear anything wrong with it, Sergeant – put it "serviceable" and I'll fly it'. (But it was really rough!) That was the kind of man he was.

As an aside, Bolt adds: 'The girls loved him and, from what I remember, he loved them!'

In fact, it was about this time – actually 21 February – that Kut met the woman who was to become his wife.

Beryl Ruby Thomas – she was always known by her second name – was born on 3 April 1918 at Garnant, north of Swansea in South Wales. Her father was David John Thomas, a 6' 2" police sergeant with his own station in the small village of Tumble, to the west of Garnant, and her mother was Annie Richards from Llanelli. Early on in the war, Ruby's parents separated and she moved with her mother to live on the west of London in Ruislip with her sister Vera and brother-in-law Horace. She took a job as a comptometer operator on the buildings side of an insurance office in the City.

Kut and Ruby first met at a Friday evening dance in Ruislip while he was on leave in London. Apparently she was not keen to go out that evening but was persuaded to do so by her sister, Vera. Ruby, then aged 23, was a remarkable person – full of zest, bright, talkative, confident and friendly. Above all, she was such fun and it is not surprising that Kut was attracted to her. For her part, Ruby was drawn by his self-assurance and worldliness and rapidly perceived his intelligence and strength tempered by a certain charm.

Ruby spoke her native Welsh fluently, was competent at French and even had some Danish from a recuperative period spent in Denmark four years earlier, so she was probably more interested in foreigners than other girls of her age and more willing to struggle with Kut's very broken English and then the complexities of the Czech language with its Latin-like declensions. At first, their lively conversations were a strange and varying hybrid of English, French and Czech.

Certainly Kut was immediately taken by Ruby. Back in the Sergeants' Mess at 11.30 pm, he penned a hurried letter and it is clear from this that the Czech was as fast on the ground as he was in the air: 'I don't know exactly at present what it will be – may be the friendship – even the love.' Yet, already, having such a friend seemed to give a new dimension to his flying: 'Everybody is glad to see us again because at once tomorrow afternoon we shall go on duty. But I like it – it's for us – for everybody – everybody must work – you work for us in your office.' He concluded: 'P.S. Darling – excuse my bad English!'

From that beginning rapidly blossomed a friendship and then a love that was not always troublefree given the strength of character and different backgrounds of the two personalities involved.

On 1 March, Kut was promoted to temporary flight sergeant. Coming so soon after meeting Ruby, this was a special joy to him and it was the first of what came to seem a pattern of occasions when the RAF appeared to mark an important occasion in his private life by granting him a new promotion. On the same day, he had his first flight in a Hurricane II. Powered by the Merlin XX engine, this had a higher speed and rate of climb than the original machine. No 1 Squadron's Operational Records Book noted: 'There were no adverse criticisms. In fact the pilots were impressed by the all-round performance.'

Then two days later, Kut had his first ever experience of flying a Hurricane at night, when for 45 minutes he practised landings. In view of his outstanding success at night intrusion a year later, it is perhaps ironic that he was with the RAF almost six months before he had the chance to fly in the dark.

Meanwhile the escort patrols flown by the squadron sometimes encountered heavy German opposition and on 19 March Kut lost another comrade. Three No 1 Squadron pilots – Pilot Officer Tony Kershaw in Hurricane Z 2759 accompanied by two Czechs, Sergeants Štefan and Zavoral – were escorting a convoy moving west between Dungeness and Hastings when three Bf 109s advanced from the south and were immediately engaged by the Hurricanes. Five Spitfires entered the fray and a dog fight ensued. Kershaw must have been hit because his screaming aircraft went into a dive and he baled out but too late. The body was picked up by one of our whalers and landed at Newhaven after dusk the following day. A few days later, on 24 March, Jean Demozay avenged his colleague when, with a long twelve-second burst, he destroyed another Bf 109 over the Channel south of Hastings.

From Kenley, No 1 Squadron moved temporarily to Croydon in south London on 8 April. That very morning Kut achieved that for which he had been yearning.

It was 8.15 am when four Hurricanes from B Flight left Croydon with instructions to patrol Mayfield at 15,000 feet. Flying Officer Robinson was leading three Czech Sergeants, Kuttelwascher, Pavlů and Plášil. Otto Pavlů soon had to return with magneto trouble. The others were later ordered to patrol Dungeness at 25,000 feet and then vectored to mid-Channel at 30,000 feet to intercept 'Raid 89'. About 9 am they encountred three Bf 109s about five miles north of Cap Gris Nez.

The German machines were painted black all over, except for yellow noses and white swastikas, and they were set out in a very wide vic arrow-head formation. As soon as the Luftwaffe pilots spotted the Hurricanes, they divided, two remaining on the port and one moving into the sun on the starboard. Two of the Messerschmitts then attacked Robinson and Plášil and a fierce dogfight ensued. Robinson seemed to be singled out for attention by a particularly tenacious German because a series of diving and head-on attacks were made upon him. During one of these, he noticed smoke puffs from the enemy's shells bursting only 50 yards away. By this time, Robinson was over Dover where there was cloud. He managed to lose the 109 and returned to Croydon. Meanwhile Jan Plášil had followed his own attacker down and gave him a short burst from about 150 yards. He missed, but turned to attack the third Messerschmitt before returning to base.

In the course of this aerial mêlée, Kut – in Hurricane Z2464 – observed that the aircraft which first attacked his compatriot Plášil remained orbiting below him and he noticed a wisp of white smoke from the starboard wing root. Like a hunter sensing a weakness in his prey, Kut dived and attacked the German from the rear. The Hurricane's wings flickered with flames as he gave him two short bursts from his Browning machine guns at no less than 30 yards. As a result of this swift and savage attack, the smoke given off from the wing root increased in volume and a piece of the port side of the fuselage fell away. Strangely the Luftwaffe pilot took no evasive action – perhaps he was hit – and, firing now from 150 yards, his Czech opponent mercilessly gave him a further two short bursts with slight deflection from the rear port quarter. The Messerschmitt continued in a gentle dive southwards and Kut followed it down to 1,000 feet. Moments later, he saw this funereal descent conclude with a crash in a small wood fifteen miles south of Cap Gris Nez. But it was no time for self congratulation: four Bf 109s suddenly appeared at about 600 feet. Kut caught cloud cover and made a dash for home.

It was Kut's first victory with the RAF and it won him a Czech medal. What he did not know at the time – and indeed would never learn – was that, according to the researcher John Foreman, he had killed Leutnant Horst Reeh from II Gruppe Jagdgeschwader 26 (II/JG26). On both sides, most pilots thought of themselves as destroying a machine rather than killing a man and a victorious flier would rarely think of his opponent as an individual, still less know his name.

On 17 April, the squadron was scrambled for a patrol over Tangmere. Kut and the others were attacked by six Bf 109s but no kills were scored. The month continued to be eventful and 21 April provided further illustration of the mettle of the Czech pilots with the squadron. During a six-man patrol over Maidstone, Sergeant Josef Příhoda was attacked head-on by a Bf 109. As the opposing aircraft sped towards one another, both sides were firing furiously, but the Czech refused to give way and the German was compelled to pull up to avoid a crash. Příhoda dived onto the enemy aircraft's tail and then gave chase across the Channel. He eventually managed to give it a short burst, saw black and white smoke, and claimed a probable. Only a week later, Příhoda was near Dungeness when he was shot down by another Messerschmitt. He baled out and landed safely in a marsh at

New Romney. Though his comrades were naturally delighted to see˙ him return, it meant a revival of his practice of moulding and shaving into rings burnt scraps of perspex from old canopies. A member of the squadron insists: 'The smell was vile.'

Meanwhile, on 22 April, the squadron lost a pilot through an accident. Sergeant G.M. Stocken used Magister T9680 without prior permission from operations, the weather was unsuitable for flying, and he paid the ultimate price for his impetuosity. A court of enquiry followed.

At the end of April, both No 1 Squadron's flight commanders 'Darkey' Clowes and Pete Matthews were awarded the DFC and sent to OTUs. A and B Flights were taken over by Ken Jackman and Bill Sizer respectively. Only a couple of weeks later, the CO was off too. 'Hilly' Brown was promoted to Wing Commander and went to head No 58 OTU at Grangemouth. Later in the year, he was awarded a Bar to his DFC and then, on 12 November, he was killed while leading 249 Squadron on a sweep over Sicily. Meanwhile command of No 1 was assumed by Squadron Leader Richard Brooker. He had flown with 56 Squadron during the Battle of Britain and had just completed his rest tour as a gunnery instructor at Sutton Bridge.

A dance and cabaret was held on 25 April to mark the departure of the top three: Brown, Clowes and Matthews. Since they were the last of the RAF's peace-time regular pilots to leave No 1, it was seen as a psychological turning point in the war-time development of the squadron. Pete Matthews went on to command several squadrons of his own and clock up a total of eight victories. Unfortunately his days on combat duty came to an abrupt end when, over in Naples during a blackout, he contrived to drive a massive German personnel carrier into the back of an American tank. It is hard to say which was damaged most, his knee or his career. He at least never forgot Kut:

I was Air Attaché in Prague from 1961 to 1963 and mentioning Kut's name nearly got me shot. He was still remembered with pride among the Czech Air Force but had to be spoken of very quietly.

From Croydon, the squadron moved on 1 May south to Redhill, the satellite to Kenley. Here it was the daily job of Alfred Jones to pick up the pilots and take them from their billets to dispersal in a Commer truck or Standard van. After working in Redhill for 30 years after the war, he still lives in that village and remembers Kut well:

He was such a dedicated and meticulous man. However early I called – sometimes at the crack of dawn – he would be the first out, fully dressed in his neat uniform.

After months of relative inaction, May saw Hitler stepping up the night bombing attacks on England. During the spring, as an addition to its daylight activities, No 1 Squadron had flown many hundreds of hours by night and so it was ready for the counter-attack against the German night bombers.

The last really massive raid on London by the Luftwaffe came on the night of 10/11 May when a total of 550 aircraft were employed. Good weather and a full moon made visibility excellent for the German bombers – and for the British fighters. The Luftwaffe lost over 30 aircraft to the RAF that ferocious night. No 1 Squadron sent up thirteen Hurricanes and destroyed at least six enemy aircraft plus one probably destroyed and a further two damaged. The hero of the night was Kut's compatriot Sergeant Josef Dygrýn, a short but debonair man with a thin moustache and wide smile who was known to the public under his *nom-de-guerre* of Ligotický, the name of a village near his birthplace of Humpolec. In three stunning sorties, he destroyed two Heinkel He 111s and a Junkers Ju 88. Another Czech with the squadron, Sergeant Bedřich Krátkoruký, damaged an unidentified bomber, while the Frenchman Jean Demozay destroyed an He 111 and the new CO obtained a further Heinkel. The other successful pilots were Flight Lieutenant Ken Jackman who downed a Heinkel bomber, Pilot Officer W. Raymond with a probable and Flying Officer J. C. Robinson who damaged a Heinkel.

It was an incredible night's work by a squadron of day fighters, but marred by the loss of Pilot Officer František Běhal. It was assumed that his Hurricane Z2921 was hit by enemy fire, as he was heard to shout over his radio that he intended to bale out. Sadly he was obviously unable to do so because next day his body was found slumped in the wreck of his aircraft at Selsdon Park, Croydon. The bearers at the funeral were six of his Czech colleagues from the squadron, but Kut felt the loss more personally than most: in France he and Běhal had trained together at Chartres and fought together with III/3 Squadron.

Squadron Leader Brooker received the DFC for the night's action; Demozay obtained another Palm to his Croix de Guerre and the French Medal of Libération; and Dygrýn went to London to meet the Czech President Beneš and take possession of the Czech

War Cross and the Medal for Gallantry. To his fierce disappointment, Kut had not been on the detail that night – he had flown the
night before and was up the night after – but he would not have
to wait long for more action and another victory. First, it was
Dygrýn's turn again: on 16 May he was vectored onto an enemy raid
and downed a Bf 109 over the Channel. Then came Kut's action.

Circus No 10 of 21 May – the only successful one that month –
involved nine Blenheim bombers each from 21, 82 and 110 Squadrons
attacking targets in France while a total of thirteen fighter squadrons
were in attendance. No 1 Squadron's role was to escort eighteen
Blenheims to Gosnay to bomb the oil refinery and power station.
Twelve Hurricanes from No 1 left Redhill at 4.55 pm and
rendezvoused over Kenley with the bombers and with fighters from
258 (New Zealand) and 302 (Polish) Squadrons who were providing
the rest of the escort wing. No 1 Squadron was rear top escort at 15,000
feet.

They all crossed the English coast south of Dungeness and the
French coast at Le Touquet. The weather throughout was haze up to
9,000 feet with very high cirrus cloud. Then, halfway from the French
coast to Gosnay, eight enemy aircraft were observed climbing from
the rear of the squadron and they attacked the bombers over the
target. The port engine of one of the Blenheims caught fire and the
bomber was lost. From then on, the sky was a confused mass of
machines with lots of dogfights in a huge aerial arena. No 1's pilots
were right in the thick of it.

Pilot Officer W. Raymond attacked a Bf 109 from dead astern with
two good bursts and saw black smoke coming from one side. He
thought he might have destroyed the Messerschmitt, but could not
follow it because of the arrival of more enemy aircraft. He only escaped
them by making a steep dive practically down to sea level. The Czech
Flying Officer Antonín Velebnovský was attacked from below by a
109. He half rolled and came behind the enemy aircraft giving a short
burst from about 70 yards. He had the satisfaction of seeing pieces
break away from the wings and fuselage.

Another of the Czechs, Sergeant Josef Dygrýn, saw a Hurricane
being attacked beneath him, so he dived on the German and, firing a
fairly long burst from 100 yards, pulled out at very close range. He saw
his bullets striking the cockpit and fuselage all the way and the Bf 109
became very unsteady and dived steeply, but the Czech could only
claim the aircraft as damaged. He then climbed and engaged another
Messerschmitt, giving it a couple of fairly long bursts until he found

still another 109 on his tail. He put his nose up and the German overshot him.

Meanwhile at about 5.45 pm Kut himself – flying as Black 1 weaving in Hurricane Z3160 – found himself at 12,000 feet about seven miles north-west of Béthune when he noted a British fighter being attacked by four Bf 109s in line astern. Zooming to his colleague's aid, he engaged the rearmost of the enemy aircraft with two long bursts from very close – pumping in 650 rounds from 100 yards – and saw smoke pouring from the Messerschmitt's wing roots. The German immediately fell into a death spin, crashing down out of control and on fire. Kut had several further engagements with enemy aircraft without any particular result. Then he in turn was attacked by three Bf 109s, but a Spitfire joined him and the RAF duo managed to shake off the Germans.

Still another Czech, Sergeant Bedřich Krátkoruký, saw two Bf 109s dive through the squadron to attack the bombers and got in a short burst at one of them from 50 yards. The Messerschmitt's tail unit dropped off and the German pilot baled out. Then Krátkoruký noticed a Hurricane being attacked by two aircraft and turned to help, but the British machine had already caught fire and was diving gently seaward and he himself was very short of fuel and unable to assist. Inside that falling Hurricane Z2764 was a No 1 pilot: Flying Officer J. C. Robinson. He was never seen or heard of again. It had been Robinson who had led Kut on his first victorious sortie six weeks previously and his loss certainly took the gilt off Kut's second victory.

On 25 May, the Frenchman Jean Demozay took his score to five when he made a lone trip over the Channel and destroyed a Bf 110 over the Goodwin lightship. Yet another Palm leaf was added to his Croix de Guerre which created so much vegetation on his left breast that his *nom-de-guerre* of Moses was replaced by the nickname Oasis! Shortly afterwards, on 18 June, he was transferred to 242 Squadron, but he was far from forgotten by his former comrades at No 1. Throughout the war, the squadron diaries continued to include press cuttings of his most recent exploit and his latest Palm.

By the end of the war, he had an amazing total of sixteen Palms – not so much an oasis now, more a tropical forest! He was credited with no less than 21 victories which made him the second highest scoring French pilot (after Marcel Albert). Apparently he planned to go into politics after the war, but a week before Christmas 1945 he was killed when his aircraft crashed.

On 1 June, No 1 moved from Redhill back to the main base at Kenley and – just two weeks later – on 14 June back to Redhill again. While No 1 was away from Redhill, its place was taken by No 258 (New Zealand) Squadron to give the Kiwis some experience of night defence. It was about this time that No 1 Squadron took delivery of the Hurricane IIB. This was better armed: twelve instead of eight Browning machine guns with the increased rate of fire of 14,400 rounds per minute.

An indication of the rapid turnover in the unit's pilots at this time was the departure early in June of Flight Lieutenants Jackman and Sizer who had only been with the squadron six weeks. One of the replacement flight commanders was the New Zealand ace Colin Gray, who came from RAF Hornchurch where he had been serving with 54 Squadron. He already had a tally of sixteen which made him one of the highest-scoring participants in the Battle of Britain.

On 15 June, Kut temporarily exchanged his Hurricane for a Miles Magister, the two-seater trainer known by all the pilots as 'Maggie'. He took his brother Jan – who had made his own escape to England and was now serving as a captain in the Czech Military Police – back to his army base at Wellesbourne, near Stratford-on-Avon. Between these flights and 25 June, Kut did not fly so he missed some exciting action.

On 16 June, twelve Hurricanes from No 1 were involved in a tremendous dogfight with Bf 109s in mid Channel. A Heinkel He 59 seaplane was destroyed off Folkestone. So were three of the 109s, all of these by Czech pilots – Pilot Officer Václav Kopecký, Sergeant Jarda Novák and Sergeant Josef Příhoda. The Czech Sergeant Albín Nassveter, flying Hurricane Z3460, became detached from the rest of the squadron and was pounced upon by a reinforcing group of enemy fighters. He crashed into the sea, was rescued and taken to Dover hospital, but died next day. The same day that Nassveter died, the Czechs on No 1 Squadron had their revenge. While on a circus operation (No 13) to Béthune, the Czech Sergeant Josef Dygrýn shot down a Bf 109 which fell into the sea off Boulogne. This was the Czech's fifth kill, making him an ace, something he had achieved in only five weeks.

Then, on 21 June, No 1 Squadron joined with No 258 (New Zealand) and No 312 (Czech) for a circus operation (No 17) to Desvres airfield in Brittany. On the return journey, over 30 Messerschmitts – some of them the new Bf 109F – attacked and a violent and long-running fight ensued. At the end of it, four Bf 109s had been destroyed, another four probably destroyed and two damaged. The Czech Pilot Officer Václav Kopecký was attacked by two Messerschmitts, force landed in the sea and was picked up by a rescue launch, but Pilot Officer N. Maranz, an American flying Hurricane Z3461, failed to return. The American had arrived from No 121 Squadron a mere nine days previously.

Next day, 22 June, Germany launched Operation Barbarossa, the invasion of Russia, and from then on an important role of the circus operations was to tie up German fighters on the Channel coast so that they could not be used to reinforce the Luftwaffe on the eastern front.

Back to flying, and once more in a trusty Hurricane (this time Z 3449), Kut achieved another kill of his own on 27 June. This was on Circus No 25 when 22 Blenheims from 18, 21, 139 and 226 Squadrons attacked a factory at Lille with fifteen fighter squadrons in support. At 8.45 pm, twelve Hurricanes from No 1 Squadron – no less than seven of them piloted by Czechs – left Redhill together with Spitfires from No 41 Squadron. They rendezvoused over Kenley with the Hurricanes of 258 (New Zealand) and 312 (Czech) Squadrons and together these squadrons comprised the rear cover wing for the operation. The wing was led by Squadron Leader Lionel Gaunce, a Canadian.

The English coast was crossed over Beachy Head and, once over the Channel, No 1 Squadron climbed to 29,000 feet with 312 above and 258 below. No 1 proceeded to Gravelines between Calais and Dunkirk where the anti-aircraft fire was uncomfortably accurate as the Hurricanes orbited between 25,000 and 30,000 feet. The problem was that the squadron had become split up before it reached Gravelines. Kut and his fellow Czech Sergeant Josef Dygrýn – flying as Yellow 1 and 2 respectively – had become separated from their colleagues and, when they saw aircraft towards the French coast, decided to investigate. It was about 9.50 pm as they crossed the coast at 30,000 feet between Cap Gris Nez and Boulogne.

At first, they observed only Spitfires. Then Kut saw two of the new Bf 109Fs swooping down upon a couple of the RAF aircraft. In an instant, the Czech had chosen his man and gave chase after one of the Luftwaffe aircraft. While diving, he managed to fire two bursts of about three seconds each from dead astern and about 80 yards. Bullets from twelve machine guns ripped into the 109 and pieces immediately fell away, including what appeared to Kut to be the cockpit hood. Now down to about 10,000 feet, the Luftwaffe pilot tried to abandon his stricken plane and clamber out of the cockpit. Kut was giving absolutely no quarter: he fired a third burst as the German jumped out. The Czech did not actually see a parachute open, but shortly afterwards observed several small boats–possibly rescue craft–setting out from the French coast.

On looking behind him, Kut found that Dygrýn was no longer there but another aircraft was: fortunately it was a Spitfire. He returned to Hawkinge to refuel and rearm (he had fired 2,060 rounds). Several of the Spitfire pilots landed there as well and one of them confirmed having seen his attack and the destruction of the Bf 109F. It was his third kill in as many months.

Later in the war, Kut explained to the Canadian broadcaster Bob Bowman one of his rules for aerial combat:

You must learn to be quick, and it's waiting for the right time. When you see that, you go in for kill. You must be quick to the one-hundredth of a second. You come in among them. You mustn't go after two of them this side and that, or you are missing them all. You must decide quick which is yours. I had a friend and I took him up, and when we were in among them I could see he was bewildered, and he did not pick off his plane. He gets nothing. I question him that he must decide on his plane quickly, and then to go for it. Next time we go up, he gets one. To act quickly, that is the thing.

On 29 June, six pilots from No 1 Squadron–all but one of them Czech, including Kut–joined with the Czech 312 Squadron to make a sweep over France, but no enemy aircraft were encountered. A little later the same day, one of the other Czechs on No 1 Squadron, Pilot Officer Bohumil Horák, was killed in an accident when he crashed Hurricane Z3240 at Horley while flying from Redhill to Gatwick. Like the American Maranz, he had barely arrived at the squadron before losing his life: he had come from No 55 OTU sixteen days previously. Horák was the second Czech to be lost in a fortnight.

It was now time for No 1 Squadron to return 'home' where it would soon be joined by a Commanding Officer with a difference.

CHAPTER FIVE

One-armed Mac

On 1 July, No 1 Squadron transferred to Tangmere, three miles east of Chichester, where it remained for the next year which included the entire night intruder phase. Here No 1 had the responsibility of defending Portsmouth and Southampton by night.

Tangmere had been built in 1917–18 but then closed from 1919–25. From then until 1939, it was the home of No 1 and No 43 Fighter Squadrons, famous for many years for their formation aerobatic displays. In the last week of August 1939, No 1 went to France where it distinguished itself brilliantly. Back in England, it spent the Battle of Britain at Northolt before moving to Wittering where Kut had joined it.

Returning now to the ancestral home of Tangmere after an absence of almost two years, No 1 Squadron found it a rather different place. On 16 August 1940, the airfield had been the target for a large force of Junkers Ju 87 dive-bombers which had caused immense damage and throughout March, April and May 1941 the Luftwaffe made a succession of bombing raids on the airfield. So the ground personnel had to be billeted off the base at Goodwood race course.

One of these was young Dick Corser on his first posting after initial training. He worked on B Flight with Kut and recalls the atmosphere of the time:

A and B Flights were alternately doing 24 hours on and 24 hours off from midday each day. As a mere erk, of course, my duties were varied. I can remember such things as cleaning the perspex cockpit cowlings to make sure that there was not one speck of dirt, otherwise to the pilot no doubt it could look like something in the distance. Of course, there was always a great air of expectancy and the pilots were always at 100% readiness even when playing cards. Once the tannoy announced 'scramble', everyone would dash to the dispersal point and the aircraft were airborne in what seemed like seconds. Then there was the long wait to hear the welcome sound of the aircraft returning and of course to see how many there were. On the black days when one was missing, that of course was all that was talked about all through that 24 hours on duty.

Another member of the squadron's ground crew at this time was Lionel Baggs, a veteran of the Battle of France who eventually became a shift NCO on Kut's B Flight:

We were all so busy servicing aircraft we had little time to talk to the aircrew. However, I had a conversation with Kut when I was posted on my engineering commission course having turned down aircrew training. He said I would regret it and I do, but then I probably wouldn't be here today. As a man, I found Kut to be very pleasant, very polite and the perfect gentleman. At the time, we were thrilled with his successes and thought he was the greatest.

During the night, No 1 Squadron now embarked on a very intensive course of interception training. A lot of time was spent working with the 'Turbinlite' Douglas Havoc aircraft of No 1455 Flight. Kut's first log entry 'Co-op with Havoc' in red ink (indicating a night time flight) was on 30 July.

The black-painted Havoc was a modified Boston II light bomber in which the bomb aimer's nose position was replaced by a powerful searchlight and the bomb bay was loaded with over 2,000 lbs of electrical batteries. One or two 'satellite' Hurricanes would fly in formation with each Havoc. The idea was that the Havoc – which carried no guns because of the weight of the searchlight – would locate an enemy bomber with its radar and then illuminate it with the huge searchlight for the Hurricane to shoot down. A large number of flying hours was consumed in training for this complicated exercise but it had no success at all. Indeed a rigger with No 1 Squadron at this time, Sydney Sharp, comments: 'We used to call it going out on petrol-wasting cruises.'

A pilot who remembers such 'cruises' with evident frustration is Jack Torrance who served with 43 Squadron, the unit that took over night intrusion from No 1 Squadron when it left Tangmere:

I recall distinctly the Havoc Turbinlite débâcle – lining up behind the right hand mainplane of a Havoc with just a pencil of light directed from the fuselage along the trailing edge on which to formate. The first problem was that, when the pilot of the Havoc opened the throttles, his acceleration was so much greater than that of the Hurricane, that usually, by the time one was over the airfield boundary, the Havoc had disappeared in the murk and, in spite of the controller's best efforts, was seldom to be located again until one was back on the ground. Why they didn't just put four cannons in the nose of the Havoc, instead of a ruddy great searchlight, I'll never know.

During daylight, No 1 Squadron flew a number of convoy escorts. They were often deployed to Merston to stand by for top cover duties with a squadron of Westland Lysanders, the air-sea rescue aircraft allocated to each circus over the Channel. In early July, Kut's flight log has several 'Escort Lysander' entries. In fact, quite separately and unknown to most people even today, Tangmere itself was from 1941 to 1944 the advanced base from which Lysanders performed a very different type of operation: carrying the agents of the Special Operations Executive and other resistance organisations into and out of occupied Europe.

Since No 1 Squadron was basically on night duty but also had daytime responsibilities, its pilots had to adopt strange patterns for obtaining sleep (or 'horizontal refreshment' as some of them called it), as Kut explained in one of his regular letters to Ruby:

> Usually I am going to bed at 8 o'clock and up at 13.00. Again to bed at 2.30 pm. and up at 20.00. All night 'on' and day for the sleep. It is much better but still sometimes during day we are 'on'.

Nevertheless he continued to write to Ruby about once a week and visited her as often as he could. On one such trip to London, he mislaid a ring at Ruby's place, but fortunately it was discovered later by her sister Vera. In a subsequent letter, Kut wrote:

> Many kisses and thanks to Vera – she found the ring. Darling well she will go with me in a Hurricane. Only one question – no place for two. Well she will take a place on the tail.

Subsequent correspondence does not record what Vera thought of this original suggestion.

Only a couple of weeks after the move to Tangmere, on 16 July Kut lost yet another Czech friend. Flight Lieutenant Antonín Velebnovský was flying Hurricane Z3902 as one of two air crew on searchlight cooperation around midnight. After requesting and receiving two vectors to base, nothing more was heard of him and a search party was organised but failed to locate him. Late in the day, his body was found in a smashed aircraft in a wood near Gaffham about eight miles from base. He had apparently flown into the wooded top of a hill. Velebnovský was the fourth No 1 Squadron Czech to be killed in a little over two months. Kut allowed only a brief non-emotive mention of the incident in his next letter to Ruby on 19 July:

Once again the death took place in our squadron. One Czech, our flight commander, was killed during night. Next Monday will be his funeral.

In the course of July and August, the squadron's Hurricane Mark IIBs were gradually replaced with Mark IICs which brandished four powerful 20 mm cannon instead of machine guns, although No 1 had a mixture of IIBs and IICs until mid September. The night training continued on the new aircraft, but August, September and October were quiet months with little contact with the enemy in spite of regular sorties.

One exception was the experience of the New Zealander Colin Gray who had joined No 1 Squadron as a flight commander back in June. On 22 August, he attached himself to a 41 Squadron patrol and destroyed a Bf 109F east of Le Havre. It was Gray's seventeenth officially credited combat victory and the following month he was awarded a bar to his DFC. By the end of the war, he was officially credited with a combat tally of 28, a magnificent performance which made him the top-scoring Kiwi of the war.

The nearest Kut himself came to any real action at this time occurred after yet another weekend with Ruby. On 19 August, Flight Lieutenant Raymond – known to his men as Ray – led Kut and three other Czechs to Manston for operational flying. While there, they were detailed to attack an enemy convoy off Ostend. They carried out a low attack with both cannon and machine gun fire. According to Kut's flight log, a member of 242 Squadron had to bale out, but he and his No 2 claimed two E-boats. He wrote to Ruby on 21 August:

Karel is well. He arrived safely back and at once was in action over Ostend. But he is alright and working again every day over a cold sea.

He explained that their next weekend together would have to be short: 'I can get only two days now – busy – everybody is very busy – everyday twice, even three times, up and over F.'

A few days later, on 27 August, the squadron lost Sergeant E. Bloor. Flying Hurricane Z3843, he was engaged on searchlight cooperation when he crashed and was killed near Horsham. It was the second night training accident in little over a month. In fact, since its arrival at Tangmere, No 1 Squadron had done little actual operational flying and the Operational Records Book opened September with the comment:

In the nature of things, pilots prefer operational activity. They realise, however, lack of this is unavoidable, since the Luftwaffe fight shy of giving them the opportunities they long for.

Towards the end of September, Kut lost the companionship of another four Czechs who were posted from the squadron. Their departure served to underline the scarcity of Czechs still with No 1 Squadron. Gradually the Czechs with the unit had been reassigned, either to one of the Czech fighter squadrons 310, 312 and 313 or to one of the OTUs and, in each case, their experience was much appreciated.

Another Czech serving a brief period with the squadron at this time provided a more light-hearted occasion for Kut. Pilot Officer Antonín Liška, who now lives back in Czechoslovakia, had a more obvious sense of humour than his colleague, as is clear from this particular anecdote:

Karel was courageous, sure, yet equally cautious and disciplined. One day I was up with him on a convoy patrol over the Channel. We were returning back to base and located the Carters' cottage. I then noticed quite an amount of people in the back garden. 'Yes of course! There is a wedding there ...' I suddenly remembered. In fact I got the invitation to that celebration a couple of days ago, but the Jerries were first of all, of course.

In the enthusiastic mood I was in, the most stupid idea

overwhelmed my mind. 'Why not have a look?' I didn't dare to
warn Karel on the R/T; I merely gave him an appropriate sign
with my thumb and immediately after, steep banking, I put my
Hurricane into a dive towards the Carters' 'Tile House'. The
lively motion in the garden all of a sudden stopped and, for a
short while, ovals of faces all turned in the same direction:
towards the sky, towards me ... But it didn't take a minute!
Something set all the figures in motion again, in frantic, chaotic
agitation in all possible directions. Some of them dropped on the
ground right on the spot. The group having dispersed, two
distinctly marked patches were left: white and black across one
another. Obviously the chivalrous groom was trying to protect
with his own manly body the fragile body of the bride who had
unluckily fallen to the ground. Oh hell, I knew all at once! They
took me for a Jerry. How stupid of me to go so low in a region
fearstricken by German air-raids.

After having landed at base, I tried to look unconcerned.
'There is a wedding party at Carters, did you notice?' I asked
Karel on our way to dispersal. 'Did you say a wedding party?' he
looked at me wildly. 'Certainly not, but a rodeo, by what I had
seen!' His sarcasm was quite real. I pretended having missed
noticing it. 'Didn't you get the invitation from Carters?' 'Most
certainly I didn't, but you'll soon get one from our Wing
Commander, you bet!' 'Don't exaggerate, Karel!' I opposed him
with a smile. 'Carters are good friends, they wouldn't get me in
trouble.' 'Carters ...? Why the hell Carters?' he shouted out with
staring eyes. 'That's me ...' he sank his thumb into his chest,
'that's me who is going to have a say in this affair.'

Kut kept Liška on tenterhooks for days and obviously relished his
colleague's discomfort: 'Karel was watchful and never missed a
moment to send me a meaningful glance.' At last, however, Kut
revealed to Liška that he had no intention of betraying a friend: 'As
far as I know, my queer participation in the Carters' wedding party
was our mutual secret till the end of Karel's days.'

On 7 October, Kut – now just 25 – was granted 'a commission
for the emergency as a pilot officer on probation in the General
Duties Branch of the RAF Volunteer Reserve'. His new service
number was 111519. A week later, on 15 October, he celebrated his
promotion by taking a Miles Magister from the nearby base of
Ford and flying to Wellesbourne, where he collected his brother

Jan and brought him over to Tangmere. After a couple of days at the base, they travelled to London where Kut was able at last to introduce his brother to Ruby.

No 1 Squadron continued to suffer losses. On 21 October, Sergeant R. H. Oakley was killed while on detachment from the squadron to No 1 Delivery Flight at Hendon. It was the fourth accidental death in as many months during which time the squadron had hardly seen the Luftwaffe.

In November – after four months of intensive training – No 1 was finally declared fully operational as a night fighter unit, but there was little to fight. The Germans were coming over in much smaller groups and were much harder to intercept on this side of the Channel. So eventually someone decided to take the fight to the enemy in a new tactical style. This was the birth of the idea of night intrusion. What was needed was a new kind of leader for a new kind of operation.

On 18 October, No 1 Squadron had been joined by the legendary Flight Lieutenant James Archibald Findlay MacLachlan, DFC and Bar, or Mac as he was known to all his colleagues, from RAF Station Hunsdon. On 3 November, he was promoted to become the Commanding Officer, taking over from Squadron Leader Brooker who was posted to the Far East to take charge of No 232 Squadron, where he distinguished himself in the defence of Singapore and the retreat through Java.

Born at Styal in Cheshire in 1919, Mac stood around 6 ft with a wiry frame, topped by sandy hair, a prominent nose, and a closely cropped little moustache. He joined the RAF in 1937, and received a DFC for his skill and courage while serving as a light bomber pilot in a squadron (No 88) of Fairey Battles in France, where he was shot down twice. Back in England, he transferred to fighters and, during the Battle of Britain, he scored six kills – four of them on one day – with Nos 73 and 145 Squadrons. Then he was posted as a flight commander to 261 Squadron on Malta where he destroyed two more enemy aircraft. However, on 16 February 1941, he was in a Hurricane when he was shot down by a more powerful Bf 109, baling out with his left arm shattered by a cannon shell and with shrapnel in both legs. The arm had to be amputated above the elbow.

Nevertheless – like Douglas Bader with his artificial legs – Mac returned to the air. Amazingly, within fifteen days of the amputation he had flown solo in a Magister. He was sent to East

Africa where he recuperated by clocking up 250 flying hours with 73 Squadron. Once back in England, he persuaded the artificial limb centre at Roehampton to build him an artificial arm that would fit the controls of a Hurricane. In October the arm was ready – it was described as 'wizard' – and within weeks he had talked the RAF into giving him command of No 1. At the same time he received a Bar to his DFC.

Mac's disability meant that he required a little more assistance than the other pilots in strapping himself into the Hurricane's cockpit. However, he resented too much concern. His rigger, Sydney Sharp – known appropriately enough as 'Tiny' because he was such a very big chap – recounts that Mac would shout: 'Don't think I'm bloody helpless.' The CO's piloting of the aircraft was a wonder to all. He used a three-pronged adjustable claw attached to his left arm to hold the throttle lever permanently in position and then, when he needed to adjust the trim, leaned over and used his right hand. When not flying, he would exchange his clawed hook for a gloved hand. These two appendages were screwed into a leather arm and – according to one of his colleagues – when he had scored in the air, he would rush from his Hurricane, remove the false arm, and excitedly throw it into the air.

Mac was a born leader who was revered by officers and men alike.

One of No 1's pilots in the intruder phase, the flamboyant Frenchman André Jubelin, later wrote: 'We loved and admired him . . . MacLachlan added a new significance to our notions of human valour. He was cast in the heroic mould.' Certainly Jubelin's admiration seemed to have no bounds: 'Of all single-minded men Mac seemed to me the purest and loftiest I had ever met.' He insisted: 'He was worshipped by everyone in the squadron.' These last words are echoed by a member of No 1's maintenance flight, Tommy Atkins: 'Mac was idolized by everyone on the Squadron.' One of the squadron's armourers, Frank Churchett, confirms this assessment: 'Mac was an incredible leader who really inspired people. We would work until we dropped for him.'

Another member of the groundcrew, Stan Greenwood – who was a flight mechanic on engines on Mac's B Flight – has good reason to remember the CO because he appeared before him on a 'fizzer', the disciplinary charge being 'causing damage to one of His Majesty's aircraft', since he had run an engine test with the

Hurricane in the bay instead of on the grass and a bit of tarmac had taken a piece out of one of the propeller's airscrews. Mac imposed a punishment of seven days confined to camp but, when he heard that Greenwood had himself reported the damage, he had second thoughts: 'I know they all do it, but you broke an order. Nevertheless, under the circumstances, seven days is a bit steep. We'll make it three.' Greenwood comments: 'You couldn't wish for a better bloke.'

Yet Mac was not simply a figure of authority, he was full of fun. He flew wearing a dirty cheese-cutter hat; on the ground he loved to go clay pigeon shooting with a 12-bore shotgun; and his car driving was a hair-raising adventure for any passengers because he could not change gear without letting go of the wheel. Wilf Merry, a member of No 1 Squadron's groundcrew for virtually the entire war, has a particularly enjoyable reminiscence:

> One evening Mac took us down to Brighton for a dance where he got pretty well oiled. One of us took advantage of this to ask if we could stay on and he agreed. It was a very good do and went on all night. Our NCOs wondered where we were and Mac said: 'You buggers, you got me drunk!'

Mac and his older Czech colleague, whom he always called 'Old Kuttel', soon became great friends and – during the night intruder operations which were to follow – keen rivals. In some respects, they were very different: the tall Mac the more exuberant, almost boyish, and the shortish Kut the more calculating and controlled. Kut acted as a foil to Mac – against the rather sober and taciturn Czech, the CO appeared all the more vibrant and dashing. Yet, for all their different national backgrounds and personalities, they had fundamental characteristics in common: peacetime training in a professional airforce, tough combat experience abroad, coolness in the air and modesty on the ground, and an unusually easy relationship with the maintenance men as well as fellow officers. As a result, there was a special kind of empathy between the two men. As Tommy Atkins puts it: 'To me they were a pair.' Kut himself insisted to a radio interviewer: 'We are rivals only in the air.'

Kut and Mac shared a sense of mischievousness. Before he died, one member of the squadron's erks, Frank Wooley claimed: 'I'm pretty sure it was Kut and another officer, probably MacLachlan, who cleared the cockpit of a Hurricane one day, dispensed with their parachutes and other clobber and flew, one sitting on the other's lap, one with his feet on the rudder bar and the other holding the stick, from Tangmere to another station.' At first this story sounds like just that, uncharacteristic of Kut's cautious and disciplined approach to life. Yet it is independently confirmed by another member of the ground crew, Tommy Atkins:

> I actually saw Kut at the controls with a passenger taking off in a Hurricane without parachutes from Tangmere for an airfield in London. Perhaps he was on his way to see Ruby and giving a colleague a lift!

Atkins – who moved from Kut's A Flight to the squadron's Maintenance Flight – mentions another incident involving the Czech:

> We kept a goat at Tangmere tethered in the maintenance unit. Kut was involved in an occasion when we let the goat free to chase a particularly unpopular Warrant Officer. The rest of us were confined to camp for that, but Kut was all right because he was flying that night.

In fact, the conclusion of this tale is a sad one indeed. Lionel Baggs confesses:

> We had our own 'intruder' – namely the squadron mascot, a billy goat that had been sprayed red, white and blue. It became a nuisance because it used to interfere with night flying by butting all and sundry on the aircraft dispersals when everyone was concentrating on refuelling and rearming. Anyway one particular day when I was on shift, I got so fed up with this goat that I arranged a firing squad – six airmen with rifles and any aircraft ammunition that was available, for example, ball, armour piercing, incendiary. We tied the goat to a stake and shot it.

During the inclement winter months at the end of 1941 and the start of 1942, the squadron continued to carry out the training for night intruder operations whenever weather permitted. A letter to Ruby (30 November) captured the frustration of the pilots:

> Every night waiting at readiness but until today no any luck. The

weather is here very bad – all day all night foggy – and we are going round and watching the sun if will come bright and break this low clouds. But no and no. You can imagine how 12 men are sitting and looking forwards for some good nights. After we shall be gay – gay everything double – if will be any opportunity. I think so because otherwise we shall be down.

Kut had a week's break from flying over Christmas. Ruby came down to Tangmere for the riotous Christmas dinner and dance at the Officers' Mess and then Kut accompanied her back to Mill Hill where he spent five days' leave.

The year closed with some excitement for Kut when, on the night of 28/29 December, he made an eventful anti-shipping patrol. Operating from Manston, just outside Ramsgate, he took off at 11.25 pm, flew over to Dunkirk, and then followed the coastline a mile off-shore proceeding in the direction of Ostend. Around midnight, he spotted two vessels about two miles off Ostend proceeding in a north-easterly direction in line astern. One was a tanker of around 700 tons and the other was a flak ship to defend it. Kut immediately reported the position of the ships and two Bristol Beaufort bombers were despatched to intercept the small convoy, but they failed to locate it. So he returned to the ships and decided to carry out a low level attack.

Kut came down to 700 feet intending to attack the flak ship but it had already seen him and threw up an intimidating blanket of heavy fire. As shells burst all around his Hurricane, he was forced to swerve to port which took him between the ship and the coast and allowed him to attack the tanker from the direction of the coast with the moon slightly behind him. Kut opened fire from 700 yards and continued to pump his blazing cannons at the tanker until he was actually over it. He saw strikes burst on the deck. Wheeling round the Hurricane, he pressed in for another attack, this time towards the coast. There were further strikes on the tanker but it was too dark to make a realistic estimate of the damage. During this second attack, medium flak had come from coastal batteries and burst approximately 3,000 feet above the Hurricane. In any event, Kut had completely expended his ammunition, so he turned for base, flying at sea level until he reached the English coast.

This was a rare occasion when Kut mentioned a particular sortie in one of his regular letters to Ruby (29 December):

Karel is back again and busy – very busy – last night very successful. I got one ship off Ostend and damaged one other. It was nice change again but heavy enough. Lots of fire everywhere. More I will tell you when home again.

No 1 Squadron pilots were now desperate for some real action. All these long months of night training, convoy escorts, and defensive patrols had been just too quiet. The weather was still dreadful with lots of snow and ice, but – thanks to the boldness of a German Dash – events were about to take a sudden and dramatic turn and present some excitement for a good deal more than this particular unit.

CHAPTER SIX

The Channel Dash

It was about this time that No 1 Squadron suffered an incident of some embarrassment. Stan Greenwood narrates:

My mate, Alan Dodson, who was a rigger was returning from leave in London and hitched a lift back to Tangmere in a car driven by an officer with a strange foreign accent. This officer drove straight into the camp and strolled into the mess where he drank and chatted to the officers. Only a little later did we learn that the 'officer' was dressed in a German uniform and it was a security test on the camp. The man wasn't wearing a hat, no one recognised the uniform, and there had been so many Czechs and others around nobody paid much attention to the accent. Old Dodson managed to escape a charge, but the security police on the gate got a rocket and security at the camp then tightened up like mad!

It is certainly true that there had been many Czechs on the base, but this was no longer the case. The start of 1942 saw the departure of Kut's close friend and compatriot Pilot Officer Bedřich Krátkoruký to No 61 OTU at Rednal in Shropshire. Like Běhal, who was now dead, Krátkoruký had trained and fought with Kut in the French Air Force and so the latter was particularly sorry to see him go. It meant that – for the next two months anyway – at No 1 Squadron Kut was now the only Czech. Instead the unit was now being filled with colonials and the New Year saw the arrival of a succession of Canadians and New Zealanders.

Kut had always enjoyed visiting Krátkoruký because his friend's wife was such an excellent cook and towards the end of January Kut himself decided to marry. His fiancée was, of course, Ruby, his sweetheart of almost a year now. The date was arranged for a month hence and the invitations were quickly dispatched. Back came the acceptances. Next door neighbours Lilian and Joe made a light-hearted response to the happy couple: 'The enclosed brings with it our sincere congratulations and good wishes for your future and here's hoping Karel's most important and comprehensive "take-off" will be completely successful and that the crew will soon be delighting in the "Victory Roll"!' For his part, Mac wrote more soberly to Ruby's mother: 'Many thanks for the invitation to your daughter's wedding which I shall be delighted to accept. I sincerely hope no unforeseen circumstance will arise to prevent my coming.' The CO would make it all right, but that would not be true of all Kut's comrades who accepted the invitation.

February 1942 was a traumatic month for No 1 Squadron. In the space of a mere six days, no less than four pilots were lost, two through mishaps and another two in combat.

On 11 February, Sergeant E. G. Parsons, a Canadian, was killed in a particularly silly accident. Since the weather favoured night flying, seven pilots of A Flight went on searchlight cooperation flights. It was slightly hazy near the ground but visibility was good. Yet, on his return from one of these searchlight cooperation trips, Parsons somehow overshot the flare path. He bounced and then opened up his throttle to go round again, but when he was still quite near the ground he selected 'flaps up' instead of 'wheels up'. The Hurricane stalled, touched a tree and then some obstruction wires, and crashed with the engine full on in a field just outside the south-east corner of the airfield. Parsons was killed immediately.

The very next day, Thursday 12 February, No 1 and Kut were involved in the famous Channel Dash. Mac was away for three days at the School of Anti-Aircraft Defence at Shrivenham for a course on searchlight interception procedure and to his chagrin missed all the action.

The Channel Dash was the occasion when Hitler, with amazing boldness, ordered the two battle-cruisers, *Scharnhorst* and *Gneisenau*, and the heavy cruiser, *Prinz Eugen*, to race out of the French port of Brest – where they had been since March 1941 – and sail to Norway which he was convinced the British intended to invade. They were accompanied by a force of six destroyers, 34 E boats and numerous flak ships. Fighter cover was provided by Jagdgeschwader 2 and 26, the sole elements of the Luftwaffe fighter arm left in France after the invasion of Russia in June 1941. They were under the command of Generalleutnant Adolf Galland whose victory score at this time was a staggering 104.

It was an exceptionally well-planned exercise code-named Operation Thunderbolt. So as to achieve surprise, the force left

Brest by night, but this meant passing through the Straits of Dover in daylight. Coastal Command experienced radar faults in both the reconnaissance Hudsons and ashore, so that it was 10.35 am before two Spitfire pilots of 91 Squadron – Group Captain Victor Beamish and Wing Commander Finlay Boyd – on a fighter sweep accidentally spotted the German battle fleet near Le Touquet. The British had long expected such an attempt and had a contingency plan for it called Operation Fuller.

Rather than shout the code-word Fuller which would have saved half an hour, Beamish and Boyd obeyed the rules on radio silence and only upon landing reported their amazing discovery. It was not until 12.25 pm that the British managed to launch the first attack. Six Fairey Swordfish torpedo bombers from the Fleet Air Arm's 825 Squadron took off from Manston and flew at the German ships. No torpedo hits were registered and all of the old bi-planes were destroyed. The leader of the heroic assault, Lieutenant-Commander Eugene Esmonde, was awarded a posthumous Victoria Cross. Throughout the afternoon and on into the evening, a whole series of further attacks were made by the RAF's Coastal, Fighter and Bomber Commands, but a succession of errors, accidents and misfortunes plus low cloud and drizzling rain helped to defeat all efforts.

No 1 Squadron's own involvement in the Channel Dash fiasco came very early in this afternoon and evening of confusion, combat, and casualties. Almost as soon as Beamish and Boyd landed and reported their astonishing find, at 11.40 am the whole squadron was brought into readiness. Less than an hour after Esmonde started his doomed attack, at 1.40 pm part of No 1 Squadron roared off from Tangmere to do its best to stop that formidable fleet. The type of operation was known as a 'roadstead' i.e. a low-level attack on ships.

Six Hurricanes were involved, comprising all the members of A Flight, and a heterogeneous crew it was too: two from Commonwealth countries, two from occupied Europe and two from Britain. In command was the New Zealander Flight Lieutenant W. Raymond. Then there was the South African Flight Sergeant E.F.G. Blair, the only Lithuanian in the RAF Pilot Officer Romas Marcinkus, and the Czech Pilot Officer Karel Kuttelwascher. The only British pilots were Pilot Officers Eustace Sweeting and G.R. Halbeard (known as Ginger).

Twenty-five minutes after take-off, the six Hurricanes

rendezvoused over Hawkinge in Kent with their escort of twelve Spitfires from 129 (Mysore) Squadron from the satellite field at Westhampnett. The formation of eighteen aircraft set a course for 100° and flew together over the Straits of Dover, each of three sections of four Spitfires providing cover to two Hurricanes, flying above and behind them. After only ten minutes, Raymond was heard to announce: 'Target ahead.' There below them were four German ships in line astern steaming north-east. As the Hurricanes swung to the port to attack, the leading vessel sent up a two-colour signal, so the aircraft passed to starboard and flew on for another two or three minutes.

At this point, just north of Dunkirk, three more ships were sighted to the port and like the others were steaming north-east. The difference was that these were destroyers. The RAF pilots were in no position to identify the actual ships now below them, but they were half of the six destroyers of the German Navy's 5th Destroyer Flotilla assigned to the battle fleet: *Richard Beitzen, Paul Jacobi, Friedrich Ihn, Hermann Schoemann, Z.25* and *Z.29.* No sooner had 1 and 129 Squadrons discovered the destroyers than the ships opened fire on the aircraft.

It was 2.30 pm when the Hurricanes launched their attack from the Belgian coast side towards the north-west. The flight of six gradually lost height to a mere 50 feet above the waves as they commenced the fearsome run-in towards the destroyers. They dived to attack from the sides in three sections of two while the Spitfires continued to provide cover, still four of them clinging protectively to each of the sections. As the three German vessels loomed larger and larger, No 1 Squadron's pilots maintained a careful line abreast formation of three pairs. In the centre was the flight commander Raymond accompanied by Sweeting as Red 1 and 2; to port were Kut and Halbeard as Yellow 1 and 2; to starboard were Marcinkus and Blair as White 1 and 2.

The destroyers opened a terrific barrage and the air around the Hurricanes exploded with fire and metal, but No 1 pressed on the attack. As the vessels came racing into close view, each of the sections took one destroyer, opened fire at long range, and closed to less than 100 yards. Wave cutting and cannons blazing, the Hurricanes roared straight on at the ever-closer vessels. Cannon fire raked the sides, decks and superstructure of the ships and many strikes were seen. The most successful of the six was Kut: he clearly saw his shells exploding in the structure just beneath the bridge of his target and back home he claimed the destroyer damaged category III.

At the very last moment, the Hurricanes pulled up and zoomed over the ships, weaving wildly to avoid the shells which mercilessly pursued them. But no one saw White section again and only four Hurricanes landed back at Tangmere at 3.15 pm.

A year or so later, Kut was persuaded to write an article about some of his exploits for a publication called *The Saturday Book*. It is clear from handwritten drafts which the family possess and from the fluency of the English used by the Czech pilot that Ruby gave him a good deal of assistance with the project. The article took the form of a diary – he did not actually keep one – and his first entry was for the Dash. Having set the scene, he went on:

We suddenly saw some destroyers steaming N.E.-wards, and the near one fired some recognition rockets. [Actually the rockets had been fired a few minutes earlier by some other ships.] At that moment one of our flight called out, 'OK Kuttel – they are ours.' I was trying in very bad weather conditions to identify them when suddenly beyond these destroyers I caught sight of some battleships. Above them some fierce fighting was going on between our fighters and some Mes. To our right was the French coast, from where we were already being fired on by A.A. guns, and I realised that the ships were not ours at all, but German ones. Here was our predicament. Should we attack the destroyers or join the fight over the battleships? Our mission was anti-shipping, so we decided to attack the destroyers immediately. Quickly turning to the left and switching on my cannons, I led my section towards the destroyers, flying in open formation.

By now the destroyers had opened fire on us and I could see clearly that the particular destroyer which I was attacking had six guns blazing away at us. My good old Hurricane rocked rather a lot as some shells burst around me, but there is no turning back in a fight and I just kept going straight ahead until I had the whole ship beautifully in my gun sight. I was almost 800 yards away when I first fired, but unfortunately it was a little bit short and hit the water near the destroyer. Pulling the plane up a little and firing with all my cannons, I let the destroyer have it, and saw one of our boys crashing into the sea before I hopped the nose of the destroyer and went dodging from side to side to avoid the shells which were pursuing us relentlessly.

Taken somewhere in the South of England in late 1940 or early 1941 at No. 1 Squadron. Back row: Clowes, Zavoral (Czech), Příhoda (Czech), Elkington, Middle row: Demozay (French), Kuttelwascher (Czech), Novák (Czech), Štefan (Czech), Front row: Hancock, Brown, Chetham, Plášil (Czech).

(*Left*) Arthur Victor 'Darkey' Clowes with his Hurricane I, P3365 JX:B. The wasp motif on the nose had a new stripe added to it for each enemy aircraft he shot down. By the end of the war, his total score was at least 12. (*Right*) Lieutenant Jean Demozay (alias Moses Morlaix) at the controls of his Hawker Hurricane while serving with No. 1 Squadron. By the end of the war he had been awarded the Croix de Guerre with 16 Palms.

(*Right*) Karel Kuttelwascher with his state board for B flight of No. 1 Squadron. Kenley, Jan-March 1941.

(*Below*) State board for B flight of No. 1 Squadron as maintained by Karel Kuttelwascher. Kenley, Jan-March 1941.

(*Facing page*) Karel Kuttelwascher wearing flying gear, probably at Kenley in the early months of 1941.

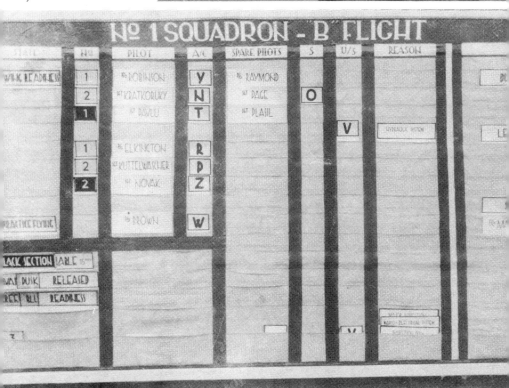

Six Hawker Hurricane IICs o
No. 1 Squadron
photographed over Tangm∈
in September 1941.

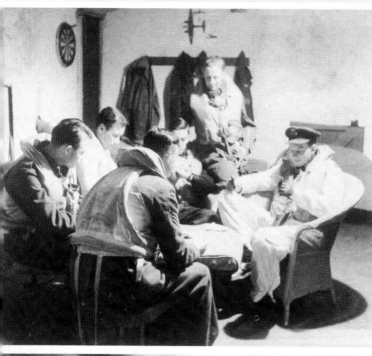

Squadron Leader James
MacLachlan (seated, far rigl
playing cards with some of h
pilots on No. 1 Squadron wh
waiting to go on night
operations.

Squadron Leader James
MacLachlan, DSO, DFC and
Bar, the one-armed
Commanding Officer of No.
Squadron from November
1941 to July 1942. He is seer
here in front of his Hawker
Hurricane IIC, BD983 JX:Q,
decorated with a reminder of
his shooting down over Malta
in February 1941.

On my right, Ginger clung to my tail faithfully and it was not until I tried to call him that I realised my wireless had gone. I wanted to tell him to open formation as we afforded the gunners too good a target by flying together, but Ginger stuck to me like glue. All my ammunition was gone, so the only thing to do now was to make tracks for home, with Ginger following. We had to be careful in beating a retreat, as there were plenty of enemy fighters around. We kept a sharp look out in all directions. I must say I was perturbed to see two Mes flying in the same direction as us about 500 yards to our left. This was certainly a tight corner, but we were very lucky, and the Mes turned to the left, apparently without having seen us. I can imagine now what an easy prey we would have been with no ammo, no wireless and very little petrol. The prospect of an icy bath in the North Sea did not appeal to me at all and what a relief it was to see the two Mes turning left and making their way back towards the French coast.

Without any further incident, Ginger and I reached the English coast and before very long arrived at our base. I was very anxious to know whether all our flight was safe, as I had lost sight of them since we first went in to attack. After reporting to the Intelligence Officer, I waited for a couple of hours, hoping that maybe they would turn up. Two of our boys came back soon after Ginger and me, but we heard later that one of the two who didn't return was a prisoner of war, and the other missing.

Kut noted flatly in his flight log: 'We lost Marcinkus and Blair.'

As he made his own attack, Flight Lieutenant Raymond had noticed a great ball of fire around Hurricane Z3774 as Blair, the South African, went down in flames. One of the squadron's groundcrew, Stan Greenwood, remembers the occasion:

> You didn't dwell on deaths. In fact we were all wondering what had happened to Blair's badge. He was very well off and had a squadron badge made in London: there was a ruby on the central figure '1' and diamonds on the wings sprouting from either side. It was rumoured to be worth £500 at the time. Blair always wore the badge on his jacket and I presume he had it with him when he was shot down.

The Lithuanian Romas Marcinkus had written to Ruby's mother only seven days previously: 'P/O R. Marcinkus has much pleasure in accepting Mr & Mrs Thomas' so very kind invitation to the wedding of their daughter Ruby and hopes that his duties will permit him to be present.' Regretfully it was now apparent that they would not.

Marcinkus was thought at the time to have ditched his Hurricane BD949 into the Channel. However, recent research by Bryan Philpott has unearthed photographs in the Bundesarchiv Koblenz indicating that in fact the Lithuanian managed to make the French coast, so it seems likely that he was able to avoid serious damage. It is suggested that he became disorientated during the charge and, following his attack, became separated from the rest of the flight and in the resultant confusion flew a reciprocal bearing. His damaged Hurricane was recovered from the sea by a German salvage team and broken down for scrap in France.

Marcinkus himself was taken prisoner and two years later, on 25 March 1944, he was one of 80 Allied prisoners-of-war involved in 'the Great Escape' from Tunnel Harry at Stalag Luft III. Once free of the prison camp, Marcinkus travelled north towards the Baltic and home, but he was recaptured near Danzig (nowadays called Gdanzk). In fact the great majority of those involved in the escape were recaptured and some 50 of them, including Marcinkus, were brutally executed by the Gestapo.

While the six Hurricanes of No 1 Squadron's A Flight were tackling the destroyers, the twelve Spitfires of 129 Squadron were doing their best to protect their charges but they too sustained casualties; one pilot and two aircraft were lost.

Elsewhere over the Channel, No 1 Squadron's B Flight had a much less eventful involvement in the Dash. A quarter of an hour after the rest of the squadron had left Tangmere, five Hurricanes from B Flight – there were three British and two Canadian pilots – took off and set course for Hawkinge, but they could not locate the main fleet or the rest of the squadron. They opened up an attack on some E-boats accompanying the flotilla and then landed at Manston, considering that they would be of more use at this forward field if required again.

In the Channel Dash incident, the Royal Air Force and the Fleet Air Arm flung into the air no less than 675 aircraft. They lost a total of 21 bombers, 6 torpedo bombers and 17 fighters, while claiming to have destroyed 17 of the Luftwaffe's fighters.

As for the *Scharnhorst* and *Gneisenau*, they were both damaged by mines before being forced to seek the refuge of Kiel. The *Gneisenau* never did put to sea again because two weeks later Bomber Command reduced her to a wreck, while two years after the Dash the *Scharnhorst* was sunk in action in the Barents Sea. That February only the *Prinz Eugen* succeeded in reaching Norway and a short time later it was then crippled by a submarine's torpedo and had to limp back to base. In any event, Hitler was wrong to be so concerned about the defence of Norway: the Allies never intended to attack there.

Four days after the Dash, on 16 February, the Mayor of Brighton lunched in the Officers' Mess of No 1 Squadron and afterwards he was invited to view his town from the air. Mac – now back from his course – used a Miles Magister, a dual control machine designed for training purposes, for the flight. It was then agreed that the Mayor's secretary, George Martin, undertake a similar sight-seeing exercise and so Pilot Officer Eustace Sweeting took him up for a short ten-minute trip. On the landing approach, however, something went wrong with the aircraft and it crashed in a field just west of the airfield killing instantly both Sweeting and Martin. A particular irony of this awful accident was that only days before Sweeting had followed his section leader and flight commander Raymond into the metallic hail thrown up by the German destroyers and survived.

A few days after the Channel Dash incident, Flight Lieutenant Raymond was posted to No 61 OTU so, on 17 February, Pilot Officer Kuttelwascher became 'Acting Flight Lieutenant (non-substantive)' and took command of A Flight. This meant that he had jumped the intermediate rank of flying officer and it turned out to be a wedding present from the RAF that could not have been more welcome.

Kut and Ruby were married at 11.30 am on Saturday, 21 February 1942, exactly one year to the day after they had first met. The ceremony was held at the Union Church, Mill Hill in North London with a reception in the 'Hunters Horn'. Best man was Kut's brother Jan and the groomsmen were Ruby's two brothers, Ken and Phil Thomas, and her brother-in-law, Horace Evans. Among the guests were Kut's Commanding Officer and friend, Squadron Leader James MacLachlan, the other flight commander, J.M. Crabb, and three other officers from the squadron. Among the many telegrams, that from friends Floss and Walter was particularly tongue-in-cheek: 'Here's to a perfect take-off, a smooth flight and no engine trouble.'

The couple honeymooned with Ruby's brother Ken and his wife Ivy at Barry, South Wales, about 50 miles south-east of the village where Ruby spent her childhood, but it was a short sojourn because a week later Kut was back at Tangmere and in the air once more.

It is clear that, right from the beginning of his marriage, Kut brought the same sort of discipline to relations with his wife that he experienced in his service with the RAF. In a radio broadcast made by Kut and Ruby two years later, he explained why he insisted that from the start his wife live in London rather than on the base:

Ruby: The first question to decide was where should we live. One of my friends had moved to live near the station where her husband was based. I felt that I also would like to be somewhere near Karel, but on this he was quite firm.

Kut: If I wasn't flying there'd be nothing I'd like better but, as things are, I'd prefer you to stay in London.

Friend: That's nonsense, Karel. What about me? I'm flying but it makes life a lot more bearable to know that Sheila will be there when I get back from a trip.

Kut: We're probably different, John. I can only speak for myself, and I know in this job that I must be firm with myself if I'm to do it well.

Friend: Well, anyway, I think you're being very unfair to Ruby.

Ruby: I don't agree, John. I think Karel is perfectly right. If it helps him to be a better pilot by my staying away, then I'm quite willing.

Friend: I don't follow his argument at all. After all, it isn't as if you were the hysterical sort who'd make things difficult for him . . .

Kut: That's not the point, John. I'd find it quite impossible to dissociate myself from any personal relationship for a couple of hours, so my mind would be divided during that time and I'd be a less efficient pilot.

Friend: As an intellectual theory, all that sounds very clever, but I don't think it means anything.

Kut: All right, we'll just leave it at that. But another thing I feel is that if there should be . . . well, an accident . . . it makes things a lot more difficult for the wife and for the officers who have to break the news to her.

Sheila: That's where I think you're quite wrong, Karel. I'd rather know the worst right away than have it second-hand.

Ruby: I wouldn't . . . it would't be quite such a blow I think if one got it second-hand. And I'm sure I wouldn't want to be a nuisance to the station officers if anything did happen.
Kut: All right then, we decide on London, and I'll fly home to see you as often as I can.

In the circumstances, Ruby had little choice but to remain at Mill Hill with her mother and a fox terrier called Connor for company. It seems that she knew what to expect. A reporter with the *People* noted about an interview with Kut:

He does not smile often, but he did when I asked him what Mrs Kuttelwascher thought of his flying. 'That was arranged before we were married,' he said. 'I told her I must be a flier first and a husband afterwards.' He has kept to that arrangement. 'I feel restless if I am away,' he said. 'The only time I am happy at home is when the weather is too bad for flying. Then I know I am not missing anything.'

A month after the wedding, No 1 Squadron commenced the hazardous night intruder operations for which they had been training for so long and which were to make Kut's name so well-known throughout the homes of Britain.

CHAPTER SEVEN

Night Intruder Tactics

The night intruder operation was a specialist exercise requiring a pilot with keen eyesight, cool nerves, and the ability to seize a chance that would only last seconds. It involved flying a lone fighter over to the enemy's own airfields and seeking to destroy his bombers as they were landing or taking off. As such, it was a particularly furtive activity where success came from striking an opponent in the back when he was least expecting it.

It was actually the Germans who started night intrusion in July 1940. The concept came from a report filed a few weeks earlier by Hauptmann Wolfgang Falck who was put in charge of the Luftwaffe's first official night fighter unit, 1 Gruppe Nachtjagdgeschwader 1 (I/NJG 1). In September 1940, I/NJG 2 was formed specifically for the Fernenachtjagd role of long-range intruding: the unit's top scorer was Wilhelm Beier with 14 night victories. However, by end of 1941, the increasing number of raids on Germany caused Hitler to order the cessation of the Luftwaffe's night intruding over Britain.

As the war progressed and the Allies took more of the offensive, the RAF started its own night intruder operations. These were started by the Hurricanes of 87 Squadron in March 1941. They were then continued by several different squadrons throughout the remainder of the year and well into 1942. One particularly able pilot at the task was Flight Lieutenant John Shaw who flew with No 3 Squadron and destroyed five enemy aircraft. However, No 1 Squadron was the unit that led the way in these sorties during 1942 and Kut soon put even Shaw's score in the shadows.

The Hurricanes of No 1 Squadron commenced their intruder operations on 1 April 1942 and continued them until 2 July 1942, when a few days later the squadron left Tangmere to move north prior to converting to Hawker Typhoons. Usually intruder activity took place during the two weeks around a full moon, known by the pilots involved as 'the moon period': the moon assisted flying as well as location of enemy bombers. During No 1's three-month period of night intrusion, there were four full moons: 1 April, 30

April, 30 May and 28 June. Such preoccupation with the moon is perhaps more characteristic of psychotics than pilots and maybe one had to be a little of a lunatic to venture alone over enemy territory, but Kut and the others delighted at the chance to visit the Germans in their own backyard and were eager to show what damage they could wreak.

As they waited for an operation, intruder pilots would tend not to read or write because the whiteness of the page would have dulled their vision. Indeed some pilots would prepare for such sorties by wearing 'dimmer' glasses – goggles with dark lenses – which protected their eyes from lights and accustomed them to the darkness which lay ahead. It was a rather bizarre sight to see aircrew sitting around casually in such forbidding facial attire. Often the time would be passed playing cards. If a No 1 pilot was slow to deal his card or appeared to be cheating, Mac would swing his artificial limb at the offending colleague, causing some pain to the recipient of the blow but tension-relieving amusement to the others.

In the course of the year or so that the RAF carried out these night intruder operations, the tactics rapidly went through various phases before settling on a combination of all of them.

At first the RAF waited for watchers on the coast to notify them that German bombers were on the way across the Channel seeking English targets. As soon as the Luftwaffe was over here, a few pilots would then set off singly and head for the Continent. They had to guess, from the direction of the bombers, which airfields the Germans were using. They would circle the enemy's bases waiting for the Luftwaffe bombers to return. When the Germans did come back, they were at their most vulnerable: low on fuel, possibly the ammunition used up, and the crews tired and unsuspecting. The navigation lights and the slow speed of the bombers as they descended to the ground and the lights on the runway all assisted the British pilot in locating and destroying the enemy.

The next phase came when it was decided to take more of the initiative, fly over to France early in the night, and try to find German bombers as they were actually taking off. This was a riskier kind of operation: the German crews were alert and the ammunition racks were full of rounds. Yet it had the marvellous advantage that, if successful, the sortie not only destroyed the enemy aircraft but its bomb load which could not then be dropped on English targets.

The third phase grew up when the intruders could not find any aircraft to hit and, rather than return with the rubber sheaths still over the protruding cannon barrels, they looked for trains to attack. Railway lines usually stood out well in the black-out because they were so much straighter than roads. Trains betrayed themselves by red and yellow sparks from the engine and by plumes of smoke which gave the pilot some indication of wind direction and strength. The RAF told its pilots that the Germans imposed a strict curfew on the French and would not allow them to travel by night, so normally pilots would have no compunction about strafing the wagons or carriages as well as the engines.

In many respects, Kut was the exception among night intruders. From the very start, he went looking for bombers taking off as well as landing and his interest was always much more in enemy aircraft than trains. His personal success was uncanny.

In fact, the chances of finding and finishing German aircraft were low. Night after night many of the pilots would not even see an enemy aircraft, let alone engage or destroy one. The errant Czech was known to visit no less than five German airfields before finding a bomber. The Luftwaffe aircraft often returned to a different airfield than the one from which they had taken off and they had something like twenty bases from which to choose. So trains were the more frequent target for the Hurricanes' cannon and beating up a locomotive would ease the pilots' disappointment at not finding something more substantial.

The intruder operation was a lonely and dangerous kind of mission which has had too little coverage in the history books. Unlike the Douglas Havocs and de Havilland Mosquitoes which also performed night intruder operations, the Hurricanes had one engine and a single crew member. If the Merlin engine failed or the aircraft was badly damaged, the pilot would have to crash-land his aircraft and he was on his own. Navigation was almost by 'feel'. The pilot had to have one hand permanently on the control column and the Hurricane only had two little red cockpit lights, so there was no way to unfold cumbersome maps or – if one could – see them at all distinctly. Each aircraft was invariably alone, flying over enemy territory in the vicinity of well-defended airfields in circumstances which made them visible to the Germans. It is astonishing that there were not more fatalities.

What was it like to fly a night intruder operation? It has not proved possible to contact any of the No 1 Squadron pilots who flew them: only nineteen were involved; four of them died in the course of this risky period of operations; others died later in the war; and the rest are either now dead or have not been traced. Nevertheless, several pilots from No 43 Squadron – the 'Fighting Cocks' – have been contacted. Of course other pilots on other squadrons flew such sorties, but the relevance to Kut's story of the experience of 43's men is that the squadron flew the same kind of operation in the same type of aircraft from the same airfield within nights of No 1 ceasing night intrusion. In 1942, No 1 flew night intrusion from Tangmere from the beginning of April to early July and then 43 Squadron took over from early July to the end of August.

One of 43's intruders was Harry Lea who, like Kut, became a BEA pilot after the war although they never met because he was based in Jersey. He now lives in Portugal and he still flies Piper Aztec G-FOTO doing air-to-air photography with Arthur Gibson as the cameraman. He outlines the basic characteristics of night intruder operations:

Our operations took place on moonlit nights only and we had our various areas to patrol. After take-off, we remained low and flew south across the Channel at about 50 ft, this of course to avoid the German radar screen. Before reaching the French coast, we climbed fairly rapidly to about 6,000 ft to cross the coastal defences and then back down to low level to our patrol area. Navigation was the big problem in a single-seat aircraft and took quite a good deal of concentration (no nav-aids or auto-pilot). However, we did become adept at finding our way around.

There were occasions weather-wise when conditions were very hazy, and you could get reflections of the moon on ground water which gave a peculiar effect and tended, if you were not careful, to cause disorientation and this was rather disconcerting. Also, you could see the blurred shadow of your own aircraft on the haze which at times upset your concentration. Trains were prime targets, and the squadron as a whole had a reasonable success rate. Very often, on our return to base, we spent a little while flying into the moon [that is, looking down the moon's reflection track on the water] along the French coast looking for shipping movements and reporting back to our intelligence. Our return again was at low level usually landing back at Tangmere without the aid of lights in case of any prowling enemy aircraft.

These ex-43 men are certainly a scattered lot and the next intruder account comes from New Zealander Jack Torrance. He indicates just how difficult was night intrusion and how exceptional were the achievements of Kut and Mac:

As I was a very new pilot on 43 Squadron when we moved from Acklington to Tangmere about the end of June 1942, I was very impressed by the charisma of Kuttelwascher and MacLachlan as the masters of the intruding art. I realised fairly soon that they were in fact the only real exponents of that particular form of night attacks on enemy aircraft. Apart from the two aces, a typical night intruder trip would be something like this.

Briefing about dusk, giving German airfields which might be in use that night, courses to fly, emergency R/T channels, met. report and so on. Strict R/T silence applied except in emergency. Across the Channel at the minimum altitude possible under the existing weather conditions, which could be a bit nerve-racking if one encountered low cloud. Never having been over France in daylight at this time, I found map-reading quite difficult. If one maintained a steady course, a series of lights appeared on the ground along one's track, operated by the German plotter organisation. This was to guide German night-fighters towards intruding aircraft, but if one did a 360° turn this temporarily confused the spotters, and the lights on the ground went out. On the occasions I was over France at night, I saw several airfields with flarepaths on, but on each occasion, as soon as I approached, all the lights of the airfield were extinguished and at no time did I see any aircraft.

Being so inexperienced then, I found each time that, after a few such manoeuvres, I was completely lost and, once out over the Channel, I had to climb until I could get a homing to Tangmere. I did not encounter it myself, but flying very low over the Channel on a clear moonlight night with the surface of the water unruffled was quite hazardous, as it was difficult to judge one's height above the water. This was evidenced by the loss of Ronnie Whitten, an experienced New Zealand flight sergeant pilot on 43, who flew into the Channel when returning on such a clear night from France.

From discussions with other pilots at that time, I think my experience was fairly typical of all except a few, like Kuttelwascher and MacLachlan, who knew the French countryside intimately by day and night and could easily find the airfields even on the darkest night. Added to this navigational expertise, of course, in the case of the two aces was their skill and determination as fighter pilots and their marksmanship. We were told at the time by the Intelligence Officers that, although we had very little in the way of concrete success with our intruding efforts, German pilots were quite disturbed by those losses they suffered just when they had felt safe at home and also by the number of diversions away from their home bases. In short, I thought then, and I still think at this distance, that the intruding efforts of most of us were mainly of psychological value and that, without the successes of Kuttelwascher and MacLachlan, even that value would have been much less.

Another former 43 Squadron intruder who is a New Zealander is Morrie Smith. His account of night intrusion emphasizes the considerable difficulties simply of navigating oneself to and from the enemy's base, let alone locating and destroying one or more of his bombers:

We flew to and from our targets using dead reckoning navigation and I found that, after stooging around my target for a time, I very easily became dis-orientated. I found that this was particularly the case when looking for railway engines around such a railway junction as Béthune. After flying up and down railway lines in all directions, I found that I really had to think: where am I and how do I get out? The reciprocal course which I had plotted way back at Tangmere was maybe originating from a location possibly 50 miles away at Béthune. Kut did not have this problem because of his familiarity with the French countryside and aerodromes. MacLachlan had a similar knowledge of France which would have assisted him to find his way around and so contribute to his success as an intruder pilot.

We pilots were each night given a target aerodrome. Each pilot would then plot a dead reckoning course both ways. For example, my intruder trips were usually to Chartres. I would plot a course to the French coast, to say le Tréport, and fly south from there using a U-shaped loop in the Seine river [at Les Andelys] as a navigational check. Homeward I would fly to the French coast near Caen (hopefully) and then fly north to Tangmere. Although on a couple of occasions I saw an aircraft fly over

the drome, by the time that I turned to intercept, their navigation lights were out and they had vanished. They were probably
trying to draw me away from the drome to allow their bombers
to land. Operations at this time stated that returning bombers
were nightly being diverted from aerodromes because of the presence of intruder aircraft around their home bases.

One lasting memory is of the solitude and complete loneliness
I felt after crossing the coast and flying deep into France. The
cockpit was blacked out except for essential flying instruments,
the radio was dead (because of the low altitudes flown), and
outside – except for the shine of rivers and railway lines and the
very occasional light – all was pitch black. At this time, 43
Squadron was both day and night operational and I know that
all we pilots had above average or exceptional night vision.
Although I would fly around for sometimes one or two hours
over France, I can say that I had extreme difficulty in identifying
anything on the ground – woods, villages or towns – and I would
think that the other pilots had the same problems. An intruder
pilot in a single-seater aircraft was certainly 'on his own' over
France.

Freddie Lister too was a night intruder pilot with 43 Squadron. He
shared the tension and the frustration of such operations:

You would sit at the dispersal hut on readiness for hours on end
wearing very dark glasses to prepare you for a 'scramble' into a
dark airfield and somehow this added to the tension. Another
form of tension was that, being a day fighter squadron and being
used to flying in pairs, when one of the squadron failed to return
nobody knew the reason. Did he fly too low and hit a power
cable, or too high and be picked up by radar and flak? On my
first mission in bright moonlight, I got the fright of my life when
I looked down and saw an aircraft below me, only to find out that
it was my own shadow. This made me feel very naked as I felt
that, if I could see myself, then the whole of the German defences
could see me. One then feels very much alone.

I found no aircraft but destroyed two trains. Being a moonlight night, it was usually cold on the ground and the steam and
smoke from the train lay on the ground and in the valley, so you
could 'track' a train for many miles and then 'prang' it. The
squadron was on intruder ops for approximately two months and

no aircraft were found or destroyed, but quite a few trains were destroyed. One can only hope that the fact that we were in the area of landing fields caused panic and hopefully some aircraft crashed. Karel was the 'master' and a very brave man. We all wished we would have been half as skilful.

The blow-by-blow account of No 1 Squadron's intruder operations which follows reveals how much Mac trusted his pilots and how much initiative he was willing to allow them. This applied especially to Kut who was allowed to fly almost whenever and wherever he wanted as a kind of freelance operator. This can be contrasted with the practice of No 43 Squadron as revealed by another of this squadron's intruder pilots, Godfrey Ball, known to all his RAF colleagues as Albert after the First World War fighter ace. At the end of the war he returned to Australia and, now in his seventies, is never happier than when flying either a Pitts Special or a Decathlon, the only aircraft now available to him with the capability of sustained inverted flight as well as other aerobatic manoeuvres. From Australia, he writes:

Kut's CO, Squadron Leader James MacLachlan, and ours, Squadron Leader Daniel du Vivier (a Belgian), did not see eye to eye with one another, so squadron contacts were kept to a minimum. There seems to have been an interesting difference in the way the two squadrons conducted their intruder operations. It would appear that No 1 Squadron pilots were allowed to roam all over France and select their own aerodromes for investigation and possible action. With us, the job was very rigidly defined. The aerodromes to be patrolled were written up on the board and the pilot detailed to 'intrude' any one of them would have his name written alongside. The time of take-off was decided by Operations Staff who would ring through to the squadron – probably on the advice of Intelligence. We were obliged to remain in or near the circuit area of our designated aerodrome for one hour. According to the fuel we had left at the end of the patrol, we could go 'train-busting' or have a go at any target which attracted us.

Of course 'Old Kut's' feats were known to us all and I know that they inspired me with hope that I too might meet with some success. But our squadron score for the two months we were at Tangmere as far as intruder work was concerned was nil! I myself enjoyed night operations and always regretted that we were given the job too late. Although the Hurricanes we used were the same noisy, manoeuvreable, fighter-designed aeroplanes which had distinguished themselves so brilliantly during the Battle of Britain, their black shapes now slipped stealthily over the enemy-held countryside. There was always the promise of being able suddenly to spring upon our prey, and momentarily to illuminate the blackness with the flames from the cannon sweeping backwards over the wing surface, and then watch the shells send the unsuspecting victim crashing into the ground. I never thought of human beings being involved, nor did I dwell upon the tragedy of death. I only relished the thrill which is instinctive in so many of us – the thrill of the hunter stalking his prey.

Clearly night intrusion was something special and it required a particular kind of aircraft. Fortunately such an aircraft was to hand in the Hurricane.

CHAPTER EIGHT

The 'Night Reaper'

At the time of its intruder operations, No 1 Squadron was equipped with the Hawker Hurricane IIC. This mark first flew on 6 February 1941 and entered service in the late spring of 1941. Of all Hurricane versions, it was the one built in greatest numbers: 4,711 were constructed in Britain, the majority at Langley. This Hurricane was powered by a Rolls-Royce Merlin XX engine and had a maximum speed of 330–336 mph and a service ceiling of 35,600 feet. No 1 had been re-equipped with the Hurricane IIC during July and August 1941.

The Hurricane was not a particular success as a night fighter but it proved very suitable as a night intruder. As one of 43 Squadron's night intruder pilots, Harry Lea, puts it:

> The Hurricane IIC was a splendid aircraft for the job in hand. It had range with its two 45 gallon wing 'drop tanks', excellent armament with four 20 mm cannon, and it was a tough, solid aircraft that could withstand a great deal of punishment and still survive. This latter point was proved at the Dieppe Raid when we suffered severely from ground fire and all but two aircraft returned, of which five sustained varying degrees of damage, one of these you would wonder how it managed to stay in the air.

His colleague, Freddie Lister, shares this enthusiasm for the Hurricane: 'It was just the aircraft for intruder operations: a good view, a wonderful engine and easy to fly.'

There were three features which particularly distinguished the intruder Hurricanes from the ones flown by 1 and 43 Squadrons in the Battle of Britain: armament, fuel, and colour.

The IIC was fitted with four 20 mm cannon, two in either wing, in place of the eight or twelve Browning machine guns on the earlier marks. These cannon were either French Hispano or Swiss Oerlikon guns. It was immediately obvious that a Hurricane was a IIC because its cannon protruded so far out of the leading edge of the wings – the overall length of the guns was 8 ft 2½ in – and the recoil springs stood out along the barrels. These protruding cannon had rubber covers like over-sized condoms, so that it was a simple matter for ground crew to see if a returning pilot had used his weapons.

On No 1's intruder aircraft, the cannon's ammunition consisted of equal quantities of high explosive (HE) and ball (20 mm or 0.787 in). The former exploded on impact to create a hole in the enemy aircraft and the latter was a solid steel missile designed to pierce the plating of the German planes. They alternated in the belt and, at a muzzle velocity of 2,880 feet per second, it did not take them long to reach their target. Many think of the fighter aircraft of the last war as having a considerable volume of ammunition. In fact, the available firing time of a Hurricane armed with cannon was even less than that of one with machine guns, although of course there was much more power in the punch. The IICs carried a total of 364 rounds (91 per cannon) which – with an approximate rate of fire of 600–650 rounds per minute – was only long enough for about nine seconds firing. So every second had to count and in Kut's case it most certainly did.

Like all fighter armament, the IIC's cannon were aligned to focus at a point some way ahead of the aircraft. The original Hurricane had its machine guns aligned to converge at a point about 650 yards ahead, but later the distance was reduced to 400 yards. Finally, at the insistence of Squadron Leader P.J.H. Halahan (the Commanding Officer of No 1 Squadron until May 1940), the alignment was further reduced to 250 yards. Consequently, Kut's combat reports tend to describe his Hurricane as at a particular position when he fired his cannon. Obviously he positioned himself behind the enemy, so as to escape observation, and a little above or below, so as to hit the fuselage, and his usual mode of attack was to tuck in close and fire from a distance of 100–200 yards.

Use of cannon could be colourful. Godfrey Ball of 43 Squadron recalls:

When shooting up trains, the cannon shells would ricochet from both the engine strikes and from the permanent way (if you undershot when aiming at the guards van) and looked remarkably like flak – blue, red, green and white. It almost seemed at times as if I were going to fly into my own bullets!

(*Right*) A wedding day photograph of Acting Flight Lieutenant Karel Kuttelwascher and his bride Ruby Thomas. The ceremony was held at the Union Church, Mill Hill in North London on 21 February 1942.

(*Below*) A Hawker Hurricane IIC with four cannon and twin drop tanks of the kind flown by Flight Lieutenant Karel Kuttelwascher on his night intruder operations. This particular aircraft belonged to No. 87 Squadron (United Provinces) and was called 'Night Duty'. Its pilot was Sergeant B. Bawden from Sydney, Australia.

A Dornier Do 217 aircraft. Karel Kuttelwascher destroyed eight aircraft of this kind.

Three Junkers Ju 88 aircraft. Karel Kuttelwascher destroyed two aircraft of this kind.

Three Heinkel He111 bombers. Karel Kuttelwascher destroyed five German aircraft of this kind, three of them on one night over St. André.

Official Air Ministry portrait of Flight Lieutenant Karel Kuttelwascher drawn by Eric
Kennington in 1942 and now held in Czechoslovakia.

Flight Lieutenant Karel Kuttlewascher shaking hands with his Commanding Officer, Squadron Leader James MacLachlan. Between them, they had just shot down 20 of the 22 night intruder kills achieved by No. 1 Squadron.

Squadron Leader Max Aitken, Commanding Officer of 68 Squadron, and Air Vice Marshal Karel Janoušek, Inspector General of the Czech Air Force, together with Squadron Leader James MacLachlan and Flight Lieutenant Karel Kuttelwascher. Note: the Czech pilots badge on the right breast pocket of all four men.

The intruder operations over the Continent required plenty of fuel and so No 1 Squadron's Hurricane IICs were fitted with two 45-gallon drop tanks, one under each wing. This additional 90 gallons of fuel, added to the 66 gallons in the two main tanks carried in the wings and the 28 gallons in the reserve tank located between the engine and the cockpit, provided a total of 184 gallons and took the overall combat weight to around 8,000 lbs. If necessary, these drop tanks could be jettisoned by pulling a lever on the starboard side of the cockpit (what American pilots on long range Mustangs would later call, in characteristically colourful language, 'punching your babies'). 43 Squadron Hurricane intruder, Harry Lea, points out: 'Before carrying out an attack, we used to jettison our long range tanks. This was because when empty, or partially empty, they were lethal when struck by enemy fire.' So invariably the pilot – having started and taken off in the normal way on the main tanks – would use the fuel in these additional tanks before switching to his main tanks in case he had later to release the drop tanks.

Another of the 43 Squadron intruder pilots, Godfrey Ball, recalls a particular problem about flying a Hurricane with drop tanks:

This extra 90 gallons just about doubled our endurance in flying time. I always aimed to use this extra fuel up first. As we had no gauges for these extra tanks, it was necessary to time how long they had been in use very carefully for, if they ran dry, one was likely to get an air lock in the fuel system which, while not being disastrous, was very frightening especially at night. The Hurricane was fitted with a 28 gallon gravity tank which, when turned on, got rid of air locks very quickly, and it was fitted mainly for this purpose as air locks could also be caused by draining the main wing tanks. I allowed for a consumption of 60 gallons per hour so, when they had been on for an hour and a half, I would operate on the normal tanks. When actually in an area of possible combat, I always used the wing tanks rather than the auxiliaries.

One night over France, I ran the 'long range' tanks dry by mistake and got an awful fright. I was only at about 500 feet when the red fuel warning light came on like a huge beacon in the darkened cockpit and at the same time the engine faded out. I had turned the reserve tank on in less than a 'split second' but, although the engine responded quite readily, it seemed to me that it would never come good. It was only then that I found out how long 'immediate' could be, for the good book said that under such circumstances turning the petrol cock on to 'gravity' would bring an immediate response!

The price of having drop tanks was a certain loss of manoeuvreability. As 43 Squadron pilot, Jack Torrance, notes: 'The old Hurricane gave a feeling of great reliability and steadiness, although it was sluggish in the air with the drop-tanks full.' Of course the benefit of the drop tanks was increased range. The combined fuel volume of 184 gallons enabled an operation to last – at a normal average consumption rate of around 50–60 gallons an hour – about 3–3½ hours and to cover – at an optimum cruising speed of about 170 mph – a range of around 900 miles. Since up to half the intruder pilot's fuel could be used reaching and returning from the general target area, his maximum time over the German bases would be around two hours. However, any action would increase fuel consumption and reduce the time available in the air and, in fact, a more typical sortie would be about 2–2½ hours overall. Kut's longest intruder operation lasted 3 hours 5 minutes.

Now three or more hours was quite a long time to spend sitting in the fairly confined space of a Hurricane cockpit and some of the intruder pilots used to joke that an essential characteristic of those carrying out such operations should be a tough posterior.

Fortunately, one of the attractive features of the Hurricane for its intruder role was that its cockpit was a little more spacious than that of some other fighter aircraft. Morrie Smith flew intruder operations with 43 Squadron and insists:

> The Hurricane IIC was a very easy aircraft to fly and a good gun platform. Since the cockpit was so roomy, a pilot had room to stretch – a very welcome exercise for a pilot compelled to sit for 3–4 hours on an uncomfortable dinghy attached to a parachute. For some reason the escape equipment in the dinghy seemed after a while to be all edges and most uncomfortable!

Of course, limitation of space was not the only problem for pilots flying such long sorties: there were the calls of nature. The rigger of Mac's machine, Sydney Sharp, remembers how the CO used to take the precaution of urinating near the tail of the aircraft before setting out on an intruder operation.

There is some slight doubt about the colour scheme used for the intruder version of the Hurricane IIC. Although there is no photographic evidence, it seems likely that some of No 1 Squadron's intruder aircraft were painted matt black all over (except for red spinner) and certainly this was true of the 43 Squadron intruders. It was appreciated that a matt finish on the aircraft could increase 'drag' and therefore reduce top speed, yet the intruder, unlike the interceptor, did not depend on speed but on concealment. However, most of No 1 Squadron's machines – including Kut's – were flown in a hybrid day and night scheme: upper and side surfaces in dark green and dark grey (day fighter) camouflage with lower surfaces including fuel tanks all black and no underwing roundels (night fighter). Codes were in dull red and serial numbers in black with a tail band in duck egg green. The overall effect was to turn the machines into deadly looking things: dark, forbidding, almost evil.

Nevertheless, the aircraft could still give itself away in the darkness because the exhaust manifolds used to glow red hot, so part of the maintenance routine was to apply very thick red lead paint to the manifolds. As 43 Squadron pilot, Jack Torrance, comments: 'Even with the flame-shields over the exhaust, I found the flickering blue flames strangely comforting over the water but, once over the French coast, one felt very conspicuous in the night sky.' His squadron colleague, Morrie Smith, makes the same point: 'I felt that everyone for miles around could see the exhaust stubs glowing in the night, but the anti-glare cowlings protected the pilot's night vision from this glow.'

Godfrey Ball, another 43 intruder, remembers a disturbing occasion on the return from an operation:

As I descended deeper into the cloud, I experienced a frightening phenomenon: the whole inside of the cockpit was lit up by a red glow. My immediate reaction was 'Fire!' But there was no heat and all my instruments showed everything to be in order, so I ventured to look outside. My two exhaust manifolds were belching out the usual flame, made perhaps a trifle more red and less blue from being throttled back, and this source had illuminated the surrounding very dense cloud. It was an eerie sensation but, once I knew what it was all about, it ceased to trouble me.

Kut's particular Hurricane at the time of No 1 Squadron's intruder operations had the squadron code letters JX:E – the designation of his aircraft since the beginning of June 1941. At this stage of the war, in RAF parlance E was for Edward, the christian name of the Czech President Beneš and the name chosen by Kut a few months later for his son.

Kut's mount had the serial number BE581, although by the time of the intruder operations the black rudder and wing panel were replacement components from Turbinlite flight Hurricane BD770. Hurricane BE581 started its service life on 26 October 1941 when it was taken on charge by the RAF's No 29 Maintenance Unit and then, after two months of checking and testing, it was delivered to No 1 Squadron on 28 December 1941. The first record of Kut flying it was on 22 January 1942 and three weeks later he used it on his involvement in the Channel Dash. Subsequently he flew this aircraft on every single one of his intruder operations which is a sterling tribute to the most able maintenance crew who serviced it during those tough three months.

Kut really cared for his Hurricane and for the magnificent men who worked on it. Before his death, one of the mechanics with No 1 Squadron, Frank Wooley, declared about the Czech: 'He would come to the maintenance flight frequently – most other pilots never ventured near – and ask about the aircraft, especially when his own was in for servicing.'

At perhaps the height of his success when he received his first DFC, Kut had an emblem painted on the starboard side of the engine cowling of his Hurricane. It depicted a scythe in yellow and across it a banner in red carrying the name 'Night Reaper', a gruesome image which reflected his acute sense of vengeance.

A similarly named aircraft in the war was 'Grim Reaper'. This was a Mosquito with 109 Squadron – code HS:F and serial number DK333 – which had on the nose a Father Time character carrying a scythe. It was probably this aircraft which was confused with Kut's in Michael Shaw's book *Twice Vertical* because in that publication the Czech's Hurricane is described wrongly as depicting 'an emaciated Father Time wrapped in the Czechoslovakian flag'. If Kut was not alone in using the same 'Reaper', equally other wartime aircraft carried versions of the scythe motif: Pilot Officer McKnight of 242 Squadron flew a Hurricane in the Battle of Britain which had painted on it a scythe dripping with blood.

Five weeks after night intrusion ended and Kut left the unit,

BE581 was re-assigned from No 1 Squadron – which was converted to Typhoons – to No 486 Squadron, the New Zealand night intruder unit, and then after merely a week to No 253 Squadron known as the Hyderabad Squadron. Only two weeks later, it passed to its last squadron, 532, a unit on Turbinlite duty. On 7 November 1942, the New Zealander Sergeant W.H. Carter took up the aircraft on a training flight. During an attempted landing near Mablethorpe, the aircraft's lights failed and it crashed into a hedge before overturning. Sergeant Carter was injured and the former 'Night Reaper' was finished.

The author and his wife have on their landing wall a handsomely-framed water-colour painting produced in 1942 by J.H. Striebel Jr. It depicts vividly one of Kut's successful night intruder operations. Dominating the foreground of the painting is his Hawker Hurricane IIC – complete with cannon and drop tanks – clearly identified as that of Flight Lieutenant Karel Kuttelwascher by the JX:E marking. The background shows a Dornier Do 217 bomber, its starboard engine aflame, plunging to the ground and therefore it is likely that the incident depicted in the painting is his intruder operation of the night of 3/4 June 1942. Certainly it is a graphic and powerful representation of a classic Kut moment.

Many years later, Kut's aircraft was depicted in a series of aircraft profiles published by Profile Publications Limited. The one on the Hawker Hurricane IIC by Francis K. Mason has on one of the centre pages a five-view colour drawing of the 'Night Reaper' made by James Goulding. This illustrates the Hurricane as it was on 4 May 1942 – which we shall see was Kut's greatest sortie – and is so detailed it shows red doped patches over previous battle damage on the port aileron, the rear fuselage and the tail unit.

Huw Roberts – who married a daughter of one of Kut's brothers-in-law – recalls a family reunion in Cardiff at Christmas 1971:

My stepson, Lyndon, who was then aged six, was opening his presents before Ruby and the rest of us. One of them turned out to be a plastic construction kit of Karel Kuttelwascher's actual aircraft. We were all so surprised and none more so than Ruby herself.

This construction kit was made by Frog. However, the company went out of business in 1975 and its moulds were eventually purchased by another company called Novo which operates from Russia.

Kut was not alone among No 1 pilots in personalising his aircraft with a motif. Almost as soon as he had arrived at No 1, one-armed Mac had his Hurricane decorated. His aircraft was JX:Q BD983. The port side of the Hurricane's nose now carried a picture of his left arm with a shell going through it, the fingers of the hand making a defiant V-sign. Another No 1 pilot, Flight Lieutenant L.S.B. Scott, enlivened his Hurricane with a picture of a red indian wearing a war bonnet.

These were not the only forms of decoration on the intruder Hurricanes. Kut had a neat row of white swastikas painted immediately below the cockpit on the port side, one to represent each kill. Some of the other pilots had little trains, boats and even lorries painted in red below the cockpit on the port side to indicate their success at blowing up various forms of land and sea transport, even if they had not managed to equal Kut and Mac's success at actually downing a German bomber.

The German aircraft which all the intruder pilots were seeking, and that a few members of No 1 Squadron including Kut and Mac at least found, came in three shapes: the Dornier Do 217, the Heinkel He 111 and the Junkers Ju 88. All had graceful lines, probably as a result of their mutual clandestine evolution as civilian transport aircraft in a country forbidden to build military aircraft, and all tended to be underarmed and underarmoured for battle with modern fighters, so that – once an enemy aircraft was actually located – the success rate of RAF pilots was relatively high.

The Do 217 was a progressive development and slightly larger version of the Do 17. Originally entering service as a bomber in 1941, it was subsequently modified for night fighter duties. As a bomber, it had a crew of four and it was powered by two BMW radial engines. In the darkness of the night, one of the distinguishing features of the Do 217 was the twin tail planes.

The He 111 medium bomber first saw service in the Spanish Civil War where it faced little opposition, but in the Battle of Britain it took a considerable hammering and soon it was diverted to such less hazardous duties as night bombing with a crew of five. For British citizens on the ground, the aircraft was most memorable for the ominous throb-throb of the two unsynchronised Junkers Jumo inline engines whereas, for RAF pilots tackling the bomber, a trade mark of all later He 111s was the asymmetrically-placed 'bubble' housing a nose machine gun.

The Ju 88 was the most versatile and widely used German bomber of the war. In fact, it performed a whole variety of non-bombing roles including night fighting. The types encountered by No 1 Squadron in 1942 would have had a crew of three and been powered by either two BMW radial or Jumo inline motors.

As the crews of these German bombers operating from airfields in north-west France and the Low Countries went about their destructive and deadly business of bombing English towns and cities, they little realised that about to be unleashed upon them was a special kind of Hurricane flown by a special kind of pilot. They were now to discover the heavy damage that could be inflicted by the men of the RAF's No 1 Squadron.

CHAPTER NINE

A Baptism of Fire

No 1 Squadron's night intruder operations started on the Wednesday night of 1 April 1942, appropriately enough the official birthday of the Royal Air Force. The timing was no coincidence: the moon was at its fullest and brightest and shone like a giant searchlight in the sky providing convenient illumination for the RAF pilots.

Two of the squadron's most senior and experienced pilots were selected to pioneer this new type of sortie: the Commanding Officer, James MacLachlan, and the Czech Flight Lieutenant, Karel Kuttelwascher. Technically it was Mac who made the first intruder operation. He took off at 10.15 pm and went over to France, but $2\frac{1}{4}$ hours later he was back at Tangmere with nothing to report. Kut took off only five minutes after the CO at 10.20 pm and, by dramatic contrast with Mac's disappointing experience, amazingly the Czech had immediate success.

Kut crossed the French coast slightly west of Le Havre at 3,000 feet. At first he orbited Evreux airfield but, finding no activity, he decided to press much deeper into occupied France. Eventually, another 70–80 miles on, he reached Melun-Villaroche on the far side of Paris and it was here that to his delight he discovered an illuminated flarepath with its promise of aircraft movements. After only a couple of minutes above the lit-up base, a red rocket was fired. Then there on the runway was an aircraft about to take off.

Flying at about 1,500–2,000 feet, Kut looked down on the Luftwaffe machine as it climbed to 1,500 feet on its first circuit with navigation lights on. Now he could identify it as a Junkers Ju 88. The 'Night Hawk' swooped. Tingling with excitement and closing carefully to a mere 100 yards, he gave two short bursts from astern. A lethal hail of cannon fire slammed into the enemy bomber and a bright flash erupted from its starboard engine. The Ju 88 fell into a steep diving turn before the flaming coffin crashed into the ground.

As Kut swept over the runway, he was thrilled to see another Junkers about to enter the fray, its wings glinting in the moonlight.

104

In a strafing attack, he fired five or six short bursts and saw strikes hitting the enemy aircraft. As with a bird's claws in its victim, so his cannon fire had the German in its grip, but it was not quite enough. Kut later claimed it as only damaged. At this point a battery of searchlights caught the Hurricane in its glare and flak was quick to follow. Kut swiftly took evasive action by diving to starboard as low as 500 feet and then he climbed to 3,000 feet still on a right hand orbit. Ten minutes had now elapsed and both the flarepath and searchlights had been switched off, so he decided to call it a night and left the area.

He followed the meandering line of the Seine at about 4,000 feet above thick cloud. The route took him over Paris and on to Rouen before crossing the French coast east of Fécamp. He landed back at Tangmere at 1.25 am. At over three hours, this first intruder operation would prove to be his longest and, combined with the action he saw, it meant that the 'Night Reaper' returned to base with very little fuel to spare. It had been an audacious mission, but it had achieved excellent results, and the whole of the squadron was excited to have tangible proof that this new kind of operation could be so successful.

Kut's *Saturday Book* article – the language clearly polished by Ruby – provides his own account of this baptismal intruder operation:

By dusk everything was ready and, after an hour of waiting in dispersal and a nice cup of English tea, I set off. All the boys wished me luck and told me they would wait in dispersal until I returned. It seemed to me that I had never before in my life taken off so smoothly. I felt so free and exhilarated, with the moon shining above me, and the Channel already in sight. I lowered the revs for economy's sake and with a smoothly purring engine I left the English coast behind me.

I passed over a hundred miles of calm sea before reaching the French coast, where I pinpointed my position and set my course afresh. A couple of searchlights were playing below me, but I avoided them and carried on without opposition. It seemed to me that I should by now be nearing my target but I could see no landmarks because of a slight haze beneath me. Peering down in the hope of finding my bearings, I saw a few lights and, on closer examination, I found that I had come across an aerodrome.

They must have known I was hovering around because they

immediately switched off their lights. Almost simultaneously another set of lights were switched on, which reminded me of the Christmas trees of my childhood days. Red, green, blue and yellow lights were all over the place, and I said to myself 'Crikey Moses, you can't fox me with this, boys. That's definitely a dummy.' Turning to the left, I located once more the real aerodrome with its flare path dimmed, and there I saw a plane taxiing with its navigation lights on.

He was just taking off and I swooped down to get beyond him. I passed through his slipstream and got rather a bump but, slowing my speed a little, I was able to get within firing range. With my gun sight and firing button already switched on and the plane looming up right in front of me, I gave it a long burst and saw it catch fire in a matter of seconds. I was obliged to pull out quickly to the right to avoid colliding with it and I watched it hit the ground and burst into flames. I made a half circle to the left and saw just in time another plane taking off. Again I dived, opened fire from slightly above and behind him, but at that moment I was caught by four searchlights and fired on with streams of shells from the ground defences. I had to be content with only damaging this second plane as the firing still continued from the ground. It was not very accurate firing, but it was time for me to make my way home.

Next night the Luftwaffe was in evidence with a raid on Weymouth in which two hospitals were hit and there were heavy casualties. From Tangmere the CO and the Czech carried out further intruder operations. Again Mac went off first. He found nothing over Rennes or Dinard, but on the way home carried out two low-level attacks on a goods train near Combourg and left it enveloped in steam with two trucks burning. An hour later, Kut went over to France but, after being airborne almost two hours, he had nothing at all to report.

Meanwhile, No 1 Squadron was continuing to make routine patrols and that night Pilot Officer Harry Connolly had his spirits dampened. He was patrolling Selsey when, seven miles off the coast, his engine cut. He successfully baled out and took to his rubber dinghy, but it was three hours before he attracted the attention of a trawler with the aid of his whistle!

The arrival of No 1 Squadron's night intruder operations meant that Kut's letters to Ruby, his bride of just six weeks, had to be written in odd moments and his brief visits to her in London fitted into odd days, as is clear from his letter of 4 April written in his characteristic broken English:

> Once more here is your Karel, who is thinking so much about you. It is 21.00 and I am alone in my room. The weather is at present too bad for our flying and I shouldn't be surprise if we'll go to bed tonight. Last time, I was very in hurry – I couldn't stay above longer because here was waiting lots of things.

In fact, for the next two weeks, further intruder operations were prevented by bad weather over France, but defensive patrols continued.

On 5 April, there occurred the kind of incident which reminds pilots that, however great the risks from engaging the enemy, one can never overlook the danger of accidents. A Czech flight sergeant named Zdeněk Bachůrek, who had only been with the unit a month, was on patrol in Hurricane BE647 when at midnight he crashed near the Chichester–Arundel Road at Fontwell, just two miles north-east of Tangmere. It appeared that he simply forgot to switch over from mains tank to reserve tank and as a result he suffered severe head injuries and was taken to hospital. Fortunately he recovered and now lives in Czechoslovakia.

Then on 10 April there was another tragic accident. Sergeant Jan Vlk was ordered to carry out a Z.Z. landing practice at 7 pm. Three quarters of an hour later, it was reported that he had crashed in a field near Barnham. An ambulance raced to the scene and was there within four minutes, but Vlk has obviously been killed instantly. Apparently the accident occurred as he was flying low over a railway and the aircraft, Hurricane Z3970, stalled off a turn and hit telegraph wires and a tree. Vlk struggled with the controls but his crash landing in the field was too heavy for him to survive. Again the pilot was a Czech and Kut must have felt for his much less experienced compatriots.

A couple of days later, the CO was detached to Old Sarum at Salisbury for four days for Airborne Division Tactical Week, but he was back in time for the next round of night intruder sorties. It was the night of 16/17 April when the next intruder operations were flown and again it was Mac and Kut who made them. The Squadron Leader went off first at 10.25 pm and visited no less than three areas – Evreux, Dreux and Bretigny – on two occasions each, but all to no avail. There was plenty of flak but no enemy aircraft.

Meanwhile Kut left Tangmere at 10.45 pm. There was a new moon, so the sky over the Channel was dark but clear. He crossed the French coast at Fécamp flying at 5,000 feet. Over France, there was slight haze and cloud away to the north of Fécamp, but otherwise a myriad stars glittered overhead. Like Mac, he started at Evreux where he orbited once but found nothing. So he went on to St André-de-l'Eure and then to Dreux, but there was no evidence of Luftwaffe activity at either. At Chartres he saw three white lights and back at Dreux again he encountered medium flak. Then, on the return journey, he circled St André at a speed of 180 mph and a height of 2,000 feet. At about a quarter of an hour after midnight, he came across two aircraft with navigation lights on orbiting the airfield.

One of the Luftwaffe pilots immediately switched off his lights, but Kut followed the other and resolutely closed in to 200 yards. He managed to give him a punishing total of four short bursts from dead astern, using up 140 rounds. He saw the third and fourth bursts striking the enemy aircraft with colourful flashes and sparks as the explosive ammunition tore into it. The enemy aircraft promptly nose-dived and hit the ground with a bright orange flash. Kut was not absolutely sure of the identity of the German aircraft – he thought it was a Dornier Do 217 – but there could be no doubt that it was destroyed. Kut returned to Dreux where there was a little flak and Evreux where he was met by some light flak and a searchlight which fortunately failed to illuminate him. As he crossed the coast east of Fécamp, one very bright searchlight did manage to catch the Hurricane. Kut dived away to port to escape the glare and was soon out over the Channel. He landed safely at 1.35 am.

This second night intruder kill – added to his three day-time victories of April, May and June 1941 – now made Kut an 'ace'. The status of 'ace' was never officially recognised by the RAF, but was generally applied to any pilot credited with at least five confirmed combat victories – this arbitrary figure coming from the French air services of 1914–18.

Night intrusion was interfering with Kut's letter-writing to Ruby and his plans to have a holiday with her, but he did not expect the situation to last long, as indicated in his letter of 23 April:

I received this afternoon your very nice letter and thanks very much for it my own darling. This week I am a little bit late with my letter but darling you'll always understand why. Moon is here and I am busy. Not very busy at present but any moment now. It will be over in a couple of weeks and we shall be together again for a long leave – every day, every night – Ruby and Karel. Darling I hope we'll have the same, such nice holiday if not better yet. I hope the weather will be good; I am looking forwards like a little boy for his two month holidays.

These first three weeks of No 1 Squadron's assignment to night intruder duties had – like the rest of the year so far – been a quiet period as far as activity by German bombers was concerned. However, the catalyst for change came on the night of 28/29 March when the RAF's Bomber Command sent two hundred bombers over to the Baltic port of Lübeck to try out a new system of fire raising. The beautiful old city was devastated.

The incident seems to have made a deep impression on the Führer and a couple of weeks later, on 14 April, he ordered hard-hitting reprisals. Raids were now sanctioned on British targets where attacks were likely to have the greatest possible effect on civilian life and these were called *Terrorangriffe* ('terror attacks'). Both sides soon came to call them the 'Baedeker raids' after the travel guide which included details of cathedral and historic cities. These raids started on the night of 23/24 April when Junkers Ju 88s and Dornier Do 217s were diverted from their usual tasks of laying mines and sent to bomb Exeter. Few crews found it, but the next night a repeat attack on the city was rather more successful.

The next batch of intruder operations by No 1 Squadron came at the start of the second moon period on the evening of 24/25 April, when Exeter was receiving its second visit from the Luftwaffe. Tonight the CO decided that it was time for some of the others to be blooded and so, as well as Mac and Kut, Sergeant Macháček, Sergeant Pearson, Flight Lieutenant Scott, Pilot Officer Perrin and Flight Sergeant Cooper – in that order – all took off from Tangmere at staggered intervals.

The seven had a night that was somewhat less than magnificent. After about $2\frac{1}{4}$ hours, Mac and Kut were the first back with nothing to report. Scott and Perrin had the same experience. Cooper – the last to take off – was recalled owing to bad weather. Pearson was the last home, since he lost his way and landed initially way down the coast at Exeter. But there was no sign of the Czech Sergeant

Vlastimil Macháček. He was supposed to be going to Bretigny, but his Hurricane BE573 was plotted to mid Channel and then disappeared, never to return. It was an unsettling incident for the squadron. The first time that pilots other than Mac and Kut had been given a chance on intruder operations, one had not come back. For the third time in three weeks, a Czech member of the squadron had been lost from active duty.

On the next two nights, the German bomber attacks were notably heavier and far more destructive: Bath was the primary target on both occasions. At No 1 Squadron, another confidence-boosting demonstration was required from the two experts and it came on 26/27 April when Bath was being hit again.

The CO was the first in the air at 10.05 pm. In a radio interview given a few weeks later, he rather nonchalantly described what it was like to set out on a night intruder operation:

I'm afraid the dangers and hazards on night offensive patrols have been rather exaggerated. Certainly the average intruder pilot is not the cat-eyed, carrot-eating killer that the Press sometimes makes him out to be. Most of us night fighters are too fond of our mornings in bed to go flying around in the daytime. Personally, sleeping in the sun appeals to me infinitely more than chasing Me 109s at 30,000 feet. Give me a moonlight night and my old Hurricane, and you can have your Spitfires and dawn readiness. We've no formation flying to worry about, and no bombers to escort. In fact, nothing to do but amuse ourselves once we've crossed the French coast.

I must admit that those miles of Channel with only one engine brings mixed thoughts, and one can't help listening to every little beat of the old Merlin as the English coast disappears in the darkness. I always get a feeling of relief and excitement as I cross the French coast and turn on the reflector sight, knowing that anything I see then I can take a crack at. We have to keep our eyes skinned the whole time, and occasionally glance at the compass and clock. As the minutes go by and we approach the Hun aerodrome, we look eagerly for the flare paths. More often than not we are disappointed. The flare path is switched off as soon as we arrive, and up come the searchlights and flak. But if you're lucky, it's a piece of cake.

Tonight it was Mac's turn to eat cake.

His assignment was the Evreux–Dreux group of airfields and he made visits to Bretigny, Evreux, and St André before he found any activity. At St André he saw an aircraft taking off and went in to attack, but lost it as its navigation lights were switched off. Then he attempted a head-on attack on a second aircraft, but frustratingly lost that too. This was not good enough: Old Kuttel – as the CO called him – could not have all the action, so he switched targets once more. Leaving St André, Mac travelled the short distance back to Evreux where he had more luck.

He saw an aircraft take off and climb to 500 feet and, as it became silhouetted against the sky, identified it as a Do 217. He closed to 600 yards astern and gave three short bursts without observing any effect. So he narrowed the distance considerably down to 100 yards and gave another one-second burst. Sparks now flew from the starboard engine of the Dornier and the nose of the bomber dropped as it went down into a shallow dive before crashing into a field. That would be something to tell Old Kuttel, but Mac was not finished yet. On his return to St André at 1,000 feet, he saw another Do 217 at the same height and on a converging course. He throttled back his Hurricane and allowed the enemy aircraft to pass. Then he made two short attacks from dead astern at 250 yards. He saw strikes and then smoke against the moonlight so, when he landed at 1.05 am, the CO was able to report his first victories: one Do 217 destroyed and another damaged.

Kut had not yet taken off on his own sortie and was delighted to hear of Mac's success. Now it was the Czech's turn to show what he could do.

It was 1.35 am when Kut left Tangmere. As the Hurricane pulled away from the deck, she laboured into the darkness doubly pregnant with full drop tanks. Over the English Channel there was patchy cloud at 4,000–5,000 feet, but he crossed the French coast at Fécamp at 2,000 feet, well below the cloud base. The ultimate objective of the sortie was Evreux, but Kut noticed activity at Boos airfield near Rouen where No 1 had briefly operated in June 1940. There were six white lights set in two parallel rows of three. Also visible east of the field there were other lights flashing red and green. These may have been the German *Kleine Schraube*, the equivalent of the RAF searchlight boxes with their marker beacons.

The moon was waxing, filling out the silver globe and providing more of the luminescence that was succour to the night intruder. So Kut went off to investigate, orbiting the airfield at 2,000 feet. After three minutes – at approximately 2.15 am – he saw a Dornier bomber between him and the moon. He manoeuvred his Hurricane behind and slightly below the German, closed to 100 yards, and gave one long four-second burst at the machine. His cannon shells found their target with unmistakable accuracy and had a devastating effect. The Dornier's starboard engine caught fire and the aircraft went into a steep left hand turn and dived to the earth before crashing between hangars.

He would have no difficulty back at base in claiming that one destroyed. But first he had to reach home. As he saw his Dornier crashing, he was shocked to find red tracer ammunition passing over the cockpit from behind! Damn it – he should have kept an upward eye on his rear-view mirror. One had to be looking everywhere at once in this business. Immediately he throttled back sharply with his left hand and put the Hurricane's nose down with his right. He discovered the source of the tracer fire when a Junkers Ju 88 night fighter zoomed up from behind and over-shot him just 20–30 feet above. That had certainly been a close call but this Czech was not for bouncing!

Although his engine was damaged, he quickly jettisoned his two long range tanks with the control on the starboard side of the cockpit, pulled up his Hurricane and raced after the German. When he was near enough, he fired four short bursts from short range dead astern. The ammunition hit the Ju 88 which went into a steep left hand turn, first up and then down. However, it went out of sight into the darkness south of the airfield. He would only be able to claim that one as damaged.

Some weeks later, in a radio interview Kut identified this incident as the nearest he came to losing his life on intruder operations:

> I got very easily one Dornier. I was so pleased that I forgot that something can happen to me. And the next second I see lots of tracer bullets going over my head. I manage to push down the stick, and he passes just over my head with big speed. He was sure he had me. As he passed, I managed to pull up again and go behind him. I damage him. I don't have time to be scared. It's all quick.

Flak from four anti-aircraft guns and some machine guns on the ground now opened fire, but the bursts passed well above Kut. Then two searchlights were put up, but they failed to illuminate the

Flight Lieutenant Karel Kuttelwascher, DFC and Bar, being congratulated by Jan Masaryk, the Czech Foreign Minister. London—11 July 1942.

Flight Lieutenant Karel Kuttelwascher is interviewed by Lieutenant Colonel Brož for a radio broadcast to occupied Czechoslovakia on 6 May 1942, immediately after his 'triple kill' over St. André.

Flight Lieutenant Karel Kuttelwascher together with his older brother Captain Jan Kuttelwascher during a period of leave. Autumn 1942.

Hurricane. However, clearly it was time to leave. Kut returned home over the River Seine – where there was some mist – and crossed the coast at Etretat at 2,000 feet. Once over the Channel, he climbed to 3,000 feet and touched down back at base at 3.25 am. It had been a short, sharp sortie of just over 1¾ hours, during which he had utilized 356 rounds to destroy one German aircraft and damage another.

The Saturday Book carried Kut's description of the night that was almost his last:

It was rather chilly as I took off soon after midnight, and I felt suddenly lonely as I crossed over the sea all on my own. However, I did not feel that way for long because, when I was a few miles from the French coast, I caught a glimpse of a signalling beam which aroused my interest. By this time, I had crossed the coast at a low altitude to avoid detection and saw a few lights turning in the distance. It took me longer than I expected to reach the locality as visibility was good, making distances rather deceiving. I made sure of my position and instantly knew that there was an aerodrome here. Besides I could just see the emergency flarepath which was illuminated below me.

Something must be happening here I thought and I was right because, after hovering around for five minutes or so, I caught sight of a plane silhouetted against the moonlit sky. I did my best to close in as soon as possible but I lost him. Deciding quickly that he must be coming down, I waited for him on the side from which he would have to land. I hadn't long to wait; in a moment or so I saw him. I was in a good position to close in for the attack, being just behind him and slightly below. I gave him a long burst to make sure that I would get him first time, as I was too low to attack him repeatedly. He turned steeply to the left and then crashed among the hangars where he immediately burst into flames.

In about three seconds, I was a bit startled to see a stream of tracer bullets passing about ten feet above me. The only answer was that an enemy night fighter was on my tail, so I quickly pushed my stick forward and he went roaring over my head at a terrific speed. Instantly hurrying my plane up, the position was reversed and I was now on his tail firing madly at him. He started to climb but, with his extra speed, I could not catch him and finally I lost sight of him as he climbed to the left on the dark side of the sky. By now I was rather short of ammo and, without reaching my original target, I decided to return to base. On the way home, I fell to thinking how near I had been to becoming an 'also ran'. If the night fighter had made the most of his opportunities, he could – I realised – easily have got me. As it was, I reached base with news for the boys of an additional obstacle in our new game of intruding – the presence of night fighters.

In both his flight log and combat report, Kut claimed to have destroyed a Dornier Do 17 and the squadron's Operations Record Book makes the same identification. In fact, this particular make of aircraft had been withdrawn from most bomber operations by 1942. Therefore, it was probably a Do 217, the only difference being in size. In 1971, Michael Shaw in *Twice Vertical* challenged the make of aircraft destroyed by Kut that night. He too believes that it is doubtful whether a Do 17 was around so late in the war and therefore describes the German aircraft as a Heinkel He 111. This seems unlikely since the He 111 ought not to have been confused by Kut with the very different Do 17 and Do 217 with their distinctive twin tail fins. However, he obviously had no time for checking because of the immediate arrival of the Ju 88.

Towards the end of the first month of No 1 Squadron's intruder sorties, the score was: Kut 3, Mac 1. A signal was received from the AOC 11 Group addressed to the two of them: 'Heartiest congratulations on highly successful intruder operations last night. Well done.' For his part, Mac too sent a telegram. He had made a promise to the Roehampton designers of his artificial arm that each time he destroyed an enemy aircraft, he would let them know. It was to be only the first of several such telegrams.

CHAPTER TEN

The Triple Kill

Over the next three nights, the Luftwaffe was even more accurate in its bombing than at Bath, only this time the targets were Norwich, York and then Norwich again. Down at Tangmere, over a couple of these nights, Sergeant Pearson was allowed to have a go and three other pilots – Pilot Officer Murray, Warrant Officer Scott, and Pilot Officer Corbet – were sent on their first intruder operations. They patrolled the same areas of north-west France as those where the CO and his A Flight Commander had achieved such early kills, but none of them even saw a German aircraft. Another later trip by Mac equally failed to find any Luftwaffe aircraft, but on the return journey he obtained some satisfaction by shooting up two trains and a tug.

Rear-Admiral André Jubelin later wrote about the frustration of these intruder operations in *The Flying Sailor*. Jubelin – or Old Ju as he became known – was a member of the Free French Navy who escaped from the Japanese in Indo-China in 1940 by flying a light aircraft to the Philippines. On arrival in England, he was attached to the RAF, first with 118 Squadron – where he was involved in the Channel Dash of February 1942 – and then with No 1 in the last days of its intruder phase.

In his book, Jubelin captured the hit-and-miss nature of night intrusion:

Would one pilot be near the airfield concerned? That was the first throw in the game of chance, involving the whole squadron. It might very well be that all would return empty-handed. The next chance would be the one each of us had to take. One man might see nothing and circle for hours over a base that would be fast asleep till daylight. Another might be delayed too long by searchlights or flak and so prevented from arriving in time for the bombers' return. Another might grow tired of waiting and leave too soon. Still another might be deceived by the lure of dummy runways marked out in open country, while the bombers touched down on the real airfield in a less conspicuous place five miles away. Then again, there would be the man whom destiny had marked for its own. For him the night would suddenly change to a place of perilous enchantment. And when the runway flares lit up for the great moment, the few seconds' fire of his heavy and light weapons might be all too short for the numbers of the quarry revealed.

Once again, it was Kut who – to use Jubelin's phrase – was marked by destiny when, a mere four nights after his last success, the Czech achieved an even more spectacular performance. The occasion was the night of 30 April/1 May. There was a second full moon, so conditions were ideal for night intrusion, and Mac decided to make it the biggest effort so far. Like latter-day Valkyries, no less than eight No 1 pilots took to the air that evening.

Mac himself was first off at 11.05 pm and Kut followed 25 minutes later, the two of them heading for German airfields in France. At staggered intervals over the next few hours, the other six less experienced pilots flew off, avoiding the well-defended airfields and concentrating on the easier targets of trains. Mac tried a succession of different airfields but found no aircraft, so he picked up a railway line and followed it until he discovered a goods train. He attacked the engine with one long burst from 500 yards closing to 200 yards at which point the boiler appeared to explode.

Kut took off half an hour before midnight and this time flew further west than usual: his destination was Rennes, some 40 miles inland from the Brittany coast. The moon was now full again and the Hurricane was caressed by a milky lunar light. He flew on a direct course from base to target crossing the Channel at 5,000 feet and then, on reaching the French coast, swooping down to 2,000 feet. He experienced an unusually strong interference hum in his earphones while passing Cherbourg.

Once he reached the target area, he circled Rennes airfield on a right hand orbit at a distance of about two miles, watching, waiting, wondering. It was a clear moonlight night with no cloud and only a little haze. But there were no lights and no activity. So he flew north back to the coast and then returned to the east side of the airfield about 1.20 am. Now there were two white lights near the runway and another one moving on the runway. The moving white spot turned out to be a navigation light in the nose of an aircraft – at that point unidentifiable – taking off. As soon as the

German was airborne, the light went out, but Kut was already on the machine. Like a bird of prey, he swooped fast and low.

Kut tucked his Hurricane neatly behind the enemy aircraft and manoeuvred to put it between him and the moon. Now he could identify his victim as a Dornier Do 217 bomber. He closed to 150 yards dead astern and attacked with three short bursts of blazing cannon fire. The first two bursts seemed to have no effect, but the third was obviously too much for the trapped Luftwaffe aircraft. The Dornier's nose fell down and the aircraft dived steeply, soon to explode in an intense conflagration on the ground.

Kut decided to remain on the scene for a time and orbited Rennes for another five minutes, but there was no further activity. He still had fuel and it was too soon to go home. So he flew north to Dinard airfield on the coast and orbited it at a distance of approximately four miles at height of around 2,000 feet. Soon he saw another enemy aircraft with one white tail light take off but, as soon as the light was switched off, he lost sight of the German in the dark.

However, it was Kut's lucky night. For, after orbiting for a further five minutes, he spotted a Heinkel He 111 bomber taking off with full navigation lights on. He could not see if there was a light in the nose, but the white light in the tail, the green on the starboard wing and the red on the port wing presented him with a glittering target. In fact, the lights were switched off while the Heinkel was still on the runway, but it was too late for the German who was now silhouetted against the moon.

Kut followed the enemy aircraft and, when it had climbed to 1,000 feet, he closed in to 150 yards dead astern and attacked with unerring accuracy in a series of two-second bursts. A large chunk of metal flew off the starboard engine of the Heinkel, but the stricken bomber still lumbered on. Both aircraft were now travelling at about 180 mph and had reached the sea. Kut gave the German two more short bursts and at this point the He 111 plummeted straight into the sea off Dinard. It disappeared immediately. There had been no return fire from it at any time. Neither had there been any searchlights or flak. It was almost too easy.

This was Kut's first double – two in a single night – and certainly enough for one evening. He set course for base, passing west of Jersey at 2,000 feet, climbing to 5,000 feet past Cherbourg, and crossing the Channel back at 2,000 feet. He landed back at Tangmere at 2.20 am, having expended 300 rounds of ammunition.

Underneath the note of this flight in Kut's log book, the CO wrote in his flamboyant hand and characteristic language 'A bloody fine show!'

Again *The Saturday Book* offers a more personal account of this particular nefarious enterprise:

My destination tonight was W. France. My main object was to wreak vengeance on these blessed Jerries for having in the early evening blitzed one of the most beautiful of English towns which was purely a non-military objective. [This was probably a reference to the attack on Norwich which in fact occurred the evening before.] I took off well before midnight in bright moonlight, and flew on a direct course from base to target. I came right over the target, and was obliged to fly south to confuse the ground defences as they had already detected my presence there. On the almost completely blacked out aerodrome, I spotted a plane with its navigation lights on. As he was taking off, I dived after him and manoeuvred so that he was between me and the moon. He immediately switched off his navigation lights, but he was too late as he was already well placed in my gun sight.

I fired three short bursts. There was no result from the first two but after the third the aircraft turned steeply downwards and exploded on the ground. My plane rocked violently as if in a terrific gale. The enemy plane must have been loaded with bombs to have exploded like this and it gave me great satisfaction to know that he at least would never again deliver any of his loads on English soil. I waited there for about five minutes and seeing no activity I decided to fly north to another drome near the coast. There I saw a plane with its tail navigation lights on, but unfortunately lost him when he switched off his lights. I then flew around for another ten minutes and saw a second plane fully lit up and about to take off. Its lights were switched off before becoming airborne, but I followed the direction in which he went. After a few minutes I saw him against the moon just above me, and managed to come dead astern. Giving him two bursts from short range, I saw his starboard engine was shot to pieces. By now we had crossed the coast and after two short bursts the plane plunged straight into the sea, sinking immediately.

Meanwhile, in the course of the night, No 1 Squadron's train-busting six had considerable success in various parts of

Normandy and Brittany. Flight Sergeant Bland excelled by attacking the engines of no less than five goods trains before exhausting his ammunition. In every case, he left them stopped and engulfed in steam. Sergeant Pearson too attacked five trains, disabling two and breaking away from the last only because his ammunition was totally expended as well. Sergeant Campbell took on four trains and damaged them all before his ammunition ran out. Pilot Officer Perrin blasted two trains to a dead stop. For his part, Flight Lieutenant Scott made six attacks on the engine and down the length of a large goods train with evident damage. Even Pilot Officer Corbet – who could find no trains – fired a burst at a row of covered trucks in a siding, a signal box and a signal gantry, putting out the light on the last!

It had not been a bad night's work. Mac had said that, if one was lucky, night intrusion was 'a piece of cake'. If Kut's two additional aircraft destroyed was the cake, then a total of fifteen trains disabled was a good icing.

The next night was much quieter with only the two Scotts – the British flight lieutenant and the Canadian warrant officer – going over to France. The only incident was the former's successful attack on another train. The following night – 2/3 May – was hardly more eventful. Four pilots performed intruder operations, but the only one who found anything was Kut and even he could discover nothing with wings.

Crossing the French coast just east of the Cherbourg peninsula, he decided to try his hand at this train-busting lark. So he flew inland to St Lô and found a goods train puffing slowly up the valley. He put the Hurricane into a screaming dive and opened fire at 700 feet. He gave the locomotive two short bursts before pulling out at 500 feet, leaving below an engine billowing with steam. This was too easy and he proceeded on to the real target, Caen airfield about 35 miles to the east. Nothing was happening at Caen, but he noticed that further over to the east at Lisieux bombs were being dropped and a fire was starting.

He recrossed the French coast north of Caen at 1,000 feet. About a mile off the coast near St Aubin-sur-Mer, he found a small motor boat – possibly an E-boat – travelling east. He made three short attacks, from 1,000 feet down to 500 feet, and had the quiet satisfaction of seeing the launch stop and list badly while a patch of oil began to spread from it across the sea. Kut was back at Tangmere after $2\frac{1}{4}$ hours. In his flight log, he drew child-like pictures of a train adorned with smoke and a boat riding some waves.

The next evening (3/4 May) saw the most devastating of the 'Baedeker raids'. The Luftwaffe returned to finish the job half done at Exeter at the start of the raids. There was clear moonlight and an almost cloudless sky making visibility excellent. About two hours after midnight, the leading bombers marked the target with flares and a shower of incendiaries and in the next three-quarters of an hour further waves dropped on the city some 50 tons of high explosive and many thousands of incendiaries. Exeter went up in flames, the cathedral and nine churches were wrecked, and firemen and ARP personnel were machine-gunned.

That same evening, five No 1 Squadron pilots took off on intruder operations. Kut was heading for Dinard but for the first time experienced problems with his Hurricane. There was trouble with the engine and about mid-Channel he was forced to return, landing only 35 minutes after having left. Three other pilots had uneventful flights, but it really was Mac's night.

Taking off just as the German bombers were arriving over Exeter, the CO's excitement came at Dinard and he described the occasion almost boyishly in a radio interview given shortly afterwards:

The other night I saw the Jerries when I was still some distance away. They were flying round at about 2,000 feet. I chose the nearest and followed him round. He was batting along at about 200 miles an hour, but I soon caught him, and got him beautifully lined up in my sights before letting him have it. The effect of our four cannon is incredible, after the eight machine-guns I had previously been used to. Scarcely had I pressed the button when a cluster of flashes appeared on the bomber and a spurt of dark red flame came from its starboard engine. The whole thing seemed to fold up then and fall out of the sky, burning beautifully.

I turned steeply to watch it crash, and as I did so I saw another Hun about a mile away, coming straight for me. In half a minute he was in my sights, and a second later his port petrol tank was blazing. I gave him another short burst for luck and then flew beside him. It was just like watching a film. A moment before he hit the ground, I could see trees and houses lit up by the dark red glow from the burning machine. Suddenly there was a terrific sheet of flame, and little bits of burning Heinkel flew in all directions. I was beginning to enjoy myself by this time and flew straight back to the aerodrome to find another. Unfortunately, all the lights had been switched off and, though I circled for some time, I found nothing.

So I cracked off for home. I looked back once and could still see the two bombers burning in the distance, and a few searchlights trying vainly to find me. On the way back I spotted a train. They're easy to see in the moonlight, as the trail of steam shows up nicely against the dark background. I made sure it was a goods train before attacking the engine, which I left enveloped in a cloud of steam. My squadron has rather specialised in this train-wrecking racket. During the April–May full moon we blew up seventeen engines for certain, and probably several others.

In the course of the day, the squadron leader received a signal from Leigh-Mallory: 'Heartiest congratulations on your splendid show last night.' Mac's double – a Do 217 and a He 111 – had been achieved only three nights after Kut's own double and put the whole squadron into a state of high excitement. The air was almost electric with the good-natured rivalry that was now beginning to evolve between these two crack pilots.

Next night – 4/5 May – the Germans made an attack on Cowes which was reasonably successful, but fortunately for the British it would prove to be a turning point for the Baedeker offensive; from then on, almost everything went wrong for the Luftwaffe bombers. That night another five intruder operations were conducted by No 1 Squadron, all but one of the Hurricanes departing more-or-less together.

This time Mac saw nothing, let alone hit it. At Rennes, then Dinard and finally Caen, fog blanketed the whole area. The Australian Sergeant Dennis briefly saw an aircraft landing at Boos but was in no position to attack. Flight Lieutenant Scott had a little more luck. He observed three aircraft landing at different intervals and managed to fire a quick burst at the last one, but it was losing speed rapidly and he overshot. It was Sergeant Campbell – who took off later than the others – who introduced a new kind of target by attacking a tanker lorry which he left spewing burning oil all over the road. For good measure, he took on two trains and disabled both. Significantly though, there were very few trains around that night. Obviously the squadron's operations of the past week had had an effect.

However, Kut – the one other No 1 pilot over France that night – was not interested in trains; he was after bigger stuff. Just 40 minutes before midnight, the Czech took off from Tangmere and headed south across the Channel. The moon was waning, so that the golden orb looked as if a segment had been chopped off by an astral axeman. Kut crossed the French coast south of Fécamp at an altitude of 2,000 feet. Three searchlights came up at him from the town but, showing considerable presence of mind, he flashed his navigation lights on and off twice and to his relief the ploy succeeded and the searchlights were doused, those manning them clearly assuming that he was 'friendly'.

There was a slight haze and some cloud away to the east, but otherwise visibility over France was good that night. Below the canopy of stars, Kut made for his first target, the German airfield at Evreux, about 70 miles inland. Over this target, he orbited for ten minutes but he could see no lights or activity. Disappointed, he flew on a little further south to St André-de-l'Eure, where he had shot down a Dornier less than three weeks before.

Reaching St André at 0050 hours, he circled the blacked-out base for ten minutes. Then the airfield lit up with a double flare path east to west and there, ready to land, was a gaggle of no less than six enemy aircraft. He immediately identified them as Heinkel bombers, probably on their way back from a destructive mission over Cowes, their crews relieved to be in sight of the sanctuary of their base. All six showed white tail lights. They were orbiting at 1,500–2,000 feet ready to touch down and therefore vulnerable to Kut's cannon. For two minutes he circled outside the Heinkels, cautiously stalking his prey, carefully positioning himself for a kill.

He closed the Hurricane in behind one of the Germans and took a precise aim. He fired a two-second burst from about 100 yards dead astern but slightly below. Four streams of cannon fire converged into a cone of destruction and at its apex the starboard engine of the Heinkel caught fire. The German aircraft twisted grotesquely and dived to the ground north-east of the airfield. Immediately, he was able to repeat the same tactics on a second machine. A one-second burst of uncompromising accuracy caused the hit Heinkel to plunge downwards, flickering flames consuming it as it crashed into a wood east of the airfield.

Astonishingly, the remaining four Germans still seemed to be unaware of his presence so, quickly pressing on the attack, Kut lined up behind yet a third Heinkel. Ruthlessly he fired a two-second burst of ammunition from dead astern and saw his shells slam into the target. The enemy aircraft dived down steeply from 1,500 feet and then Kut lost sight of it, initially unsure whether he had secured a third kill. But 30 seconds later, sweeping round on orbit, he saw three separate fires burning on the ground. The lurid flames licked the black night. There could be no doubt about it: three bombers had been totally destroyed in a matter of just four minutes. He had only used 200 rounds of ammunition and he had certainly made them count.

At this point, airfield lighting went out and machine gun fire started. Kut later told a radio interviewer: 'They opened all the anti-aircraft fire on me and I had to fly through it. It was like going through hell.' He had no choice but to depart this malign environment. The time was 1.05 am – he had been over the airfield for only fifteen minutes but he had done enormous damage.

Yet the sortie was not finished. He flew on to his third enemy base of the night – Dreux – but he could find no activity there. So he turned north for home at last. North of Evreux, four searchlights illuminated him. He tried to repeat his earlier technique and flashed his navigation lights, but this time it did not work. The searchlights remained on him, so he had to dive steeply and to one side before he managed to escape them. Kut re-crossed the Channel at 3,000 feet. At 2.05 am – almost three hours after leaving base – he touched down at Tangmere to report his astonishing achievement to his ecstatic colleagues.

This St André massacre – there were probably fifteen men in those three Heinkels – provided the final diary entry in Kut's article for *The Saturday Book*:

In the last 24 hours I have been out twice on intruding ops. From my early morning trip, I came home without having had any luck at all and with engine trouble. This job had not in any way been to my liking – having to cross over a hundred miles of sea with a faulty engine makes one think rather a lot and anticipate quite a few unpleasant happenings. The second trip I made just before midnight and, oh boy, what a grand do it was! Knowing that a large force of enemy planes were attacking England, it was decided that the intruders should go out in strength. We did so and were fully rewarded for our work.

I took off when the attack on one of our towns was finishing. I made my way post-haste to a French aerodrome which I felt sure they must be using for this attack. Some boys had already got there ahead of me, so I hurried to join them at the last minute. What a spectacle confronted me on arriving at the aerodrome. Again I thought it resembled a Christmas tree, except that this one was suspended in mid air. About 20 Jerries were awaiting their turn to land, and, being in a hurry, they flashed on and off all the lights they had. Bounding into the mêlée with the ferocity of a tiger, I was in just the right mood for a kill, but pulled myself together knowing that, unless I was calm and calculating, I should be able to do nothing at all. I remembered also that my mother had told me 'Grab all and you gain nothing'.

The one problem now was how many of those b----s I could finish with my ammunition. I decided I had better get within close range and give my victims short bursts in order to make my cannon shells go further. Jerry knew that we were hovering around in strength and so they kept switching their navigation lights on and off to fox us. We, however, went boldly after our prey, knowing that there was no danger from the ground defences while their own planes were flying around. As I was waiting for an opportunity to get at the Jerries, I saw one pass right over my head. In a split second I had pulled my stick back slightly and had fired two short bursts at him. Flames shot instantly out of one engine, and down he went into a steep dive to hit the ground. Again pulling my plane quickly to the right, I did the same to a second one which had been simply begging for it with his navigation lights full on. He too caught fire and hit the ground with a shower of sparks flying all around me.

All this shooting had taken place in one minute, and now I had the opportunity of looking around me a little, as there was nothing in my vicinity at the moment. I saw one of our boys also doing his best and sending a Hun hurtling earthwards in flames. I once more fixed on a Hun to shoot down, but it took me three minutes to get within close range as the devil kept on switching his navigation light on and off as he waited his turn to land. At last I got into the position for the attack, but this time it took me a little bit more ammo to finish him off. He turned into a steep left hand dive, with me on his tail firing ceaselessly. I was obliged, however, to pull up my plane and climb once more to a safe height as I was too near the ground.

This dazzling display would prove to be the most outstanding intruder operation that Kut – or indeed any of No 1 Squadron's pilots – would make. In fact, it was a punitive operation of particular effectiveness that proved to be a record for all RAF intruder pilots. Given the limited rounds of ammunition carried by a Hawker Hurricane IIC, it is hard to see how any pilot could bring down more than three enemy bombers in a single sortie. In other circumstances, Kut's mode of operation might be described as elegant in the sense that it involved a pure economy of ammunition and effort. The Czech's triple kill of that night presented a new score sheet for the two No 1 Squadron rivals. It was: Kut 8, Mac 3.

However, it seems that the two pilots also had another, more comprehensive scoring technique. Mac told a newspaper reporter at this time:

We are great rivals in this night business and 'Old Kuttel' always manages to keep one jump ahead. He's a 'natural'. The other night, when I shot down two Hun bombers over there, we had a tie of eleven each, including day scores. However, 'Kuttel' just grinned when I said we were neck and neck and that night, of course, went out and shot three more.

It is not absolutely clear how the pair arrived at initial joint scores of eleven. Certainly Mac's number of aircraft destroyed – eight by day and three by night – reached that figure, but – before his triple success over St André – Kut's score could only reach eleven if one assumed a score in France of three. After St André though, they certainly were level-pegging in RAF scores – but this would not remain the case for long.

CHAPTER ELEVEN

Marking Up The Score

By this stage of No 1 Squadron's intruder operations, Kut was being built up by the press to satisfy a hero-hungry nation and the *Daily Express* had taken to calling him 'the Baedeker ace'. However, a reporter with the *People* noted:

> Of the many modest heroes I have met, 'Old Kut', as his RAF comrades call him, is the most modest. When he talks of his exploits, he might be describing a success on a fair-ground shooting range.

Understandably the Czech Government in exile was keen to use his success by broadcasting news of his morale-boosting exploits to the citizens of Czechoslovakia. His most recent operation over St André was obviously just the kind of achievement to give heart to his fellow countrymen and women and so a couple of days later he agreed to make a broadcast to home. The transmission took the form of a four-minute interview with Lieutenant-Colonel Brož. The Controller of Czech military broadcasts throughout the war was Josef Josten who is still campaigning from Britain for freedom in his country through his Committee for the Defence of the Unjustly Persecuted. Kut was one of his 'stars' and they met on a number of occasions: 'He was a really delightful chap, very cultured, very modest and with inborn intelligence. He always behaved absolutely meticulously and professionally.'

The presence of Mac and Kut in the same squadron at this time made a formidable combination that provided inspired leadership and a friendly rivalry which was now becoming legendary in both the squadron and the press.

André Jubelin's dedications in *The Flying Sailor* include Mac ('that true hero') and Kut ('the great Czech pilot') and he wrote of their competitiveness:

> The other important figure in our little group, in which all the

126

pilots were exceptional men, was Kuttelwascher, a Czech lieutenant who, after having fought in the ranks of the French Air Force, had joined the RAF. He, too, was a comrade in arms. Kuttel, as we called him, was a close competitor of Mac for the record of enemy aircraft shot down. Their rivalry caused them to spend as long a time as possible in the air over France. They took off two or three times a night and often returned after daybreak. We pulled their legs about it. 'You people come back after daybreak because you don't like landing at night.'

In fact, Jubelin indulged in a little literary licence: the squadron's Operations Record Book makes it clear that no one flew more than one intruder sortie in a night and a computer print out from the Royal Greenwich Observatory reveals that no one returned after daybreak.

The rivalry between Mac and Kut infected the whole squadron and the effect was undoubtedly beneficial. Leslie Elvidge was a Leading Aircraftman in the Instrument Section at Tangmere and, as he was attached to the CO's B Flight, he was naturally rooting for Mac: 'This keen competition between two officers did more than anything for the morale of the squadron.'

The spirit spread well beyond Tangmere. Michael Shaw in *Twice Vertical* noted about this period:

The successes of Squadron Leader MacLachlan and Flt. Lt. Kuttelwascher over the previous weeks had been widely reported in the British press. Some reporter with a good nose for an 'angle' had developed his daily reports around a supposed rivalry taking place between the two pilots for the highest score. 'Old Kuttel is three ahead now', 'Pilots duel for top score', 'One-armed Mac strikes again' the headlines read. MacLachlan, a rather shy man socially, was quietly amused by all the nonsense. The gruff Kuttelwascher just grunted at each successive news report and shrugged it off. They were only doing a job.

The squadron's second moon period was coming to a close and, as spring blossomed into early summer, further victories of any kind proved most elusive. The evening after his triple kill, Kut was out over the Isle of Wight on a night patrol. Recording this in his log book, he noted disappointedly: 'Lots of enemy aircraft – but nothing in my gunsight!'

Over the next few nights, half a dozen different pilots flew intruder operations and each visited several airfields, but the lack of moonlight and the poor weather reduced visibility to the point where all that was seen was odd kaleidoscopes of variously coloured lights. Soon the weather became so appalling that on one day no flying of any kind was possible – even the birds were grounded! If things were bad for No 1 Squadron, conditions were equally inclement for their adversaries. On the night of 8/9 May, the Luftwaffe returned to Norwich, but the absence of moonlight ensured that it failed badly.

At this interlude in intruder activities, Kut himself took a well-earned period of leave so that for eleven days he did no flying at all. He returned to London where his wife Ruby enjoyed this all too rare time with him. It was in the course of this lull in operations that Kut and Mac received some metallic recognition of their success. So intense was the interest of the squadron's supporting personnel in the heroics of this gallant pair that, as soon as the news was received on 14 May, the information was broadcast over the tannoy to the whole squadron.

The boss was awarded the Distinguished Service Order for his command of the intruder operations. It was probably to mark the award of his DSO that the CO was persuaded to make a radio broadcast at this time. Characteristically he concluded the broadcast by giving generous credit to all members of the squadron, but he singled out his friend Old Kuttel for special mention:

My whole squadron, both ground crews and pilots, are as keen as mustard, and I must say they've put up a terrific show. Since April 1st the squadron has destroyed 11 aircraft for certain and probably three more, apart from the 17 trains and the odd boat I mentioned before. The lion's share of this total goes to my Czech Flight Commander, Kuttelwascher. He and I are great rivals at the game. All the boys love him. He's a first-class pilot, and has the most uncanny gift of knowing just which aerodromes the Huns are going back to. He'll look at the map and say, 'I'll go there tonight!' – possibly it is some unobtrusive Hun aerodrome. Sure enough, even if the others see no activity, Old Kuttel certainly will. One night last week we agreed to visit a certain aerodrome, but five minutes before we took off he changed his mind and went to another. I got to my aerodrome to find it covered with fog, while he calmly knocked down three.

Flight Lieutenant Karel Kuttelwascher relaxing with a drink during his visit to the USA. The occasion was a visit to the Army Air Forces School of Applied Tactics (AAFSAT) at Orlando, Florida. 16 July 1943.

Flight Lieutenant Karel Kuttelwascher (second from the left) photographed in front of an American aircraft during his visit to AAFSAT at Orlando, Florida. 17 July 1943.

Flight Lieutenant Karel Kuttelwascher of the RAF lectures to American pilots on the night intruder tactics in which he specialised and looks beyond France and the Low Countries, the scene of his intruder missions, to the main objective of the Allies: Berlin.

On a visit to the Warner Brothers Studios in Hollywood, Flight Lieutenant Karel Kuttelwascher meets the film star Errol Flynn who was then starring in the production of 'Uncertain Glory'. September 1943.

At the same time as Mac's medal, there was an equally well-deserved one for Kut who was awarded the Distinguished Flying Cross. The official citation – which was dated 20 May – read in part:

> He has at all times shown the utmost keenness to engage the enemy, and his wide experience and powers of leadership have made him invaluable to the squadron. Both by day and by night, a pilot of outstanding ability whose enthusiasm to engage the enemy is unbounded.

However, Kut's award – like those to all Czechoslovak personnel – was not published in the *London Gazette* to reduce the risk of retaliation against relatives still in Czechoslovakia. One seems bound to wonder about the effectiveness of this exercise, since his exploits were being reported in the British press almost daily.

On 19 May, Kut returned to Tangmere just in time for No 1 Squadron's very successful dance at Merston communal site to celebrate its 30th anniversary. No RAF squadron was older or prouder. To mark this special anniversary, a certain Flying Officer 'X' of No 1 Squadron wrote an article for a national newspaper. Following a brief history of the squadron, almost inevitably the piece finished up with a comparison of Mac and Kut and a shrewd assessment of their respective characters:

> Between them Kuttelwascher and MacLachlan have brought night intruding and night fighting to a fine art. As individualists MacLachlan and Kuttelwascher are remarkable. As an example of international cooperation they are typical of the RAF in general, of their own squadron in particular. They are persons of considerable character: MacLachlan direct, unassuming, volatile, exuberant . . . . This passion is tempered on one side by intelligence, on the other by impatience. He is very English. Kuttelwascher is also intelligent, and is very Czech. MacLachlan is fair and practically six feet tall. Kuttelwascher is fair and very short. He is also exuberant and unassuming, full of that Czech sense of humour which, in its love of understatement and irony, is so very close to our own. But underneath the exuberance and fun – the Kuttelwascher accent is a joy to all – there is deliberation, extreme patience, care and, above all, a kind of natural craftiness. Both men have a considerable score to wipe

out against Germany – one of the loss of an arm, the other the loss of a country.

Meanwhile the 'Baedeker raids' were continuing to show poor results from the German point of view. On 19/20 May, Hull was saved when the Luftwaffe dropped most of its bombs outside the city; five nights later, at Poole, a decoy fire proved most effective; and on 29/30 May, there was so much rain and clouds that not one bomb hit the intended target of Grimsby.

Towards the end of the month, No 1 Squadron had a shock when it was ordered to change the frequencies of the radio telephone and to switch from night to day camouflage. The pilots wondered what on earth was going on: were the night intruder operations over already? Forty-eight hours later, the order was cancelled: night intrusion was to continue.

However, the weather remained very bad and the nights dark, so that intruder operations were not resumed until the start of the squadron's third moon period at the end of May. On the night of 28/29 May, six intruder sorties were flown and the CO let the less senior men gain some valuable experience. Between them, four pilots – Corbet, English, Murray and Williams – disabled a total of ten trains. Next night, there were three operations and a further two pilots – Campbell and Pearson – shot up another eight locomotives. These eighteen trains were the first targets for more than three weeks and it was certainly good to be back in action.

The alluring moon was now full again and No 1's most senior officers were tempted back onto night intrusion. Yet two months on in the squadron's intruder phase, most of the pilots now had some proficiency in this style of operation and interestingly the next few successes came from neither Kut nor Mac.

The first such occasion came on the night of 30/31 May. Four pilots set off that evening, all but the CO from Manston, near Margate, rather than Tangmere. This was the first such use of an alternative field and it provided the Hurricanes with a better location from which to strike at some new, more-northerly targets, St Trond, deep into Belgium, and Venlo, a Dutch town even further east next to the German border. On returning, two of No 1's pilots had nothing to report, while the CO had added four more trains to the squadron's tally, but it was the Canadian Warrant Officer 'Gerry' Scott who had the most luck.

Scott left Manston to patrol St Trond. As he crossed the Belgian coast, searchlights and flak were thrown at him without result. Arriving at St Trond he found the airfield brilliantly lit: the Visual Lorenz – a landing system in which heights were indicated by lines of different coloured lights across a line of white lights – was on and the navigation lights of a Junkers bomber were seen approaching the base as the German pilot lined up to land.

The Canadian closed his Hurricane into attack, losing height to 500 feet. From a position dead astern, he gave two one-second bursts. He observed strikes on the fuselage and then a big white flash from the German's port engine followed by long white streams of smoke from that engine. Scott was now virtually on top of the Ju 88 and the airfield lights were suddenly extinguished, so he was forced to break off the attack to avoid collision, but he claimed one enemy aircraft as damaged.

Shortly afterwards, Scott spotted another aircraft about 500 yards ahead and only 500 feet above. Maintaining a position slightly below, he followed it as far as Brussels ready to add to his night's work. The problem was that in the darkness he was not sure whether the aircraft was hostile and he finally decided that this fleeing spectre was probably a Blenheim!

In fact, that night there was a veritable swarm of British aircraft over the European continent, since it was the first of the so-called '1,000 bomber raids'. Actually no less than 1,046 RAF aircraft dropped a total of 1,455 tons of bombs devastating a third of Cologne. The civilian casualties were almost 500 killed, about 5,000 injured, and 60,000 homeless. Operation Millenium, as it was called, was an horrific holocaust to visit upon any civilian population, German or otherwise.

Next night, that of 31 May/1 June, the Luftwaffe launched an attack on Canterbury intended as a response to Bomber Command's raid on Cologne. The Luftwaffe could muster less than a tenth of the RAF's strength, although it managed to inflict heavy damage on the old quarter of the city. However, the 'Baedeker' offensive was now almost over. Over the past five or six weeks, the Germans had suffered heavy losses for little strategic purpose and at this point they decided to switch from targets of simply aesthetic interest to those of some industrial or maritime importance.

On the night of 31 May/1 June, No 1 Squadron again used two bases from which to conduct intruder operations. Four pilots operated from Tangmere. Flight Sergeant English had nothing to report. Mac found his windscreen obscured by what he thought was an oil leak and was forced to return to base where he found that the 'oil' was in fact blood from a bird that he had hit. Sergeant Higham managed to blow up the engine of a goods train, but Kut had the most excitement of the Tangmere lads.

Off Fécamp, the Czech pilot saw steaming north-east a convoy of twelve ships in vic formation with two large ones – which he thought were destroyers – on each wing. Leaving behind this formation, he patrolled no less than seven airfields – Evreux, St André, Dreux, Rouen, Yvetat, Balbec and Le Havre – searching for enemy aircraft. The best that the nomad could find was two goods trains between the last two towns and he made sure that he disabled these.

Reaching the French coast once more, Kut followed it round to St Valéry-en-Caux where he sighted the convoy that he had seen on the way over. Now there were two or three small boats weaving in the rear. Sweeping down to just 100 feet, he attacked one from astern with three one-second bursts. Smoke poured from the boat and oil spread over the sea, so back at Tangmere he claimed it as damaged Category III. The night's work was the occasion for more amusing little sketches in the Czech's log book: two trains billowing steam and a boat riding the waves.

It was this kind of night's work by Kut that was obviously in the mind of the late Frank Wooley – a member of the squadron's ground crew – when, shortly before his death, he commented:

Both Kut and Mac gave us a great deal of extra work especially at night, which of course we did not mind. In fact we were as excited as they were when they returned from their escapades. Kut would leap out of his cockpit and jump up and down excitedly telling everyone in earshot how he had spotted a train puffing along, the white smoke visible in the moonlight. Down he swooped with a few bursts into the engine and then there was a lot more smoke. Perhaps he would find more trains that night or a convoy of lorries. No one on the squadron would forget these general remembrances for the morale of the whole unit at that time was extremely high because of this action. I do remember on the long summer evenings not being able to slip out to our little local pub when Kut was on the prowl for we never knew when he would reappear for refuelling and rearming.

Meanwhile three other pilots from No 1 were operating from

Manston. The New Zealander, Pilot Officer Perrin, went over to France, while the Australian Sergeant Dennis flew to the Netherlands. In both cases, all they could claim was a boat slightly damaged. However, Sergeant G.S.M. Pearson had a terrific time.

Pearson too was sent to the Netherlands and reached Gilze-Rijen at 2,500 feet. Underneath a roof of stars, he found the airfield lit up and the Visual Lorenz on, so he started to circuit the base. Half way round, he saw an unidentifiable enemy aircraft on circuit at a height of about 1,500–2,000 feet. The German's navigation lights were on but they were repeatedly switched on and off. Pearson followed the black enigma and, when he was about 300 yards away, he started an attack from a quarter port astern. As he gave a two-second burst, he closed in to 150 yards. Now dead astern, he gave a total of five further bursts, exhausting his ammunition. He clearly observed strikes on the fuselage before pieces blew off and the starboard engine caught fire. The enemy aircraft went into a spiral dive to the right and hit the ground about five miles south of the airfield. It exploded and burning fragments were seen over a wide area.

There was absolutely no doubt about Pearson's destruction of the German aircraft and it was the first night intruder kill made by No 1 Squadron which was not by Kut or Mac. What was not certain was the nature of the Luftwaffe machine destroyed. Pearson was unable to identify it with certainty and claimed it as either a Ju 88 or a He 111. He was right: thanks to contemporary research by the Dutchmen Leo Zwaaf and J. Thuring, it is now known that the destroyed aircraft was a Junkers Ju 88 C-4 from the night fighter unit, VI/Nachtjagdgeschwader 2. The young German crew killed was Oberfeldwebel Dieter Schade, Unteroffizier Jacob Cezanne, and Unteroffizier Adolf Jansen.

The following evening, 1/2 June, Luftwaffe bombers were over Ipswich, but heath fires diverted many of the bombs. Meanwhile, the RAF made a second '1,000 bomber raid' when 950 aircraft attacked Essen and the Ruhr, but cloud hampered the bombing. That night the focus of No 1 Squadron's own activity was again on the Low Countries. Although one pilot took off from Tangmere and patrolled French bases, more members of the squadron – five of them – used Manston to launch intruder operations to Belgium and Holland and these were the ones who saw action.

Pilot Officer Harry Connolly was sent to St Trond in Belgium. Just before he reached the base, he saw a Ju 88 against the moon.

The enemy aircraft was flying at the same height as himself, about 1,500 feet. Connolly made an astern attack from 100 yards' range, firing one short burst and observing strikes. Just then the Hurricane's port guns jammed and the aircraft side-slipped. While Connolly manoeuvred back into position, what he believed to be another Junkers was seen behind him. The German aircraft opened fire and for several tense minutes the Hurricane and the Ju 88 circled, trying to catch each other's tail cat-and-mouse style before contact was lost. So Connolly was able to claim an enemy aircraft damaged, but he was lucky to be alive to report the encounter.

The Canadian, Flight Sergeant G.C. English, had an even more successful night. He was sent off to Venlo in Holland. However, he could not find the airfield and, rather than waste his time, he attacked and stopped a long goods train. Abandoning the search for Venlo, he made now for Eindhoven which he orbited at 1,500 feet. Soon he saw a Do 217 circling at the same height. It had no navigation lights on and irritatingly he lost it in the inky blackness. Then he found it again and pulled up behind. The Dornier's pilot knew that he was in trouble and put his machine into a dive to the south, but English clung close. At a height of just 500 feet, the Hurricane fired a two-second burst from 150 closing to 100 yards dead astern. Cannon shells struck the Dornier's starboard engine and the enemy aircraft continued to dive straight into the ground where it burst into flames.

Again a night intruder kill had been made by a pilot other than Kut or Mac, but these victories made on consecutive nights by Pearson and English would prove to be the only ones achieved by the squadron in the whole intruder phase by pilots other than the Czech and the CO.

For English it was literally the night of his life. The day afterwards he was carrying out a practice camera gun attack on another aircraft of the squadron, when his aircraft – Hurricane Z3897 – stalled. At only 2,000 feet, he went into a spin and was unable to regain control before he dived into the ground at Bersted, near Bognor Regis, and was killed. It was the second accidental death of the squadron's night intruder phase and all the more poignant because – dangerous though they were – so far only one pilot had actually been lost on an intruder operation.

On the evening of 2/3 June, there were only two intruder sorties and Sergeant Pearson, still flushed by his victory of a couple of nights previously, disabled another three trains.

By now Kut had not shot down or even damaged an aircraft for almost a month and, while he certainly did not begrudge Scott, Pearson, Connolly and English their successes of recent nights, he was eager for more action of his own. But tonight, instead of night intrusion, he was one of six assigned to a patrol over Canterbury known as a 'fighter night' operation which involved free-lancing aircraft seeking German bombers above the anti-aircraft guns' maximum fire heights. The previous night another six No 1 pilots had carried out the same duty with nothing to report, so Kut was not sure what to expect. In fact, that night the Germans had returned to Canterbury after the evening away at Ipswich.

It was 2.40 am when Mac led Kut and the others into the ebony of the night. The six aircraft headed east. There was some moonlight and no cloud, so visibility was good. Before reaching the city, Kut saw numerous fires already burning there. They were too late. The German bombers had done their damage – but they were not yet home. The wily Czech decided to try to cut them off as they returned to base. Therefore he set a course for Deal at a height of 5,000 feet. To his immense annoyance, while crossing the English Channel he was fired at by the Dover defences just to the south.

Leaving behind this virulent pox now spreading across the sky, he set course for the Nieuport flashing beacon on the Belgian coast and winged his way over the Channel. After ten minutes' flying – it was now 3.25 am – he saw a Dornier Do 217 gradually overtaking him at a distance of only 4,000–5,000 yards on his starboard side. The German was at 4,000 feet and gradually losing height. Kut manoeuvred himself behind the Dornier. He opened the throttle, increased speed to 190 mph, and closed in for the kill.

He positioned the Hurricane at 150 yards dead astern and slightly below, the classic spot for an attack. The fighter's four Hispano cannon recoiled as he fired bursts of two seconds and one second – using up 140 rounds – and, after the second burst, the starboard engine of the enemy aircraft caught fire. The Do 217 went into a shallow dive, but this parlous condition did not last long before it plunged into the sea about five miles off Dunkirk on the French coast. There had been no chance for the enemy to return fire at any time. Kut continued towards the Nieuport beacon at a height of 2,000 feet, but it was becoming late, so he turned and flew back home via Deal and Beachy Head, landing at Tangmere at 4.30 am.

No 1 Squadron had now been conducting night intruder

operations for two months and, as far as the rivalry between the Czech flight lieutenant and his squadron leader was concerned, the scoreline tonight was: Kut 9, Mac 3. But the CO had no intention whatsoever of leaving matters as they were.

CHAPTER TWELVE

A Night To Remember

On the evening of 3/4 June, a time when the Germans were over Poole, a total of seven No 1 Squadron pilots – three of them Czech – were detailed to make intruder operations and it would prove to be a night that these searchers in the sky would recall vividly but with mixed emotions.

Mac was first off at 1 am. Successively he checked the airfields at Fécamp, Evreux, St André and Dreux, but found nothing. Back on the ground, he would tell a newspaper reporter:

At first I found nothing to attack. After patrolling a darkened airfield for some time, I decided to return home. Then it struck me that this was exactly the sort of place to which Old Kut himself would come sooner or later. So I turned back.

In fact Mac returned to St André which was now lit up with a full Visual Lorenz. The CO's heart leapt as he saw no less than around fifteen bombers orbiting at 1,000 feet, continually switching their navigation lights on and off, and preparing to land. No pilot could ask for a riper bunch of inviting targets but they were not without defensive armament.

Ignoring the daunting odds against him, Mac picked on the aircraft just coming in on the Visual Lorenz. He followed it down and closed to 200 yards. Just as the German crossed the last bar at a height of about 100 feet, Mac opened fire with a one-second burst from dead astern. The bomber's nose immediately went down and it crashed in a shower of sparks just short of the airfield. At that moment, the Hurricane was illuminated by six searchlights and flak opened up. Mac immediately took evasive action by diving to one side, but he was not about to leave an area so rich in potential victims.

Selecting the nearest out of about ten bombers that were still circling, he followed it at a height of 500 feet as it went down the Visual Lorenz. He gave it a two-second burst from dead astern at a range of 200 yards, observing strikes on the enemy aircraft. But he could not press his advantage. The Hurricane was picked up by searchlights again, the flak began tó come up once more, and he was obliged to break away. Things were now hot over St André and Mac took his aircraft up to 2,000 feet to avoid the flak.

Here he found a Do 217 doing a circuit with its navigation lights on. He promptly attacked it with three one-second bursts from 200 yards. Sparks began to fly from the bomber's port engine and then the port wing dropped as the enemy aircraft went into a 45° dive. After a few seconds, there was a bright red flash from the ground. Mac was not quite finished. At a height of 1,000 feet, he managed to find a fourth target and followed it until it was crossing the first bar of the Visual Lorenz. From a position dead astern and a range of 200 yards, he fired at the Luftwaffe machine and observed strikes on the fuselage. However, after about three shells had been fired from each cannon, his ammunition was totally exhausted and reluctantly but inevitably he had to pull away.

In his radio interview mentioned earlier, Mac described his feelings as he returned from an intruder operation of this kind:

> Well, when your petrol and ammunition are nearly gone, you are faced with the old Channel again. If you've got something, as I had that night, you leave the enemy territory with a sort of guilty conscience; not for what you've done – that's great fun – but somehow you feel they've got it in for you, and that everyone's going to shoot at you. It's a sort of nervous reaction, I suppose. The whole thing seems too easy to be true. Ten to one there's no Hun within shooting distance, and the ground defences are quiet. That makes it all the worse, and I generally weave about till I'm half way back across the Channel. If you've done nothing, of course, you don't get this feeling, as you're still looking for something at which to empty your ammunition – trains inland and barges and ships on the coast. We've had some of these recently, too.
>
> Out over the Channel you can hear your ground station calling the other aircraft of the squadron, and you count the minutes and look eagerly for the coast. Often it seems to take so long coming back that you feel sure the compass is wrong. At last, in the distance, you see the flashing beacon, and soon you are taxiing in to your dispersal point. I dread the look of

disappointment on my mechanic's face if my guns are unfired. But, if the rubber covers have been shot off, I've scarcely time to stop my engine before I am surrounded by the boys asking what luck I've had. Then comes the best part of the whole trip – a cup of tea and a really good line-shooting session.

For that night's work, the CO was credited with two enemy aircraft destroyed and a further two damaged, all believed to be Do 217s and one clearly identified as such. It was hard to remember that such a remarkable man only had one arm. Certainly he had more mettle than most!

Almost exactly 24 hours after his last victory, Kut was off on another, even more successful, sortie. This time he reverted to the traditional intruder operation and – as Mac had correctly anticipated – he went back to St André, the scene of his great triple kill. He took off an hour after Mac at 2 am. It was a dark night and the stars sparkled like a million fine diamonds cast upon a black cloth. He had only been in the air about ten minutes when he observed a Dornier Do 217 at 3,500 feet flying towards France. Apparently the enemy saw him too, because the aircraft began weaving and losing height. Although Kut started to follow it down, it dived away to one side and was lost to sight.

He proceeded in slight haze but good visibility across the Channel at 2,000 feet and crossed the French coast at the same height at Cabourg, south-west of Le Havre. Once over France, Kut climbed to 3,000 feet and altered course for St André. It was 3 a.m. when he arrived there. He could see a single flare path and partial Visual Lorenz. After a quarter of an hour, two enemy aircraft were seen orbiting at 1,500 feet with navigation lights on. Kut soon identified them as the familiar Heinkel He 111 bombers. The 'Night Reaper' sliced through the blackness and swept towards its harvest in a smooth arc of certain death.

Kut selected one of the bombers for attack. Coming behind the German aircraft, he squeezed the trigger and felt the kick of the cannon, firing two one-second bursts from dead astern at 200 yards. The starboard engine caught fire and the bomber dived steeply before crashing to the ground in a blazing pyre of twisted metal and high octane fuel. One down. Kut brought the Hurricane back on to orbit and saw a Do 217 at about the same height of 1,500 feet. He gave it a two-second burst from the unusually long range of

300 yards, astern and slightly below, observing strikes. It turned sharply to starboard, dived away and was lost to sight. It could only be claimed as damaged.

But the night and the operation were still not over. After orbiting for three or four minutes longer, Kut found more enemy aircraft, this time a little lower at 1,000 feet. Selecting the nearest, which was another Dornier, he came up behind it and opened fire with an effective one-second burst from 200 yards. At once it burst into fire on the starboard side, but it continued flying straight and level. He was not going to let this one escape. Kut gave it a second similar burst which resulted in it going into a steep dive to starboard, finally crashing east of St André airfield. Two down for sure. Three other enemy aircraft were sighted, but understandably the frightened crews switched off their navigation lights. Although he orbited for a further ten minutes, Kut was unable to move into position to attack any of them.

The lights at the dummy airfield west of St André-de-l'Eure – at St André-le-Favril – were switched on and off twice and some light flak now came up from positions south of the main airfield. So Kut returned to the Channel via the Seine and Rouen. West of Rouen, three searchlights came on but failed to illuminate him. However, north of Le Havre, he observed very intense flak for two minutes. He re-crossed the Channel at 3,000 feet – by now the weather was clear – and landed back at base at 4.40 am, this time having expended 236 rounds. Back at Tangmere, he learned that Warrant Officer Dygrýn – who was due out at about the same place as he saw flak on his return – was missing.

So, in the space of little more than 24 hours, Kut had destroyed three German aircraft and damaged another one. Of course, the Czech's two latest kills had come on the same night that Mac had added to his own score, and it would appear that he had seen ample evidence of the CO's success a little earlier in the evening.

This is indicated by an incident recalled by André Jubelin in *The Flying Sailor* which almost certainly occurred on 3/4 June (because on the only other occasion that Mac downed two enemy aircraft, Kut had to return after only reaching mid-Channel):

Outside the hut, the purring of an aircraft moving on wheels was heard approaching. 'That's Lieutenant Kuttel,' said Blick. [This was his nickname for the telephone operator/clerk in the pilots' crew room, Corporal Mitchell, most others calling him Mitch.] The Czech pilot was returning from a mission to Dinard and

Caen. [In fact, Jubelin – who admits in the text that he was relying solely on a fallible memory – had the destination of this operation wrong.] As a rule, with the precision of an acrobat, he touched down with all petrol shut off. One used to have to listen hard to hear him. 'Terrific' he announced as he came in. 'Nothing at Dinard, nothing at Caen. I was going to pay a call on Fanny [a light near Breteuil] when I saw, from the top of the cliff at Conges, two magnificent fires on the plain. I dived. Two ships had crashed on the airfield. Probably a collision.' Mac, beside himself with delight, leapt at the Czech pilot, thumped him on the shoulders with his one sound hand and shouted 'Yes! A collision with my shells! What an amazing bloke you are! Bloody good ideas you have, going to see that girl-friend of ours!' In a twinkling, all the pilots surrounded Mac's triumphant figure. 'I gave the firemen what for, I can tell you,' Kuttel added.

It is not clear what Jubelin meant by the Czech giving the firemen 'what for'. Maybe he simply buzzed them in devilment, although a Hurricane shooting down bombers as low as 1,000 feet would have been enough to make them move anyway. Other reports suggest that he strafed some Germans attempting to put out the wreckage of one of his victims. All one can say for certain is that, if there was any such incident, he chose not to mention it in his combat report.

Incidentally, the reason why the Breteuil light came to be called 'Fanny' is typical of the boyish humour of these young pilots in the face of so much personal danger. The light had been used as a guide to St André-de-l'Eure for some time when – according to the tale – a No 1 Hurricane passed nearby one morning flying at low level and the pilot saw through a window a beautiful half-dressed girl opening the shutters. For a reasonable if risqué reason, someone christened the (no doubt imaginary) girl 'Fanny' and the name soon came to be associated with the helpful beacon.

This latest night's success for the No 1 Squadron intruders resulted in a rash of further press reports. The *Daily Express* – always good for a lurid phrase – dubbed Kut and Mac 'the killers who stalk by night' and 'the two terrors who stalk in the dark'. A subsequent news item included a photograph of the Czech's face headlined: 'Eyes that kill in the night.' Now the score between the squadron's friendly rivals had been transformed to: Kut 11, Mac 5. However, if one adopts the wider scoring technique apparently used by the two pilots (which included victories prior to night intruding), then – excluding Kut's uncertain French victories – the

Czech and the CO were still virtually neck and neck at 14 and 13 respectively. But from now on Kut would leave the boss behind by any reckoning.

Certainly it had been a veritable night to remember. It would prove to be Mac's best night in the intruder phase and – combining his victories with those of Kut – the most successful night in the whole of the squadron's intruder operations.

Marring the night, however, was Josef Dygrýn's failure to return. It may be recalled that Dygrýn – a Czech – was an experienced night fighter pilot who while with the squadron had once shot down three bombers in a single night before soon becoming an ace. However, he was not a hardened practitioner of the very different art of night intrusion. In September 1941, he had left No 1 Squadron for a spell with the Czech 310 Squadron and had only returned two weeks ago. This was in fact his first – and last – intruder operation. Flying Hurricane Z3183, he has been assigned to patrol the Evreux group of airfields, but was probably hit as he returned across the French coast at the point where Kut observed flak. It was some three months later before his decomposed body was recovered from the beach at Worthing, so that he was not buried until 14 September.

It had been a sensational week for No 1 Squadron: seven enemy aircraft destroyed and another five damaged. The congratulations flowed into Tangmere.

A signal was received from HQ 11 Group passing on one received from the new Head of Bomber Command, Arthur Harris, who referred specifically to the recent '1,000 bomber raids':

> The exceptionally light casualties during the Cologne and Essen raids were undoubtedly in large measure due to the very effective intruding and special fighter arrangements made to cover the operations. I should be obliged if you would convey to the crews concerned the thanks of the bomber crews for the very efficient protection provided.

It seems that the Germans were so troubled by the RAF's night intruder operations that they had diverted much of their night fighter effort in an attempt to cope with the Hurricanes. As a result, the heavy Bomber Command raids – which included the Czech 311 Squadron – had reached their targets with little trouble. This was certainly news to the pilots of No 1: only one night fighter had actually been met.

As well as the signal from 'Bomber' Harris, there was a message from Sir Archibald Sinclair, the Secretary of State for Air: 'Congratulations on your fine exploit last night.' The Czechoslovak Air Force Inspector in London had been following closely the deeds of No 1 Squadron since Czechs began to fill the squadron's ranks and the CO now received a signal from Air Vice Marshal Karel Janoušek which read: 'Heartiest congratulations on your squadron's last night's great success. Good luck in future hunting to you and "Old Kut".'

After this outstanding night, things became very, very much quieter. The pilots would fill their time gathered round a table playing the usual games. Even here though, Kut's acute sense of propriety was in evidence as is clear from an interview:

> We take our full rest, and then we have some little amusement, like shove ha'penny and even bridge, but I like it without money. I don't like any game with money because it is cheating. With money you see, you are not my friend, because I am trying to fight you.

For him, fighting was confined to the air.

It was during this respite that Czechoslovakia burst into the British headlines as a result of the Heydrich incident.

Ironically it had all started at Kut's own base of Tangmere. Totally unknown to him, on 28 December 1941 a Halifax had taken off from the airfield carrying three teams of parachutists who were dropped into his homeland. One of the teams, 'The Anthropoid', consisted of a Czech, Jan Kubiš, and a Slovak, Josef Gabčík, who on 27 May 1942 ambushed the car of the SS Obergruppenführer Reinhard Heydrich, the Deputy 'Protector' of Bohemia and Moravia, known as 'the Hangman' for his brutal treatment of the Czechs. A bomb attack on the outskirts of Prague wounded Heydrich and he died of blood poisoning on 4 June.

The retaliation was immediate, massive and savage. The Germans obliterated the villages of Lidice and Ležáky, murdering all the men, incarcerating the women in concentration camps and deporting the children. Other brutal 'actions' followed and the death toll eventually amounted to something like 3,000. Kut was shocked and horrified by the news and, if ever he needed a sharper cutting edge to his sense of vengeance, he had it now.

Following the 'night to remember', over the next two and a half weeks – when there was little moonlight and sometimes poor weather – a total of a dozen more intruder operations were performed on various nights by a number of No 1 Squadron pilots. Kut was not among them and no one had anything of interest to report. It was time for the Czech avenger – his fierce hatred of the Nazis now fuelled to a new intensity by the Heydrich incident – to show once more how it was done and the opportunity soon arose during the start of the fourth and last moon period of the squadron's intruder operations.

On the evening of 21/22 June, the Luftwaffe's bombers attacked Southampton for the first time in over two months. Fortunately, the port received only about a fifth of the load intended for it. That night, four No 1 Squadron pilots carried out intruder duties. The CO had no action and Pilot Officer Murray lost contact with an enemy aircraft after a dogged 25 minute chase.

By contrast, Flight Sergeant Pearson – the only surviving No 1 pilot besides Mac and Kut to have shot down an aircraft on an intruder operation – had more success. He flew over to Evreux and, just as he reached it, the airfield lighting conveniently came on – a double flarepath and red perimeter lights. He circled at 1,000 feet at a distance of about three miles, until he saw a twin-engined aircraft with navigation lights on, flying at the same height. A red Very light was fired from the airfield and answered by a green one from the aircraft which now prepared to land.

Pearson manoeuvred onto the tail of the aircraft, guided by the tail light and other white lights which appeared on the Luftwaffe machine. In his eagerness, he pulled up exceptionally close and gave a one-second burst from dead astern. The flak from his guns illuminated the aircraft brilliantly and he estimated that he must have been within a mere 30 yards' range. There was no return fire, but a red rocket, which split into four parts, was fired from the enemy aircraft. Pearson throttled back to avoid overshooting and fixed his sights on the enemy aircraft for a second burst of two seconds from further back at 200 yards astern, very slightly to port. This time strikes were seen on the fuselage.

Then he gave a third and a fourth burst of two seconds each and, although no strikes were observed, there was a bright glow and billowing smoke from the port engine. Suddenly the German aircraft climbed and was swallowed by the night. Pearson was credited with an enemy aircraft damaged. However, in view of the heavy fire from close range and the glow from the engine, the

Assistant Air Attaché, Squadron Leader Josef Jaške (left), Squadron Leader Douglas Annan, Liaison Officer RCAF (centre), and Karel Kuttelwascher (right) at RCAF Headquarters, Ottawa, Canada. October 1943.

Flight Lieutenant Karel Kuttelwascher photograhed in front of a North American Harvard at No. 13 Senior Flying Training School, Royal Canadian Air Force at St. Hubert, together with Squadron Leader Douglas Annan, Liaison Officer RCAF (right). October 1943.

More tranquil days on a Test Flight at RAF St. Athan, South Wales, 1945. From right to left: F/Lt Karel Kuttelwascher, F/Sergeant Don Hilton, W/O Wright, unknown, W/O Norris CGM, unknown.

The triumphant march through Prague of the home-coming Czech Air Force led by Karel Náprstek with Karel Kuttelwascher five rows behind. 21 August 1945.

squadron asked Fighter Command to consider stepping up this claim to be a probable – the request was refused. As with his last victory, Pearson did not manage to identify the German aircraft.

But again it was Kut who had the most exciting night by boosting his score still higher. For the fourth occasion, it was over St André. The Germans there must have grown to dread the arrival of the 'Night Reaper'.

Take-off was 0055 am. That night there was no cloud and only a slight haze, so visibility was good. Leaving Tangmere behind, Kut climbed to 3,000 feet for the Channel crossing and maintained this height as he passed over the coast just north of Le Havre. His intended target was St André and he flew there directly to find the red flashing beacon and a few white lights. He passed the airfield on the west side, noticing that once more the dummy field at St André-le-Favril was lit up. Since he could not see any aircraft, he flew on towards Dreux and then, ten minutes later, circled back on the east side of St André at a height of 2,000 feet.

Now more white lights – about nine altogether – were on and so was the Visual Lorenz. Kut decided to lose height and came down to 1,000 feet before stooging around for about fifteen minutes. It was 2.10 am when he saw a Junkers Ju 88, with its navigation lights on, slightly below him on the opposite side of the airfield. He nipped quickly across the field and took the Hurricane up to the enemy's tail. As the Junkers came through the last bar of the Visual Lorenz at a mere 200 feet, Kut opened fire from 100 yards, dead astern and slightly above.

The unfortunate German did not stand a chance. As Kut's cannon crashed into action, momentarily night became day. After a two-second burst from the Hurricane's guns, the starboard engine and the fuselage of the Ju 88 caught fire. As the law of gravity exercised its irresistible, deadly grip, the aircraft crashed into the ground and spread itself out in flames along the runway. Obviously the incident immediately attracted the enemy's searchlights. There were four of them, but they failed to illuminate the Hurricane. Then Kut saw another Ju 88 with its navigation lights on. It was opposite the end of the runway and flying at 1,000 feet.

He chased the German aircraft and gave two two-second bursts from 200 yards dead astern. As the four cannon spoke in unison, he observed strikes but no flames. So he went to pump more ammunition into the enemy, but – to his intense frustration – both his port cannon had stoppages. The German's navigation lights went out and it dived away to starboard. So Kut lost contact and only claimed it as damaged. The Hurricane swung away as more searchlights came on and flak opened up. In spite of the cannon failures, Kut continued to orbit for a further 40 minutes, but there was no further activity. Meanwhile, throughout all this time the lights remained on at the dummy airfield.

Kut returned to base, landing at 3.45 am. He had only managed to use 175 rounds and had to report the failed port cannon. In fact, a number of intruders were having difficulties with cannon stoppages at this time. New ammunition was in use and the charge in some rounds was faulty, being insufficient to re-cock the weapon with the next round. The problem was overcome by using weaker recoil springs.

Later that day – 22 June – Kut was at last presented with his first DFC at Tangmere, but so prolific and so proficient were his victories becoming that the Czech would soon receive a second medal.

CHAPTER THIRTEEN

The Flaming Finale

No 1 Squadron was now entering the final week or so of night intrusion. On the night of 23/24 June, four pilots went over to France, but thick haze made it impossible for these hunters in the sky to see anything on the ground even from 500 feet. Next night, it was the turn of the Germans to suffer from the weather. Indeed it was so foul that not one bomb hit the intended target of Birmingham.

The following evening there was another '1,000 bomber raid' by the RAF: this time 1,006 aircraft were dispatched against Bremen and the Focke-Wulf works took a pasting. That same night, 25/26 June, six men from No 1 Squadron flew intruder operations and it was a rather more eventful night than two evenings previously, but in a mixed manner. This occasion saw the unit pressing deeper than ever into enemy territory and, in order to enable them to do so, once more Manston was used as the take-off point.

Mac went over to the Low Countries and patrolled between Gilze and Antwerp, but he was unable to locate his target (Gilze) as, before crossing the coast, his map had blown overboard! Meanwhile Kut too went out to the Netherlands and patrolled Flushing, Gilze and Walcheren, noting in his log book: 'Nothing to report! The weather is very bad!' Sergeant Pearson saw two burning aircraft and momentarily chased a Bf 110 over Holland. Sergeant Campbell had a similar experience: over Holland, he saw two aircraft and chased another, before blowing up the engines of two trains – the first locomotives to be attacked for over three weeks.

However, it was the New Zealander, Pilot Officer Des Perrin, who won the plaudits that night when, in a flight lasting 3 hours 35 minutes, he went to Gilze, next Eindhoven, then Venlo, and finally – pressing still further east across the German border – to Düsseldorf, landing at Manston with virtually dry tanks. This was the first time that any No 1 Squadron intruder had penetrated to

Germany and this bold thrust into the fatherland further boosted the already high morale of the squadron.

Unfortunately the sixth intruder pilot that night, the Canadian Warrant Officer 'Gerry' Scott, was lost. He took off from Manston in Hurricane HL589 at a quarter of an hour after midnight and set off for Eindhoven, but did not return. No news was ever received about pilot or aircraft. Unlike the two Czechs, Vlastimil Macháček and Josef Dygrýn, who failed to come back from their first intruder operation, Scott was one of the most experienced intruders on the squadron: this was his tenth such sortie.

That night was the first occasion that Kut had flown from Manston, 100 miles further east than Tangmere and therefore much more suitable for flights to the Low Countries. Sid Turner, a flight mechanic with No 23 Squadron, returned to Manston from a week's compassionate leave to find that No 23 had gone to Ford and he and a colleague, Maurice Noakes, were assigned to service the Hurricanes of No 1. Turner himself was required to look after Kut's machine.

Still living near Manston at Folkestone and now a civil engineer with British Rail, he recalls:

I remember so well one night going out to 'my' Hurricane and helping the pilot into the cockpit, chocks away, aircraft off, then – after hearing the take off and the dead silence after the aircraft had gone – walking back to the ground crewroom with the rigger. I recall hearing a piece of music coming across the airfield, most appropriately the 'Warsaw Concerto'. I thought how apt the music was and it has haunted me ever since. However, after a hot cup of tea, we would then settle down until our aircraft came back. I used to listen to the chatter of the pilots over the radio-telephone but Kuttelwascher was virtually silent. We got the call that the aircraft was in circuit and went out with our blue torches to marshal in the plane. I remember helping Kuttelwascher out and getting on with refuelling and so on when the armourer said: 'Blimey, every magazine empty!' This happened on several nights.

On the night of 26/27 June – while German bombers were over Norwich – Sergeants Campbell and Higham took off from Tangmere and between them disabled the engines of four goods trains on intruder operations over France. Meanwhile six

Hurricanes were ordered up on a roadstead operation to look for E boats 40 miles out to sea. Kut was involved in the latter exercise, but heavy cloud prevented anyone from seeing any enemy craft.

Later that day, a mere five days after Kut being actually presented with his first DFC, the squadron received the following signal: 'H.M. the King on the recommendation of the AOC in C has been graciously pleased to award a bar to the Distinguished Flying Cross to F/Lt K. Kuttelwascher, No. 1 Squadron. This award is not, repeat not, to be published. Please convey AOC's congratulations.' The official citation – which was dated 1 July – concluded: 'He has displayed exceptional skill as a night fighter pilot and his enthusiasm to engage the enemy is outstanding.' Working on the basis of the dates of the actual citations, it was just 42 days since Kut was first awarded the medal and by any reckoning to win the DFC twice in six weeks was a remarkable achievement.

As the squadron embarked on its final night intruder operations, Kut was not finished yet. On the night of 27/28 June, when German bombers were over Weston-super-Mare causing serious fire damage, two intruder sorties were flown without result. Next right, when the Luftwaffe was hitting Weston-super-Mare again, six pilots went over to France. On his last intruder operation, Mac chased an enemy aircraft for a couple of minutes but the cloud beat him. In fact – except for Kut – the only success was Sergeant Campbell's blowing up of the engine of a goods train.

It was 1.55 am when Kut set off on his intruder operation to the Dinard and Rennes area of France, further west than he usually operated. For the last time on a Hurricane intruder operation, he had a full moon and the air was so clear it looked like a golden orb in a jewelled sky. Crossing the Channel at 2,000 feet, he passed west of the Cherbourg peninsula and noticed a flashing red and white beacon at Jersey. Over St Malo, he found very different weather conditions with cloud down to 500 feet. At Dinard there was no activity, so he decided to explore an alternative target area. He flew north for ten minutes and started to patrol the base of the Cherbourg peninsula in an east-to-west direction. The weather was almost as bad as over St Malo with 10/10 cloud, the base varying from 500–1,500 feet.

Eyes narrowed slightly, Kut peered all around him, scanning the skies, searching for tell-tale navigation lights of enemy aircraft approaching base or a betraying black silhouette against the white moonlight. He covered the patrol line at a height of 2,500 feet no less than four times before he saw an aircraft. It was 3.20 am. There, about three miles to the south of him and 500 feet below, was a Dornier Do 217 bomber. For ten minutes he chased it in a south-easterly direction towards Bayeux. The Luftwaffe aircraft struggled to escape, but whatever it did Kut was still marking it in his own version of Czech-mate. Eventually he was able to close in to 150 yards astern and slightly above, carefully lining up the bomber in his sights.

There was a brief burst of fire from the Dornier's dorsal turret, but at that moment Kut opened his attack with a half-second burst and the return fire was effectively silenced. As the German in desperation began to dive, Kut clung to him and gave a second burst of two seconds from slightly further back at 200 yards dead astern. The Dornier caught fire at once. When Kut last saw it, the enemy aircraft was still diving steeply through cloud at 500 feet with wings and fuselage well alight. It was heading for the ground in the neighbourhood of Trévières, west of Bayeux. Therefore, he claimed it as destroyed.

Kut now turned towards the sea and, as he flew round towards Barfleur, he sighted seven E boats at 3.4 am. The E boats were putting up intense flak and back at Tangmere he would find that their likely target was Pilot Officer Corbet of his own squadron. He manoeuvred the Hurricane to put the boats between him and the moon and then dived to attack. Below the scudding Hurricane, its shadow flickered and shimmered on the undulating water like a silent sceptre. Ahead considerable return fire was coming at Kut, but he pressed on the valiant assault.

After a long three-second cannonade from 200 feet, one of the E boats began to belch out smoke and was seen to have a heavy list to starboard. Later he claimed it as a Category II. Another E boat received a two-second burst and was seen to be hit, but Kut's ammunition was exhausted and he could not continue the attack. Back at base, he claimed the second boat as Category III. At 4.15 am he was back home. For the first time on an intruder operation, all his 350 rounds were expended.

Next night, three pilots returned to France. Pilot Officer Corbet disabled three goods trains and Sergeant Higham knocked out two engines, in one case setting the trucks on fire as well. So to the last the No 1 intruders were taking every opportunity to disrupt the passage of equipment along the French railway system.

As the month of June closed, the Operations Record Book for

No 1 Squadron showed that the total flying hours by the squadron on all types of activities in that month came to 1,008 hours 20 minutes. This was believed to be the squadron record for any one month. According to his flight log, Kut's contribution was a total of 63 hours 25 minutes, just over a third of the time night flying.

The last intruder operations flown by No 1 Squadron occurred on the night of 1/2 July 1942 – an evening of heavy electrical storms – and it proved to be a flaming finale to the overall phase of night intrusion. Pilot Officer Perrin had nothing to report, but Sergeant Campbell and Flight Sergeant Pearson each saw successful action.

Sergeant J.R. Campbell was sent to Rennes and had to battle through a thunderstorm to reach it. Finding no activity there, he decided to patrol the railway line running north. Campbell – who had already knocked out twice as many trains as any other pilot on the squadron – now disabled three more goods trains, one going north, another south, and the third in a junction on the outskirts of town. He then set course for home, but on the way he spotted a Do 217 about 1,000 feet above him travelling towards St Lô.

Guided by the German's tell-tale exhaust, he dashed after it and opened fire with a ½-second burst from 200 yards dead astern and had the satisfaction of seeing strikes on the fuselage and port wing and engine. The Luftwaffe machine climbed, but Campbell – in spite of his port cannon having jammed – relentlessly pursued the German, giving him four more short bursts of about ½ second each from the starboard cannon. At this point, the enemy aircraft escaped into cloud but, when last seen, there was a glow from the port engine and therefore it was claimed as damaged.

In the case of Flight Sergeant G.S.M. Pearson, he failed to locate his target base of Rennes, but near Carteret he saw a Dornier travelling inland slightly above him. He chased it for five minutes, closed to 200 yards dead astern, and gave it a very short burst. The German did not seem to be hit but he obviously did not welcome the attention and dropped into a 30° dive. The Hurricane went after the enemy aircraft and at 350 yards a second burst of two seconds was made. This time strikes were observed and one member of the crew clearly decided that things were a little too hot because he promptly baled out. Pearson pressed on his attack with one more short burst, but then visual contact was lost.

Back at Tangmere, his combat report noted that, shortly after the engagement, he witnessed a bright flash on the ground where the enemy aircraft might have crashed. This led the squadron's

Intelligence Officer to consider stepping up Pearson's claim, but in the event it was left as simply damaged.

Characteristically, however, it was Kut who provided the real fireworks on this final night. After three months experience, his senses and skills were honed to a special sharpness and with unabated vigour he embarked on his latest and last intruder operation. At 2.10 am the Czech marauder took off from Tangmere. Once more the need to carry extra fuel in the twin drop tanks provided a bulbous underbelly to the Hurricane as it dragged itself from the airfield and made for the coast. Tonight, as on the previous occasion, Kut was off to Dinard and Rennes.

Flying at 3,000 feet, he crossed the Channel almost due south and passed over the French coast at Carentan on the Cherbourg peninsula. Above 5,000 feet there was heavy cloud and below mist hung low like a grey curtain of gauze. About 20 minutes after crossing the coast, his perennial quest for Luftwaffe bombers found him south of Dinard. The airfield was lit up with a flarepath and two bars of the Visual Lorenz. He turned to starboard and flew out to sea, orbiting over the estuary near St Malo.

At 3.25 am – he was then about five miles north of Dinard airfield – Kut saw on his starboard side the sinister silhouette of a Dornier Do 217. It was flying at 1,000 feet and had its navigation lights on, but these were soon switched off. Then on his port side and close, he found two more Do 217s. Again they were at about 1,000 feet and lights on. Kut decided to tackle the nearest of the enemy aircraft. With the stealth at which he had become practised, he closed to 200 yards dead astern and slightly below. Four cannon spat a metal stream of armour-piercing and incendiary shells, as he gave the Dornier an accurate half-second burst, followed by an equally devastating one-second burst. Fire broke out in the fuselage and on the starboard side and then the German plane plunged straight to the ground in a ball of flames.

The other Dornier was now slightly above him and still had its navigation lights on. As the Hurricane approached, the lights were switched off and Kut passed 100 feet beneath the fleeing shadow. As he turned to port to manoeuvre into position again, the Do 217 opened fire from a range of 300 yards, but the British plane was not hit. Unflinching, Kut managed to come astern of the German and inflicted a two-second burst from about 250 yards. He observed strikes, but then blackness enveloped the bomber and contact was lost. He would claim this one as damaged.

Remaining on the scene, Kut flew south to the airfield and saw still another Dornier at 1,000 feet with navigation lights on. He positioned himself neatly below and behind this tempting target. The German's lights went off and at that moment the Hurricane was nearly picked up by a searchlight on its starboard side. Nevertheless, Kut decided to follow the enemy aircraft and managed to obtain a new visual on it. He opened fire with two two-second bursts which sank into the German from very close range dead astern. The Czech's ammunition was now exhausted but that did it. After the first burst, the Do 217 caught fire. Then it dived steeply starboard before the downed Dornier crashed into a wood north of the airfield.

After this intimidating display of pyrotechnics, Kut set course for home, meeting some flak whilst crossing the coast near St Malo. On the way back, at about 3.45 am, he saw something burning on the ground near Trévières. He re-crossed the Channel just below the cloud base at 5,000 feet and landed at Tangmere at 4.45 am, as last time his ammunition totally spent. It had been another virtuoso performance which brought his total number of night kills to fifteen.

At this point, the existence of an historical dilemma must be confessed.

According to Kut's flight log, he shot down an extra Dornier Do 217 on 1 July and the occasion when he destroyed two Dorniers and damaged another in the same night was not 2 but 6 July. If true, this would raise his night score to sixteen and certainly in both February and April 1943 Fighter Command Headquarters put out official lists showing him with sixteen victories. To set against this account, we have the squadron's Operations Record Book which only shows one intruder operation by Kut in July: on the second night of the month, he downed two Dorniers and damaged a third. The combat report for the sortie gives the same version of events.

Neither source – the Czech or the squadron – can be regarded as infallible, since on other matters both have been found to contain the occasional mistake. Also both sets of records were written at a time of change. Kut moved on to a new squadron on a new base and consequently the relevant page of Kut's log book is not signed by the No 1 Squadron CO. For its part, No 1 Squadron changed airfield, aircraft and CO and left its Intelligence Officer behind with 43 Squadron, so the squadron's Operations Record Book for July contains none of the usual details of intruder operations.

However, the balance of evidence points in favour of the squadron's account of the conclusion of night intrusion and the author has based his own account on this assumption.

It was probably at this point that Mac met David Annand, then a wing commander and Chief Instructor at 41 OTU at Old Sarum and Oatlands Hill, and gave him a characteristically nonchalant account of night intrusion. Annand recounts:

> In July 1942, I was taking a Mustang from Sarum to Oatlands Hill near Stonehenge. Prior to landing, I saw a Hurricane painted matt-black on the ground. After landing, Squadron Leader Ian Morrin introduced me to Squadron Leader James (Mac) MacLachlan whom I had not previously met. Ian, a marvellous Scot, had trained with Mac and they were superlative people. At Oatlands Hill Ian, having introduced me to Mac, asked if he could have a first flight in a Mustang. Seeing only one arm, I said to both of them, 'Do you think it is all right?' Couldn't Mac half fly fighters! We asked Mac what his job was and what black Hurricanes did. He gave us chapter and verse about intruding over German bomber bases in France. He said it was 'money for old rope' shooting down Huns going into land and that it was 'like shooting down sitting ducks'.

For No 1 Squadron at least, night intrusion from Tangmere was now over. On 7 July, the squadron received just one day's notice that it was moving up to Acklington in Northumberland. Next day at 5 pm the Hawker Hurricanes roared off from Sussex heading north, where two weeks later they started to be replaced by Hawker Typhoons. The squadron left behind two members: Pilot Officer Connolly who went to No 32 Squadron and Kut who was off to No 23 Squadron. Up at Acklington, there were further changes and everyone was shocked when – the day after the first Typhoon arrived – Mac was posted to No 59 OTU before later being sent on a special mission to the USA.

It was the end of another glorious chapter in the long and distinguished history of No 1 Squadron and the crowning pinnacle of Kut's flying career.

In the course of three months, a total of about 140 night intruder operations had been flown by a total of nineteen different pilots (four of them Czech). Mac had made the most with twenty in his log book; then, not surprisingly, came Kut with fifteen trips;

however, Pearson managed to make the same number and Perrin flew twelve. The final score sheet for the squadron as a whole was 22 aircraft destroyed and 13 damaged, plus the bonus of a total of 67 trains, five boats and a lorry disabled.

Of course, the top scorer by far was Kut, the first and finest of No 1's intruders. He had shot down no less than 15 enemy aircraft and damaged another five, earning in the process a DFC and Bar. By any estimate, this was a remarkable achievement but, when one remembers that all but one of these 20 victories were scored on just 15 intruder sorties, one can appreciate his truly sensational success rate. His total RAF tally was now 18 kills. The other high scorer was Mac. He had downed five aircraft and damaged a further three, collecting a DSO for his magnificent leadership. His total of kills now stood at 13. Besides this dynamic duo, mention should be made of Flight Sergeant Pearson, who destroyed one aircraft and damaged another two, and Sergeant Campbell, the champion train-buster with a total of 21 to his credit.

The squadron's intruder operations had contributed to three particularly useful ends: the frustration of the Luftwaffe's 'Baedeker raids', forcing them to operate from bases further back; the diversion of the German fighter effort while the RAF's '1,000-bomber raids' had started up; and the disruption of the movement of goods by rail in the run-up to the planned Dieppe Raid. However, in the course of the intruder phase, the squadron had lost five pilots, two of them in accidents and another three actually on intruder operations.

During the last three weeks of No 1 Squadron's intruder activities, they were joined at Tangmere by No 43 Squadron, which had flown down from Acklington, where it had been operating as day and night fighter defence. Squadrons 1 and 43 had been stable companions at the airfield for fourteen years up to 1939 and, when No 1 left Tangmere at the beginning of July, 43 took over the intruder role. During July and August, unless weather was impossible, five aircraft were made available for night intruding. However, as noted earlier when the experience of some of the pilots was recounted, No 43 had no real success: the Germans had grown wise to British tactics and moved their bomber bases beyond the Hurricane's reach, so the sole result of the squadron's efforts was ten railway engines disabled.

No 43 Squadron pilot, Harry Lea, makes a relevant point:

As night intruders, we did not have the same results as 1 Squadron in air to air contact. I believe one of our main objects was to concentrate on ground attack for it was at this time that we were preparing for a major landing in Northern France [the Dieppe Raid of 19 August 1942]. The Germans, who were harassed in the movement of troops and supplies during daylight, concentrated this task in the night hours. Consequently, we were trying to disrupt this enemy movement by searching out and attacking trains, road transport and coastal shipping.

The Royal Air Force vacated Tangmere in 1970, but the spirit of those long, tense nights of 1942 still lives on today in the Military Aviation Museum at Tangmere, located just off the A27. This was created by an enthusiastic team of volunteers led by Jim Beedle, a wartime member of the ground crew with No 43 Squadron and author of the impressively-detailed history of that squadron. The Tangmere museum opened in June 1982 and one of the visitors in that first summer was Mari Rowe, Kut's younger daughter, who was surprised to find a photograph – unfortunately a rather poor one – of her father on display. Later the author was delighted to be able to let the museum have a much better photograph of the Czech which now resides at Tangmere where it is associated with a fine model of the 'Night Reaper'. Rightly the attraction of the museum has grown rapidly and it is now open daily from March to November.

Kut was now leaving No 1 Squadron after almost two years. This was an exceptional period of time for any pilot to spend with any one squadron in the turbulent conditions of wartime and probably a unique length of time for a Czech to pass with a British squadron while other compatriots were being transferred to Czech squadrons or OTUs. Of course, No 1 was a friendly home to a great many non-British pilots and by the end of the war the unit's proud boast was that its members had included the fourth highest-scoring Canadian ('Hilly' Brown), the second highest-scoring Frenchman (Jean Demozay), the top scoring New Zealander (Colin Gray) and the top-scoring Czech (Kut).

As he prepared to take his leave of No 1 Squadron, perhaps Kut took a moment or two to pause, to think, to remember once more the fresh, eager faces of all those comrades whom he would never see again. During his time there, 21 members of the squadron had died, seven of them Czech – so many young lives, so much human waste. Then again perhaps he did not allow himself to indulge in such painful memories. In war, the black hand of death is ever poised to snatch away a life of promise, but one could not afford to dwell too much on such agony. There were too many more operations to fly and another squadron awaited him.

CHAPTER FOURTEEN

The Wooden Wonder

On 9 July 1942, No 1 Squadron went north to Acklington to convert to Typhoons and No 43 Squadron took over the night intruder role at Tangmere. Meanwhile Kut remained on the south coast and the previous day he was reassigned to No 23 Squadron which involved merely a move down the road from Tangmere to Ford and his retention on the same kind of operations. It was the Czech's good fortune that, having served so closely with the charismatic one-armed Mac, he was now to have another CO who, while physically disadvantaged, was both colourful and courageous.

Wing Commander Bertie Rex O'Bryen Hoare DSO & Bar – known to his friends simply as Sam – had served with 23 Squadron since the outbreak of war and became its CO in April 1942. He sported an enormous handlebar moustache and was an outstanding night fighter pilot who only had one eye. By the time Kut met him, Sam already had several victories including one that was so close that he collided with it and returned with his wings full of debris.

No 23 had been on night intruder operations since early 1941. Originally using the Boston and then the full night fighter version the Havoc, at the time Kut joined it the unit was beginning to convert to the Mosquito, making it the first intruder squadron to operate this particular aircraft.

The matt black de Havilland Mosquito II was well-suited to the intruder role. It was powered by two Rolls-Royce Merlin 21 engines and had speed – a maximum in excess of 360 mph – and superb manoeuverability. There were four 20 mm Hispano cannon in the belly and four 0.303 in Browning machine guns in the nose. For intruder operations, it was fitted with long range fuel tanks which increased normal endurance by about $1\frac{1}{2}$ hours and produced an operational radius of around 600 miles (further than the long-range Hurricanes). Although radar equipment was not fitted at this stage, the intruder crews were always in radio contact with base. Like all Mosquitoes, it had an all-wood construction which gave it the nickname 'the wooden wonder'.

Throughout the months of July, August and September, No 23 Squadron used intruder sorties to keep watch on around two dozen different German bases at any one time, about half of them in France, others in Holland, some in Belgium, and – towards the end of the period – a couple in Germany. In the cases of the airfields in France and the Low Countries, many of the airfields were familiar territory to Kut.

While the Czech was reaching the end of his own intruder sorties with No 1 Squadron's Hurricanes, the first Mosquito intruder operation was undertaken by 23 Squadron on the night of 5/6 July: Sam Hoare went over to Caen but found nothing. However, the following night, he was patrolling Avord when, east of Chartres, he spotted a Do 217 and after three bursts of cannon fire sent it crashing in flames near Montdidier. His combat report noted: 'During the last burst, there was a dull thud on the windscreen and from the mess it left it is thought to have been a piece of the rear gunner.'

Following Kut's re-assignment to this unit, other squadron members achieved reasonable success throughout July. Only two nights after the CO's victory, on 8/9 July Squadron Leader Salusbury-Hughes destroyed a Do 217 near Chartres and an He 111 in the Evreux area. In the final week of the month, Flying Officer McCulloch destroyed a Heinkel as it came into land at Bretigny and the CO shot down an unidentified enemy aircraft while patrolling Orléans. The same week, however, saw the first loss from Mosquito intrusion: on the night of 28/29 July, Flight Sergeant K. Hawkins with Sergeant N. Gregory as observer flew off to patrol Eindhoven but failed to return.

At first Kut was simply on supply to No 23, and then on 13 July he was assigned to flying duties. In fact, this was a period of some well-earned leave. On 11 July, he was photographed in London being congratulated by Jan Masaryk, the Czech Foreign Minister. A few days later on 16 July, Kut and Ruby attended a British–Czechoslovak Friendship Rally at Kenwood in north London where he was photographed giving autographs to English boys.

It was not just reporters and photographers that were in touch. Kut had to give a long interview to Bob Bowman of the Canadian Broadcasting Corporation for transmission on the BBC's North

American service and such was the interest that the text was printed in the magazine *London Calling*. The interview revealed how his dedication to flying led him to be careful about eating and drinking:

> I always feel in the mood for flying, night flying does not tire me at all. Of course special foods help. I take all the vitamins that we have from the doctor regularly, but the main thing is just to be in good condition. I don't smoke and I don't drink. They tell me I don't miss much. Wartime beer is very bad. It is like water. Then I like English food. I like English vegetables. We grow our own vegetables.

It was not until 28 July that Kut actually started to fly the Mosquito. After a couple of flights with someone else at the controls, he practised landings solo and tested the cannon.

The following year Kut told the *Vancouver Sun* that, of all the aircraft he had flown, the Mosquito was the finest. Of course this might have had something to do with the fact that the aircraft was built of the local Queen Charlotte Islands spruce. Nevertheless, Kut was certainly thrilled with the sleekness and speed of the Mosquito and rather cheekily took the first opportunity that he could to fly over his and Ruby's home at Mill Hill in north-west London. On 2 August, he wrote to his now pregnant wife:

> I would like to be home to be care of you but as you know the same time I must be on duty – and as you saw today and yesterday I have a beautiful plane – don't you think? Did you see me? I will come over more often to show you how nice one is.

Once more he had to explain that he did not know when he would be able to snatch some leave:

> It is so difficult, darling – you know I would like run home and stay as long as possible – but duty here! Bloody war – but it will finish one day and I will be very happy.

On 6 August, No 23 Squadron left the remaining Bostons and Havocs at Ford and moved to Manston. In the course of the next two months, the unit alternated between here and Bradwell Bay, respectively south and north of the Thames estuary. Soon after the

The badge of the Czechoslovak pilots in Britain during World War II.

(*Left*) Sergeant Josef František, the Czech fighter ace who flew with the Polish 303 Squadron. He scored 17 victories in September 1940 making him the top scoring RAF pilot of the Battle of Britain. (*Right*) Warrant Officer Josef Dygrýn (nom-de-guerre Ligotický) who was credited with five victories—three in one night—all achieved while flying with No. 1 Squadron. The Czech was killed on a night intruder operation on 4 June 1942.

Karel Kuttelwascher at Herlify, his home in Czechoslovakia, wearing the badges of the Czech, French and Royal Air Forces together with medals awarded him by the Czech, French and British.

transfer to Manston, Squadron Leader Salusbury-Hughes added to his score when he probably destroyed a Do 217 over Beauvais.

At last it was time for Kut to carry out an intruder operation in the Mosquito. Unlike the Hurricane, of course, the 'wooden wonder' had a crew of two and on all the Czech's intruder flights with 23 Squadron his observer was Pilot Officer G.E. Palmer. The first operation came on the night of 11/12 August when the moon was new and the sky black. He was sent to patrol the French towns of Châteaudun and Orléans and, although he found Orléans airfield was lit, he could detect no activity.

Although Kut himself was seeing no real action, during this period he learned of the loss of a Canadian relative of Ruby, Peter Evans, while on a sortie. The Czech's letter to Ruby on 15 August commented:

I was very sorry for Peter to hear the news about his missing. It's rather difficult for all young boys now. Everybody with few months exercises and training and going at once in actions. It will be very sad news for his people in Canada. And I didn't know him very well – if I should have more opportunity, I would like to tell him all about this job because I know these snakes very well. I hope he will be a prisoner of war – I cannot find here his combat report and therefore I can't say what to think.

It was the night of 22/23 August before Kut went on another intruder operation. He took off to patrol Gilze and Eindhoven in Holland but frustratingly was forced to return before reaching the coast, owing to electrical equipment failure and engine trouble, only being in the air 27 minutes. His third occasion of intrusion was on 25/26 August, a night of full moon when he could hope for some action. He patrolled the Dutch bases at Deelan and Soesterberg. Near Deelan the Mosquito's electrical equipment failed and the course was lost.

It was not just the intruder operations that were disappointingly uneventful. On 30 August, Kut wrote to Ruby: 'Last night I was on duty – nothing to do – because devils didn't come to play – and this morning rain and very low clouds.'

Fortunately as far as other pilots at No 23 were concerned, all was not totally quiet on the intruder front. On successive nights at the end of August, the American Sergeant Wright destroyed one aircraft on the ground at Étampes/Mondesir and then damaged another as it was landing. Also, early in September, Flying Officer Welch attacked and damaged one of two aircraft spotted as he patrolled Melun.

Kut was back in action – if it can be described as such – on 6/7 September when he flew an intruder operation to Leeuwarden in Holland. He found no activity at the base but experienced considerable flak from Texel Island. The following night he was back over Holland, this time to patrol Gilze and Eindhoven. On reaching the Dutch coast, however, he was forced to return, after experiencing more electrical trouble. In fact, one engine went and he had to land at Bradwell Bay instead of Manston.

This concluded Kut's intruder operations on the Mosquito. His lack of luck with 23 Squadron contrasted very dramatically with his uncanny success at No 1 – indeed he never once even sighted a German aircraft. However, he had made many fewer sorties, he had not had the same freedom to roam, and he had experienced repeated electrical failure in his Mosquitoes. Actually the whole squadron was plagued with all kinds of mechanical and electrical failures and several other pilots had such severe engine trouble they were forced to crash land.

David Annand, the Chief Instructor who met Mac at Oatlands Hill, suggests:

> It was a mistake to take Kut off single-engined aircraft. He and Mac were individualists and they should have formed a Night Fighter Mustang III Squadron – much farther range and much faster than a Hurricane which in 1942 was being phased out.

The last of the Czech's nights of intrusion coincided with a triple tragedy for 23 Squadron when, on the evening of 8/9 September, the unit lost three aircraft and five men. The American Sergeant G.R. Wright with Sergeant A.M.F. Cook took off to patrol Gilze and Eindhoven, but they never returned. Flying Officer I.N. Stein with Sergeant H.G. Challicombe flew off to Soesterberg, but failed to come back, and three days later Challicombe's body was washed ashore at Felixstowe. Finally Flight Lieutenant N.A. Buchanan with Pilot Officer V.G. Brewis successfully patrolled Gilze and Eindhoven but, a fix having been made on the Mosquito fifteen miles from Harwich, nothing further was heard. Some time later, Buchanan was picked up by a naval launch but died while being brought ashore. After eight hours in a dinghy, Brewis was rescued and taken to hospital where he insisted that Buchanan, although himself badly injured, was responsible for unstrapping his harness and loosening him into the water. Eleven days later a Boston flew out to sea and Buchanan's ashes were scattered over the waves.

In spite of these dreadful incidents, operations had to continue and, only two nights after the squadron's losses, the CO Sam Hoare saw an enemy aircraft near Enschede on the Dutch border and chased it over Germany as it flew lower and lower. Without a shot having been fired, the Luftwaffe machine dived into the ground. The squadron believed it to be the first enemy aircraft to be destroyed by an intruder in Germany itself. Towards the end of September, Hoare made his last intruder trip before he was awarded the DSO and handed over command of the squadron – amazingly it was his 80th such operation.

It was time for Kut to leave No 23 . He was not going to miss anything: October, November and December saw repeated bad weather, very few intruder operations and no combats for the squadron before at Christmas 1942 it was sent to Luqa in Malta, the first unit to operate Mosquitoes from bases outside Britain.

On 10 September, Kut was presented with the Bar to his DFC at a ceremony held at Uxbridge. Then, on 1 October, he was transferred from No 23 Squadron to No 42 Group in Maintenance Command to act as liaison with the Czech Inspectorate-General, something of a 'desk flying' job.

As a result, he did not pilot an aircraft at all for four months, yet his wife did not benefit much from his time on the ground. An article in the *Sunday Dispatch* reported:

Mrs Ruby Kuttelwascher, Welsh wife of Flight Lieut. Karel Kuttelwascher, Czech ace night fighter pilot, realises that, as long as the war lasts, she must take second place to the RAF. 'When we were married just over a year ago, it was on condition that my flying must always come first,' said Kut yesterday. 'My wife was quite willing to agree to this.'

It went on:

Although he is now on leave at their home in Mill Hill, London, Mrs Kuttelwascher has so far hardly seen him. All day yesterday he was out on official visits. Tomorrow morning newsreel cameramen will arive at Mill Hill to make a picture of the Kuttelwaschers at home.

One day a little later that autumn, the heavily pregnant Ruby sat through all 3 hours 42 minutes of the wonderful film of *Gone With The Wind*. The final line of this moving film comes from Scarlett O'Hara who declares: 'Tomorrow is another day'. For Ruby it certainly was, for she gave birth to a son. The child was born on 18 September 1942 – only five days off his father's 26th birthday – and weighed 8¼ lb. He was called Eduard Huw Kuttelwascher, the first of his christian names coming from Dr Eduard Beneš (the President of Czechoslovakia and – as Ruby once put it – 'Karel's great hero') and the second coming from Wales (Ruby's home country). In fact he was always known by the second of these names, Huw.

A message was sent to Kut's former comrades at No 1 Squadron, still remembered by those who survive. It read: 'I have arrived. My name is Huw Eduard. I have selected Mr and Mrs Kuttelwascher to be my parents.' The baby was sent a sterling silver spoon inscribed: 'Best wishes from No. 1 Squadron'. There was a lot of press interest and one photograph of the proud father was headlined: 'Kuttel pilots a pram'.

Congratulations came from many quarters. Among salutations from family friends, the Collins family sent a telegram playing upon the name of Kut's Hurricane: 'Heartiest congratulations on arrival of the night disturber.' The 'official' telegrams included one from the Inspector-General of the Czech Air Force, Air Vice Marshal Karel Janoušek: 'Congratulations and best wishes to all three of you.'

On 17 October, Ruby received a hand-written letter from the Czech Foreign Minister, Jan Masaryk, who belatedly sent best wishes to her on the birth:

Forgive me for not having written before to congratulate you on Huw Eduard's arrival. I am enclosing a tiny bank account for your son. Will you ask your husband to sign the enclosed according to the bank's instructions. It seems all very complicated, uselessly so to me, but them's the rules. I hope and pray that this horror will end soon and that your little family will be able to live in a world fit for human beings to live in.

Another letter (20 October) came from Hana Beneš, the wife of the Czech President:

We would like your little son to have this small gift which we hope he will be pleased to keep as a souvenir. We also wish to pay a tribute to the wonderful skill and daring with which your husband fights for the cause of freedom. May your baby grow up to possess the same fine courage and devotion to duty.

Shortly afterwards, Kut had a different kind of letter from his former CO at No 1 Squadron. It was dated 20 October and Mac wrote from the Eglin Field Officers' Mess, Valparaiso, Florida in the USA. It provided a cheerful foretaste of Kut's own visit to the States the following summer and autumn:

Just a line to let you know I'm still going strong, and shooting an even bigger line than usual. I'm having a simply wizard time over here – I only wish you and the rest of the boys were here with me. I'm stationed at the American equivalent of the A.F.D.U. [Air Fighting Development Unit] at Duxford, and can fly any type of aircraft I want. I have already got in eleven different types here including the Thunderbolt and Lightning. I have to go up to Washington fairly after [sic], and have had some simply wizard parties with G/Capt Hess [the Czech Air Attaché]. He's been damn good to me Kuttel – he treats me as if I were his son: by God we get pissed! Do drop me a line and let me know what you're doing and what things are like at home. These Yanks just don't know there's a war on, but they're damn kind and hospitable. I have a Mohawk of my own which I fly round in and give lectures and teach the boys aerobatics and odd things. I shall probably be coming back next Spring – I hope to get another squadron.

At the time that Mac's letter reached Kut, the two intruder pilots were featured in an Exhibition of New War Pictures held at the National Gallery in London. The Exhibition opened on 23 October and a week later a reviewer wrote in *Aeronautics*: 'Eric Kennington's posters of flying personnel are strongly represented and many famous "aces" watch silently over the scenes of past glories. "Old Kut" and his friend Squadron Leader MacLachlan DSO especially caught my eye.' Kennington was an Air Ministry artist. His portrait of Mac is now in the Imperial War Museum but, according to the Air Historical Branch of the Ministry of Defence, that of Kut was – in accordance with the normal practice for Commonwealth and Allied personnel – passed to the Czech Government after the war.

Then, in the same way that the RAF had seemingly marked both Kut's first meeting with Ruby and his marriage to her by promotion, shortly after their son's birth and before the christening – actually 7 November – the service confirmed his appointment to the RAFVR and promoted him to 'Flying Officer (War Substantive)'.

Next month, son Huw was christened at the Union Church in Mill Hill, north London where his parents had been married. He could hardly have had more distinguished godparents: the Czech President, Eduard Beneš, and the Czech Foreign Minister, Jan Masaryk. Beneš himself was not there: he wrote a letter to Kut explaining that, if he attended this event, he would have to be present at so many others and so he operated a strict rule on such matters. Nevertheless he was delighted to be godfather and sent along an official representative. The other godparent – Masaryk – was at the ceremony.

Indeed the christening was mentioned by Masaryk in his next radio broadcast in the weekly series which he made during the war to his fellow countrymen and women in Czechoslovakia. The broadcast on 23 December 1942 sent Christmas and New Year wishes to all Czechs and noted:

Here I have christened Kuttelwascher's baby, a delightful child – eyes like pinheads and he hardly wept at all – he behaved as was fitting for the son of a father who is not afraid – a father who has shot down 24 Germans [this total could only be achieved by accepting Kut's claim of six aircraft destroyed in France] and never talks about it.

Kut's former colleagues at No 1 Squadron continued to follow the press coverage of him and items were regularly mounted in the squadron scrap books. When photographs of Kut and Ruby with baby Huw started to appear, one wit wrote opposite the cuttings in the scrapbook: 'Another score. Known as a probable. Now confirmed.'

Meanwhile more members of the family were entering the fray. Towards the end of 1942, Kut's cousins, eighteen year-old twin brothers William and Henry, left Brazil to join the RAF. Off the coast of Africa, their ship was torpedoed and they spent six days in a rudderless lifeboat before being picked up and eventually reaching Britain.

However, the New Year of 1943 opened with some particularly sorrowful news for Kut: it concerned his old Czech friend Bedřich Krátkoruký. It may be recalled that Krátkoruký had fought in the Battle of France in the same squadron as Kut and then served in No 1 Squadron with him before leaving a year previously to join an OTU. By now, he was a flying officer with 313 (Czech) Squadron.

On 16 January, Krátkoruký was flying Spitfire AR546 as part of the Czech Wing escorting Boston aircraft on a bombing operation against the docks at Cherbourg. Ten miles north of Cap de la Haig, there was a sweep into the sun and he collided with Spitfire VB449 piloted by a member of the same flight, Flight Sergeant J. Blaha. The two smashed aircraft fell spinning from the sky with neither pilot baling out. However, Warrant Officer Vavrinek observed Krátkoruký's Spitfire positioning for a landing, as the pilot evidently struggled with the controls, and he followed down his compatriot to witness the desperate attempt at survival. About 10–15 miles south of Portland, Krátkoruký successfully ditched into the sea, but shortly afterwards his aircraft turned on its nose and sank, taking him to a watery grave. Blaha too was dead.

On 15 February, the RAF's Fighter Command Headquarters issued one of its periodic lists of pilots with a high record of 'confirmed victories obtained while serving in Fighter Command'. It was classified 'Secret' and set out the position up to 31 January 1943.

On his personal copy, Kut proudly over- and underlined his name with red ink. He was credited with 19 victories (16 at night) and ranked 16th – in fact he was joint 14th with three others with the same score – but, according to this list anyway, no one had more night victories (his closest rival was John Cunningham with 15 victories at night). In fact, as we have seen, this score of the Czech was probably exaggerated by one night victory owing to administrative confusion, so that his true total was 18, 15 of them at night. This still made him joint top-scoring night fighter with Cunningham, the only other pilot with a night score in double figures at this time being John Braham with 12.

But Kut's 'shooting in anger days' were now over. Indeed he was doing very little flying at all at this stage. Having made his last flight in a 23 Squadron Mosquito on 8 September, he did not take to the air again until 21 January and then in the infinitely more leisurely Miles Mentor, basically a training and communications aircraft. Over the next few months, this was the only aircraft which he flew.

During this period, Kut spent some time as ADC to the AOC on his tours of Britain. By contrast, that spring and early summer saw Kut being required to act in a public relations role in exercises organised to raise much-needed cash for the war effort. It may not have come naturally to a man who was much more at home in the air and still not particularly fluent in English, but it delighted his wife Ruby because all the events were in her own part of the world, South Wales.

The eight days of 3–10 April were 'Wings For Victory Week' in Barry. The aim was to raise £250,000 to purchase four Lancasters at £200,000 and ten Hurricanes at £50,000. Throughout the week, the night fighter ace visited schools, cinemas and meetings in Barry while staying with Ruby's relatives in the town. Two months later – the week of 29 May–5 June – it was the turn of Llanelli and district to have their 'Wings For Victory Week'. Here the target was £350,000. At the dance and cabaret held at the Ritz Ballroom on the eve of the week, Kut was the guest of honour and during the week he appeared at more functions. Meanwhile, on 17 May, the RAF had enhanced his official status and made him 'Flight Lieutenant (War Substantive)'.

As if the death of Bedřich Krátkoruký in January was not bad enough, during these months of late spring and early summer in 1943 Kut lost three more of his special Czech friends from the days at No 1 Squadron.

First, on 6 March, Flying Officer Josef Příhoda was on a ramrod operation with the Czech 313 Squadron when enemy aircraft were encountered near Brest. Příhoda and his Spitfire BP862 were never seen again and he was classified as lost at sea. Then, on 28 April, Flying Officer Otto Pavlů flew Spitfire EE635 on a roadstead operation – an anti-shipping strike – with another Czech squadron, 310. A convoy was attacked from mast height, intense flak was thrown up, and Pavlů was hit and crashed into the sea. Finally, it was the turn of Jarda Novák – another Flying Officer flying another Spitfire (EP539) with another Czech Squadron (312) – to meet a similar fate. On 14 May, he was on a fighter roadstead operation against enemy vessels at St Peter Port harbour, Guernsey, when intense flak from ships and shore caught him and he fell into the sea.

Meanwhile, over in Czechoslovakia, the Kuttelwascher family –
like so many others – was suffering brutally at the hands of the
Germans. Since the Heydrich incident, there had been a series of
'actions' in which the relatives of those Czechs who had fled the
country were arrested and detained. On 4 May 1943, it was the
turn of Kut's parents and brother Miroslav to be arrested by the
Gestapo and in their case taken to an internment camp at
Svatobořice near Kyjov.

More and more Kut was conscious of being lucky to be still alive
and free. For her part, over the past eight months Ruby had been
delighted to be able to see very much more of her husband than was
the case in the earlier months of her marriage – but it was not to
last. The New World was calling.

CHAPTER FIFTEEN

New Worlds

On 10 June 1943, Kut was re-assigned to special duties with the Inspectorate-General of the Czech Air Force. The head of this unit was still Air Vice Marshal Karel Janoušek, a small and slight man with a ruddy complexion and crisp hair.

At this point in the war, the Czech Air Force was facing a manpower crisis. Unlike most RAF squadrons, the four Czech squadrons had no national pool from which to draw replacement pilots for those killed or missing or needing a rest. A secret report prepared for the War Cabinet described starkly the position for the quarter ending 30 June 1943:

> During the last 3 months, only 17 air crews have been obtained. The monthly requirement for aircrew alone is about twice that number. In North America recruiting has failed, and the Czechoslovak Government appears to be adamant in refusing to allow more of their Army personnel to volunteer for their Air Force. It seems inevitable, therefore, that once Czechoslovaks now in training have passed into first line units, wastage in squadrons, slowly at first, but gathering speed, will reduce the Czechoslovak Air Force to very small proportions.

So the Czech Inspector-General decided to send his star pilot to North America in a drive to recruit fellow countrymen to the RAF's Czech squadrons. For their part, the Americans wanted him to pass on his superlative night fighter skills to the new United States Army Air Force pilots about to complete their training and go over to Europe or out to the Pacific. However, this absence must have been a tremendous strain for Ruby with a baby of only nine months.

The trans-Atlantic flight was made on 11–12 June. Kut's 'base' in America was the Czechoslovak Embassy on Massachussetts Avenue in Washington where the Ambassador was Colonel Vladimír Hurban and his deputy was Dr Červenka. Kut would prepare his speeches in the office of the Air Attaché, Group Captain Alexander Hess, who accompanied him on his extensive travels. In 1940, Hess had been CO of the first Czech fighter squadron, 310, and – then aged 41 – was believed to have been the oldest operational fighter pilot.

At the time of Kut's arrival in America, the Czech President, Eduard Beneš, was already there: Beneš spent May and June 1943 on an official visit which included an address to the Senate and House of Representatives. Kut's first letter from the USA back home to Ruby – he wrote to her at least once every week – mentioned: 'I had the opportunity to speak to Dr Beneš who just came from here and he gave me last information and instruction about here.' The letter was addressed to her at Barry in South Wales where she had moved from London, having decided to be near her brother Ken while her husband was away.

Kut had only been in the USA a few weeks when the shattering news came through that his old friend and Commanding Officer, James MacLachlan, was missing. A few days later, an NBC programmed featured Mac as 'Man Of The Day' and reporter Robert St John recalled a visit to England and the competitive spirit between Kut and Mac: 'They were rivals. I remember how, day after day, their boxscore would appear in the London newspapers. The British people followed that boxscore with as much relish as we might the score of an especially exciting World's Series baseball competition.'

Kut obviously regarded Mac as a somewhat reckless character for in a letter to Ruby (20 August) he commented: 'About MacLachlan I was reading at once here and I wasn't surprised at all because I knew him very well. I hope he is only missing but he was so difficult as young too.' However, he had no details on Mac's sortie or fate.

Following his own special mission to the United States, Mac – now 24 – was posted to an Air Fighting Development Unit, a non-operational organisation responsible for overseeing all types of fighter aircraft. In spite of the non-operational nature of the unit, he managed to obtain permission for a special low-level raid which required his North American Mustang to be painted dark green to blend with the French countryside. At the end of June, he made his first operational sortie – a ranger operation – since his return from the USA and added to his night intruder score. South of Paris with Flight Lieutenant Geoffrey Page, they shot down four Henschel

Hs 126 trainers and two Ju 88s in just ten minutes, Mac claiming
$3\frac{1}{2}$ – three of the Henschels and a half score in one Ju 88 – which
brought his total score to $16\frac{1}{2}$.

A few days after receiving a second Bar to his DFC, on 18 July
Mac took off from Tangmere on another ranger operation in
Mustang FD442 of the AFDU. He was again accompanied by Page
and, after crossing the French coast in the Dieppe area, the two
aircraft were about three miles inland when his colleague saw black
smoke swirling from the engine of Mac's machine. No enemy
aircraft or flak were observed, so the damage may have been caused
by small arms fire. Page saw Mac climb rapidly and jettison the
cockpit canopy and presumed that he was attempting to bale out.

Clearly Mac changed his mind because, having reached only
1,000 feet, he swung the Mustang round and down and tried to
crash-land in a small field near a wood at La Croix Godey. The
aircraft overshot the field and careered into the wood, the trees
tearing off both the wings and the tail. Page circled the area for five
minutes hoping helplessly that he would see his friend leave the
smashed aircraft. In fact Mac lay bleeding and broken. Thirteen
days later, he died from a fractured skull and severe head injuries in
German Field Hospital No 711 at Pont L'Evêque, Calvados in
France.

In the USA, Kut immediately had to exchange his royal blue
uniform for a much lighter khaki one because the temperatures in
Washington were the highest since 1925 and almost his first trip
outside of the capital was to the even sunnier states of the
south-east. At the Army Air Forces School of Applied Tactics
(AAFSAT) in Orlando, he lectured to USAAF pilots on his combat
experience and most especially his night intruder successes.
Apparently the Americans were attempting similar tactics against
the Japanese.

For his part, the Czech was thrilled to have the chance to study
American military aircraft at close quarters. During his time in the
USA, Kut added another seven aircraft to the list in his log book.
These included the twin-boomed Lockheed P-38 Lightning, the
rugged and dependable Curtiss P-40 Warhawk and the fast and
versatile North American P-51 Mustang fighters. After all the
Czech, French, and British aircraft that he had already
experienced, Kut delighted in the opportunity to add to his tally by
enjoying some of the best that the Americans had to offer.

Throughout July, August and September, Kut criss-crossed the

USA visiting virtually every major city. Everywhere he went, he gave press conferences and radio interviews for the local media and delivered speeches to local organisations. As a result, he received a massive amount of media coverage. Indeed, while he was in America, he was paid perhaps the ultimate accolade of twentieth century literature – he was turned into a comic strip hero! The particular comic was devoted primarily to the escapades of wartime heroes of different Allied nations such as USA, Canada, Australia and Russia. Kut's own tale occupied seven colourful pages and highlighted his triple kill over St André, the whole piece being titled: 'Czech Night Hawk'. A slightly less graphic variation on the theme came in a Los Angeles newspaper which described him as '*Der Todteule*' ('the owl of death').

At this time some 1½ million Czechoslovaks lived in America and, wherever there was a local Czech community, Kut was pleased to meet his fellow countrymen and women. In early August, Kut was in Chicago for a whole week. It was no accident that he spent so much time here because Chicago had a greater Czech population than any other city except Prague and it included several of Kut's relatives such as cousin Martinovič and cousin Růža (who named her youngest child Karel after the most famous member of the family).

By the end of August, Kut had been in the 'New World' for over two months and already he was finding that the experience was giving him a dramatically new perspective on life. On 31 August, he sent Ruby a letter from Washington with a moving section:

In these days I am rather busy with writing. There is plenty to write about and I would like to write lot, to show people in H.Q. that I am definitely doing something good. Tomorrow I am trying to go to New York to do some shopping but I cannot say yet because my time is so funny, any minute I am getting new orders and so I must be all the time at readiness. You remember very well the readiness when you were with me at Croydon, don't you? How Karel was running and a couple hours later coming back.

Now I am in my thought in Croydon and going slowly through all my good boys and do you know how many are they left? You remember there were Otto [Pavlů], Jarda Novák, [Bedřich] Krátkoruký and [Josef] Příhoda, well darling there is only one left and that is your Karel. It is only some times what I heard the news that Jarda Novák followed all the boys and didn't return from ops. Sometimes I feel so funny about all that and I think I must write some pages about them and give it to their beloved in home. I promised to them in my thought that I will write a book which will be for them. I will start very soon and when back home I think you maybe will help me, of course if you will feel so.

It is clear from these words that Kut wanted to write a book about the Czechs with the RAF. As we have seen, he and Ruby did prepare an article on a few incidents but nothing like a book ever materialised. This work can be taken as the fulfilment more than 40 years later of the spirit of that earnest wish of 1943.

Then, towards the end of September, Kut spent some time touring Texas and California and, while in California, he was able to visit Hollywood. At the studios of Warner Brothers, he met such stars as Errol Flynn, who was making *Uncertain Glory*, and Irene Manning, who was preparing a musical called *Shine On Harvest Moon*. Kut was photographed being offered a cigarette by the suave Errol Flynn and this splendid media event was spoilt only by the fact that the Czech pilot did not smoke. While in the movie capital, Kut celebrated the first birthday (18 September) of his son Huw, some 6,000 miles away. Back in Washington, on 23 September the Czech Embassy gave a party for his own birthday – he was 27.

Meanwhile, for Ruby back in Britain, the weeks had turned into months and still there was no sign of her husband's return. On the contrary, at the end of September it was decided that he should spend a month in Canada on a similar mission of recruitment of Czechs, training of aircrew, and general public relations. He started his trip in Ottawa, where the Air Attaché was Wing Commander Jan Ambruš, and throughout his time in Canada, Kut was accompanied by Squadron Leader Douglas Annan, a liaison officer with the Royal Canadian Air Force, and Squadron Leader Josef Jaške, Assistant Air Attaché with the Czech Legation in Ottawa and former CO of 313 (Czech) Squadron. Jaške had known Kut in pre-war Czechoslovakia and sailed with him from Gibraltar to Cardiff in 1940; in his letters to Ruby, Kut described him as 'one of my very good friends'. The previous November, Jaške had had an appalling accident while flying a most unusual aircraft, the Foster Wikner Wicko (ES947), to attend the funeral of a Czech colleague, and he was sent to North America to recuperate.

Now living in Oxford and still troubled by his injury, Jaške sketches Kut's special physical and personal qualities:

> The things which stood out most were the smile and the eyes. He
> was always smiling and would joke about everything. There was
> life in his eyes which were bright like the sunshine. The
> outstanding personal characteristic was his modesty. I
> remember in Canada, with the exception of his official talks and
> question times, he never entered with me into conversation about
> his success. We sometimes shared a room and he never, never
> talked about his fighting. I never asked him about it. I thought he
> had had enough talk in the day, sometimes three sessions. In the
> hotels, we talked about the future – what we would like to do and
> how. He was very proud of his wife and her photo was never far
> from him. I felt sometimes he was very shy. What he enjoyed
> most were the evenings with our countrymen after his talk in
> Czech.

Kut was accompanied by Jaške as he travelled from the capital of
Ottawa west throughout each of the Provinces of Canada and, after
the heat of southern USA, he had to face the snows of Manitoba,
Saskatchewan and Alberta. He had a busy schedule of meetings,
speeches, and broadcasts and on finally reaching Vancouver he
joined in the local celebrations of the 25th anniversary of Czech
independence held on 28 October 1943.

While in Canada, Kut visited several Royal Canadian Air Force
flying schools to give morale-boosting talks to young pilots under
training. He also managed to accumulate another five aircraft types
to note in the last page of his flight log, including the Airspeed
Oxford advanced trainer, the Avro Anson transport and the
Lockheed Hudson bomber.

Among his many press interviews in Canada was one with the
Toronto *Globe and Mail* which emphasized Kut's almost spartan
approach to life:

> I'm visiting in Canada and the United States and have
> undergone several eyesight tests in both countries at the request
> of fliers. These tests simply register 100 per cent and it is
> something over which I have no control. I don't diet, but I do
> take vitamins A, D and C every morning. I don't smoke or drink
> and I always get lots of sleep – except in the United States and
> Canada.

After a month in Canada, at the beginning of November Kut returned to the United States. On 8 November, the Czech Foreign Minister Jan Masaryk – himself in North America – wrote to Ruby suggesting that her husband, who by then had already been abroad five months, might soon be home:

> Have seen your husband in New York and Washington. He seems to be doing some very useful work and I think it was a good idea to send him over. I will see to it that he does not stay away much longer – as a matter of fact he is anxious to get back and so am I. I hope the little one is all right.

In fact, Kut's return home was delayed because, towards the end of November, he had to have his tonsils removed at the Walter Reed Hospital in Washington.

Kut's assignment in North America was now over. His tour over there might have had some positive effect on the recruitment position of the Czech squadrons in Britain, but frankly any impact was only minor and temporary. Compared to 17 recruits in the quarter before his departure, there was an increase to almost 50 in the third quarter of the year and a fall back to 18 in the last quarter. Meanwhile the training of Czech personnel had been switched to No 111 OTU in the rather sunnier climes of the Bahamas.

In spite of the manpower problems, the British Air Ministry agreed to a Czech proposal that 21 experienced Czech fighter pilots led by the bearded Squadron Leader František Fajtl should be allowed to volunteer for service in Russia where they would form a flying echelon of a fighter squadron on the Eastern Front. They eventually went in February 1944. It was feared that this move would require the disbandment of 313 Squadron where already the ground crew was British, but Karel Janoušek urged that the squadron should be allowed to remain as a Czech unit and this was agreed. So all the RAF's Czech squadrons struggled on, making increasing use of British pilots.

On Christmas Eve 1943, Kut finally flew home, travelling from Washington and arriving on Christmas Day at Prestwick – his flight log notes that he flew with three Generals. He was a stone heavier as a result of the plentiful food in America but minus the ring given him by his mother in Czechoslovakia and lost in a swimming accident. After more than six months, he was home

(*Above*) Karel Kuttelwascher's wife, Ruby, in 1945 with their three children: standing, son Huw born in September 1942 and, in her arms, twin daughters, Vera and Mari born in November 1944. The Czech and Ruby were divorced in 1951. Huw died in 1964 and Ruby died in 1982. Vera—now known as Vee—has married the author and Mari now lives close to Tangmere.

(*Right*) Just back in Czechoslovakia, Karel Kuttelwascher with his parents, Josef and Kristina. He had not seen them for more than six years, for two of which they had been interned by the Germans.

The Arado Ar 96B, an advanced two-seater trainer flown by Karel Kuttelwascher during his time with the post-war Czech Air Force in 1946.

The Aero C-4, the Czech-built version of the German Bücker 131. This was flown by Karel Kuttelwascher during his time with the post-war Czech Air Force in 1946.

again to be re-united with his long-waiting wife and their son. It had been a hard time for Ruby. What she wanted now was for Kut to have an assignment which meant that they could be together and he could see much more of their little boy Huw as he learned to walk and speak – and, if the location could be in a pleasant and safe part of the country, so much the better.

The RAF obliged handsomely when, on 24 January 1944, Kut was posted to No 32 Maintenance Unit at St Athan, about twelve miles west of Cardiff in South Wales and less than 40 miles from Ruby's birthplace of Garnant. This was just what they both wanted for it meant that their home could remain at Barry.

In service terms, however, 32 MU was another 'new world'. It was a substantial operation which deployed some 4,000 men and women. The role of the unit was to overhaul, repair, modify, and test various types of airframes and engines. So, for this last stretch of the war, Kut became a member of a Test Flight responsible for testing a wide variety of aircraft before they were taken to different RAF stations around the country.

Apart from testing the aircraft for serviceability, the main object of the flying time was to enable the special radar technicians to test the sets for correct functioning. The pilots used to fly the bombers eastwards up the mouth of the Severn and from as high as 20,000 feet these specialists would be able to 'see' – sometimes through cloud – the Clifton suspension bridge on their little boxes. Other flights were in the opposite direction westwards out to sea where the radar operators would seek to locate ships in thick sea fog at a height of only 50 feet above the waves.

Therefore the most frequent abbreviation in the 'duty' column of the pages of Kut's flight log for this period was 'S.I. test' i.e. special instrument test. The other notation that occurred often was 'A + E' i.e. airframe and engine test.

Over the next year and a half – with a three month gap from late April to late July 1944 – Kut was in the air several times a week, testing the latest marks of British bombers, mainly the Avro Lancaster, the Avro Lincoln, the Handley Page Halifax – all four-engined heavy bombers – and the Vickers Wellington or 'Wimpy', the twin-engined medium bomber that was produced in greater quantity than any other RAF bomber either before or since. At other times, he tested fighters like the Bristol Beaufighter and the Fairey Firefly and the air-sea rescue Vickers Warwick.

There were even occasional flights in his beloved Hawker

Hurricane (the last as late as 10 August 1945) and two trainers – the Miles Magister and the Miles Master – plus single flights in the four-engined Avro York transport, the Percival Proctor trainer, and a Supermarine Spitfire as well as in one American bomber, the North American B-25 Mitchell. Tested aircraft were taken to various operational squadrons around Britain. Crews were collected in the Avro Anson or 'Faithful Annie' and the de Havilland Dominie (a biplane) in both of which Kut spent many hours. So he certainly had plenty of variety in his flying.

It was very rare indeed for a fighter pilot to transfer to heavy bombers, but by all accounts Kut's remarkable versatility enabled him to fly all these different aircraft at St Athan with the minimum amount of conversion time. They were not long flights, typically around an hour. Nevertheless, he clocked up around 300 more hours' flying time while with No 32 MU.

Two of those who flew with Kut at this time were Leo Craven and Peter Pennant-Rea.

Warrant Officer Leo Craven arrived at the Maintenance Unit from a tour of operations on Special Duties in the Middle East where he was flying the Halifax I and II. He remembers his two hour-long flights as second pilot in a more advanced version of the Halifax on 31 December 1944 and he describes the laconic nature of his tutor:

On my arrival at St Athan, it soon came to my attention that we had a highly decorated Czech air ace on the Test Flight. I had previously been in the company of and flown with many highly experienced aircrew – some had even survived two tours of operations and had been duly decorated by His Majesty, King George VI – but this was the very first time I had even seen a pilot with two rows of medal ribbons on his uniform. After a preliminary interview with Squadron Leader Stanley, to my surprise a call came over the public address system for me to report back to the CO. On my entering his office, he said: 'Flight Lieutenant Kuttelwascher will show you how to fly a Halifax Mark III'.

We met outside with our flying kit and a van took us to the aircraft, PN375. More crew met us there including an engineer, wireless operator, and several specialist radar type personnel. K.K., or 'Old Kut' as he was known, hardly said a word. He walked round the outside of the aircraft, which was normal drill, to make sure that the blocks which held the ailerons and elevators against wind damage had been removed as had the pitot head cover. I followed a few feet behind looking at the same things. It was not until he was sitting in the port seat, with me in the starboard, and all four engines running satisfactorily that he said 'Do you know what to do?' There was nothing demonstrative or exaggerated in any of his flying activity – just straightforward safety as instructed in any flying manual. He was a quiet, unassuming man but held in the highest esteem for his character and ability.

Flight Lieutenant Peter Pennant-Rea, an Engineering Officer, only flew with Kut once but knew him for several months:

I was in the Flight Engineer's seat on one occasion when Kut was piloting a Lancaster bomber on a radar test. His English was fluent with a very pronounced accent, but he was good on the radio telephone. He flew the Lancaster with the verve of a Hurricane and flying in his company was most enjoyable. Kut was a popular member of the Mess, unassuming, humorous and a most attractive personality. Although we were in the same Mess for many months, I was never aware of his past at all. Certainly he never advertised the fact that he had done such remarkable things.

Kut's time at 32 MU was a welcome assignment to Ruby: she and Kut could be together and she was back in the part of the world where she was brought up. During this time, the Kuttelwascher family remained on the coast at Barry, only six miles from the RAF station. Often Ruby knew when Kut would be coming home at the end of the day because he would dive bomb the cabbages to the consternation of the neighbours.

One Sunday – it was 30 April 1944 – Kut and Ruby travelled over to Cardiff to record a piece for the BBC Home Service. The programme was called 'Trans-Atlantic Call: People to People'. The first half of the programme was produced by the Columbia Broadcasting System in the USA and dealt with the war-time problems of an American housewife. The second half was produced by the BBC and told the story of Mrs Ruby Kuttelwascher, the wife of 'the ace night fighter pilot'.

In a surviving script for the programme, Ruby explained the

abstemious life style and tough self-discipline of her husband:

> I still think that if it wasn't for the rigid discipline that Karel
> imposed on himself, he wouldn't have made such a name for
> himself, and who knows I might not have him today. He never
> smoked, drank very little and would never go to a party, if he
> thought he might be going on operations the following day. I used
> to have to think up the excuses.

She indicated the isolation and anxiety of being a pilot's wife away
from base:

> Although I guessed at times like these that some raid might be
> coming off, I never knew. He never told me anything until a long
> time afterwards. I seemed to live all my fears in retrospect, and
> worry about dangers that he'd surmounted a few weeks earlier. I
> came to accept uncertainty as the only basis for my life. Karel
> probably told me even less than the ordinary pilot tells his wife.
> He'd served in France during those difficult days before the
> capitulation when friend and enemy were indistinguishable and
> had been led into traps so many times that it made him
> suspicious of even his best friends.

Only a couple of months after Kut's return from the USA, Ruby
had become pregnant again. On 13 November 1944, she gave birth
in Cardiff to non-identical female twins – Vera (named after
Ruby's sister) and – 10 minutes later – Mari. By this time, son Huw
was two and sadly he was already suffering very badly from asthma
(a condition which would eventually kill him). So all in all Ruby
had her hands full.

Close by at Porth-y-Castell lived Ruby's elder brother, Ken
Thomas, a physical education teacher who had performed in the
1936 Olympics at Berlin, and his wife Ivy. He recollects how one
day Kut and Ruby decided to drive over to the village where she
was born, Garnant, near Ammanford, just north of Swansea:

> As they approached a railway crossing, they found the gate shut
> and a train standing at the station. They hooted the horn to
> attract the driver's attention and, when he looked out of his cab,
> Ruby explained to him in Welsh the identity of the officer beside
> her. Karel was so well known at this time and the driver was so

impressed that he moved the train out of the station before the scheduled time, enabling Karel and Ruby to continue their journey.

A visitor to the Thomas household at this time was Mrs Peggy Jeffreys who still lives near Cardiff. She remembers meeting Kut there on several occasions:

We seemed to have a party nearly every night and sometimes we would go to dances at a hall called Bindles in Cohl Knap. We felt that there was no tomorrow and used to have a marvellous time. Ruby would usually be at home looking after the children so Karel was on his own. He liked the women very much and he was a bit of a gay boy. Karel's brother, Jan, was always there surrounded by women. They certainly played hard.

The long months at St Athan – they were there more than a year and a half – were probably the best of Kut and Ruby's marriage, notwithstanding his social life. He was in no particular personal danger, test flying being considerably less hazardous than night intrusion; they were living together instead of him on the base and her in town; and they increased the family to three children. It was not to last: the war was coming to an end and Kut was enthusiastic to be back in Czechoslovakia.

In fact, Kut's brother, now Warrant Officer Jan Kuttelwascher, was at far greater risk by this stage of the war, since he was part of the Czech Army forces taking part in the Allied invasion of Europe. There was a vivid press report of an eight-man patrol which he led behind enemy lines at Dunkirk. They came across a German patrol, killed its leader, and took three prisoners.

Later, a distant relative played a much more decisive role in the war. He was Generál Karel Kutlvašr (he spelt his name the Czech way) who on 5 May 1945 led an uprising against the Germans in Prague which resulted in some 4,000 dead. On 8 May, the Generál signed an agreement with the local German commander covering German withdrawal from the capital. Next day the Red Army arrived in Prague and it certainly did not suit Communist propoganda that the Czechs themselves had freed the city so that the Red Army could not be represented as the sole liberator of Prague. It was only on 5 May 1945 that Kut's parents and brother

Miroslav walked free from their final place of interment at Planá nad Lužnicí. They had been detained for two years to the day and understandably Kut longed to see them again.

The war in Europe officially ended on 8 May 1945 and the Czech Air Force had made a special contribution to the Allied effort. The most comprehensive statistics are found in an official Czech publication of 1965 which was able to draw upon the records of the Czech Inspectorate-General that were transferred to Prague in 1945. This book ceased to be available in Czechoslovakia after the Warsaw Pact invasion of 1968 and has never been published in Britain.

The three Czech fighter squadrons, 310, 312 and 313, had completed 28,335 operational flights totalling 46,905 hours. Flying as a Czech Wing, the squadrons flew four two-hour sorties on D-Day, 6 June 1944, as part of the historic Operation Overlord. In the course of the war, the pilots with these squadrons were credited with $68\frac{1}{6}$ enemy aircraft destroyed plus 37 probable and $59\frac{1}{6}$ damaged (and four V-1 flying bombs destroyed). For its part, the Czechoslovak Flight of the night-fighting No 68 Squadron flew 1,905 missions and was credited with $18\frac{1}{2}$ enemy aircraft destroyed plus 5 probables and 7 damaged (and 2 V-1s shot down).

During service with other RAF squadrons, individual Czech pilots were credited with a total of 68 enemy aircraft destroyed plus 14 probables and $45\frac{1}{3}$ damaged. A total of 31 Czechs flew with No 1 Squadron – more than with any other British unit except 68 Squadron with its twin-crew night fighters – and while with it they destroyed $32\frac{1}{2}$ enemy aircraft, probably destroyed another 4 and damaged $13\frac{1}{2}$.

So the total number of kills achieved by the Czechs split fairly evenly between those at Czech and other RAF squadrons. Yet, if one examines the service records of the Czech aces, a fascinating picture emerges.

Easily the most successful Czech fighter pilots with the RAF were Karel Kuttelwascher with his 18 victories at 1 Squadron and Josef František with his 17 victories at the Polish 303 Squadron, both men who never flew with a Czech squadron in the war and incidentally achieved virtually all their kills while flying on their own. Although they never flew together, Kuttelwascher and František were a pair – the most successful Czechs with the wartime RAF, both most effective when operating alone, the one by night, the other by day. In fact, one suspects that, had František lived, his singular approach would have been well suited to night intrusion and he might well have reached Kut's ability at it.

The two Czechs with the next highest scores were Otto Smik who shot down nine aircraft and – on the same day – three V-1s, almost all these victories being achieved with 222 Squadron before he flew with the Czech 310 and 312 Squadrons, and Miroslav Mansfeld who is credited with $8\frac{1}{2}$ aircraft – virtually all at night – and two V-1s, all scored while with 111 and then 68 Squadrons. The other two Czech aces – that is, pilots with RAF scores of five or more – were Otmar Kučera with $5\frac{1}{2}$ victories, clocked up with the Czech 312 and then 313 Squadrons, and Josef Dygrýn with five victories, all achieved while flying with Kut on 1 Squadron, although he spent a short spell with the Czech 310 Squadron.

So the top two Czech fighter aces never flew with any Czech squadron and, except for a couple of kills by one of them, five of the six accomplished their victories with non-Czech squadrons. The most likely explanation is that the Czech fighter squadrons had much fewer opportunities for their members to achieve kills, since they joined the Battle of Britain late and served mostly north of London and, after the Battle, these squadrons operated mostly as convoy patrols and later as close escorts to bombers with orders to protect their charges rather than seek combat. In short, Kut had more chances than most of his compatriots – and he took them.

Turning to the Czech bomber squadron 311, during its two years with Bomber Command it flew 1,011 operational sorties totalling 5,192 hours. Some 1,218,375 Kg of HE bombs and 92,925 Kg of incendiary bombs were dropped on enemy territory. This included participation in one of the '1,000 bomber raids'. After it was transferred to Coastal Command in 1942, the squadron completed 2,102 operational flights totalling 21,527 hours and was credited with four enemy aircraft destroyed and three probables plus 35 attacks on U-boats and four on surface vessels.

Czech airmen served in a variety of other roles, especially Transport Command but also Ferry Command, photo reconnaissance, air-sea rescue, and last but not least No 138 Special Squadron dropping agents into enemy territory including occupied Czechoslovakia.

The total number of Czech airmen who lost their lives while serving in the RAF came to 480. The heaviest casualties were suffered by the bomber crews of 311 Squadron: of the 480 killed, 273 came from this one squadron. Furthermore, of the 51 Czech airmen taken prisoner-of-war, 34 were from the squadron. Seven Czechs gave their lives while serving with No 1 Squadron. Here in Britain, the death of all these Czech airmen is commemorated on the Sunday nearest 28 October – the Czech day of national independence – in a simple ceremony at the Czech cemetery in the village of Brookwood in Surrey.

At the end of the war, there were some 1,500 Czechs still serving in the RAF, so that the total number of Czech airmen who served in Britain was probably around 2,000. They had fought for the noblest of motives. As Kut himself put it in a post-war article on the Czech Air Force in World War II: *'Bojovali jsme za pravdu, právo a lidskost a budeme neúprosně bojovati proti lži a násili'* ('We were fighting for truth, for justice and for humanity and we will go on fighting against lies and oppression').

After an absence of six long years, all the Czech airmen surviving the war – including Kut – were now eager to go back home.

CHAPTER SIXTEEN

The Last Fight

The war was over. Yet, even as it came to a close, another very different one – the 'Cold War' – was beginning. As early as 8 May 1945 – the very day hostilities ended – the Inspector-General of the Czech Air Force, Air Marshal Karel Janoušek sought permission for his men to fly home. However, political complications ensured that it was not until July that the Consolidated B-24 Liberators of 311 Squadron started ferrying Czech personnel and stores from London to the Prague military airfield at Ruzyně and only in August were the three fighter squadrons of Spitfires able to return home. Formally, all these squadrons were regarded as on detachment from the RAF and it was 15 February 1946 before they were officially removed from RAF records.

For his part, Kut – now approaching 29 – was as keen as any of the Czechs to return home and, as soon as Prague was freed, he wrote to his uncle, the liberator Generál Karel Kutlvašr. Back came a telegram (27 June) from the Generál: 'Thanks for your letter. My congratulations upon your success. Being now in Brno, I try to help you soon return.'

In fact it was 18 August before Kut flew back to Czechoslovakia, at this stage without Ruby and the children. The previous day he had flown in an Avro Anson from St Athan to Manston. Then a Liberator of 311 Squadron, flown by a Flying Officer Beneš, took him from Manston to the Czech capital of Prague. This return to the homeland after so many years of exile was later described by one Czech as '*nejsladší cesta*' ('the sweetest journey').

Although all big parades were normally held on a Sunday, the new authorities chose to organise the triumphal march through Prague for the homecoming Czech Air Force on the working Thursday afternoon of 21 August. Nevertheless, as Air Marshal Janoušek proudly led his men through the streets of the capital, Kut – who was very close to the head of the march – and his comrades received a genuinely warm reception from the thousands of men and women gathered to cheer them. Kut's letter to Ruby next day commented: 'People gave us yesterday a very nice welcome.' Back at home, Kut was given the rank of Staff Captain and initially based at the military section of the Prague airport of Ruzyně. Then a month later he was assigned to the Air Force Military Academy at Hradec Králové, some 70 miles east of Prague. Here his enormous experience could be used in the training programmes of new young pilots, but his 'deputy' was a Russian, something he deeply resented.

A few days after Kut's return to Czechoslovakia, Ruby – together with the children, Huw, Vera and Mari – flew out to Prague where she stayed with members of Kut's family before eventually joining her husband in Hradec Králové early in October. Ruby hated the situation in which she now found herself: living in a foreign country with three young children and allegedly neglected by her husband and his family. After only a few months, towards the end of January 1946, she flew back to England, taking the children with her, and it is clear from correspondence at this time that divorce was under consideration.

In fact, Kut himself was deeply unhappy at the situation in Czechoslovakia, both on personal and political grounds. He wrote a string of letters back to Ruby in England. On 31 January, he told her: 'My pay for last month was – do sit quietly – 479.20 Crowns, that is £2.7.10. This is the biggest swindle that they can play on us – so we are treated after all those years of fighting.' He resolved to leave the country himself, but it took him months to obtain the necessary visa from the British Home Office. On 4 March, he wrote to Ruby: 'I can see that there will be many changes over there but still it must be better than here. That freedom is enough.'

Meanwhile, Kut's role as a teacher and administrator did not enable him to do much flying with the new Czech Air Force. Indeed he had been back home for almost six months before he was in the air again, making half-a-dozen trips in an Aero C-4 – the Czech-built version of the German Bücker 131 – teaching landings. Then he switched to the Arado Ar 96B – an advanced two-seater trainer which had been adopted in 1940 as a standard training aircraft for the Luftwaffe – and over a three-month period made 50 flights in this type of aircraft. However, they were rather dull occasions: his flight log simply records 'landings' and 'orientation'.

If Kut's flying duties were rather steady and serene, by contrast the political situation in Czechoslovakia was changing dramatically and dangerously. Dr Eduard Beneš, the head of the Czechoslovak government-in-exile, was a left of centre politician who would have been at home in the British Labour Party and he and his colleagues had every intention of re-creating in post war Czechoslovakia the kind of western democratic system of government that had existed there up to 1938. However, after their experience of Munich, the Czechs no longer altogether trusted the British or the Americans, so in 1943 Beneš signed a treaty of mutual assistance with the USSR. As a result, once the country was liberated the Communists were able gradually to assert a grip on all aspects of Czech society.

Kut could see the precariousness of his position only too clearly. The authorities had so much against him: he had served with the Royal Air Force and become a well-known hero, he was married to a British woman and had British children, and he was a strong personality who was willing to express critical views.

Kut's intention to leave Czechoslovakia was not something which he particularly hid, as is clear from Stanislav Berton – now resident in Australia – who met him several times shortly after the war at the family of Kut's uncle, Generál Kutlvašr:

> I remember vividly our last meeting in 1946. We were at the Kutlvašrs' for tea and walked from Hanspaulka to Prague-Dejvice. K.K. did not like the Communists. During the conversation, I deduced from his attitude to the situation at that time and various remarks that he contemplated to leave Czechoslovakia and stay in England. His wife and children were in London already. I asked him directly about his intention. He was rather surprised but admitted that I was right. I am afraid he did not guard his plan well. He mentioned to me that Pavel Tigrid published in *Obzory* a similar story. He was rather annoyed by it. He was upset with the developing situation. The Communists were in all important positions and the men who were fighting on the side of the British were suspect and considered by the Communists as unreliable.

Kut was one of those who found it impossible to reconcile his political views with the attitude of the new political regime. Though he was not particularly interested in politics, he was a patriot and a democrat who had been close to the leadership in exile of the liberal politicians Beneš and Masaryk. Furthermore he was a tough and uncompromising character who was used to speaking his mind.

Marcel Ludikar, a former wireless operator with the RAF's 311 (Czech) Squadron, remembers the meeting held in early March 1946 to form a veterans' organisation for Czechs who had served in the war. The meeting was held at Riegrovy Sady in Prague and the organisation was called Svaz zahraničních vojaků (the Union of Soldiers from Abroad). Several hundred men, most in uniform, were present, including Kut who made a special point of travelling from Hradec Králové in spite of his departure from the country now being imminent.

The Communists were trying to gain the positions of influence in all such associations, but Kut was totally opposed to such stratagems and, according to Ludikar, made a trenchant contribution:

> Kuttelwascher was strongly anti-Communist. He attacked the tactics of the Communists and warned those present in no uncertain terms of the dangers that would result. His speech was straightforward and absolutely first class. This was a very brave thing for him to do and I was so impressed with him.

Perhaps as a result of Kut's intervention, the Communist candidate for the chairmanship – a Colonel Reicin, the Russian-trained chief of political security – failed to win the post, but the Communists took other positions.

Kut resigned from the Czech Air Force on 21 May and five days later he left his country after less than a year back home and flew from Prague to Croydon in an RAF Dakota. That very day, 26 May 1946, elections were held to the new Czech National Assembly. The Communist Party obtained about 38% of the votes and, together with its allies, commanded rather more than half the seats. The Czechoslovakia Kut left behind was plunged further into darkness. The Communist election victory led to the arrest of many non-Communists, who were imprisoned in camps, and the formal basis of a police state was quickly established.

As the next election campaign of 1948 commenced, it became clear that the Communists were losing support. So, on 26 February, the Communist Party staged a coup and Eduard Beneš – one of the godfathers to Kut's son – was deposed as President. On 10 March 1948, it was announced that Jan Masaryk – the other godfather to little Huw – had committed suicide by leaping out of his window in the Cernin Palace. Like most Czechs, Kut never

believed this account, but it was years after Kut's own death before
– in the Prague Spring of 1968 – the brutal truth came out about
the alleged suicide. Evidence was then revealed that Stalin had
personally ordered the murder of Masaryk and that Soviet secret
police had assisted the Czech secret police in dragging the Minister
from his bed, shooting him behind the right ear, and throwing him
out of the window.

Immediately after the coup, a Stalinist purge began and, among
the wide range of groups under attack, were former members of the
Czech war-time forces. Indeed, within days of the coup, leading
figures were arrested and scores of officers and NCOs were
dismissed. Kut's uncle, Generál Karel Kutlvašr, was accused of
conspiracy against the Government and received a life sentence.
The Head of the Czech Inspectorate for the wartime RAF, Karel
Janoušek – for whom Kut worked – was sentenced to death,
although this sentence was later commuted to life imprisonment.
He eventually spent fifteen years in jail and, upon his eventual
release, one of the first to offer assistance was Kut's first RAF Flight
Commander, Pete Matthews, who was then the British Air Attaché
in Prague.

The coup of 1948 led to another odyssey for many Czechs as they
fled the country for the second time in a decade, but this time – as
with the third exodus of 1968 – the journey was one way. For Kut,
the coup was confirmation that he had only just left Czechoslovakia
in time and that he would never be able to return. In fact, four
months after returning to Britain in 1946, he had been naturalised.

Re-united in London, Kut and Ruby decided to remain married
after all and they set up home in Uxbridge, Middlesex. Later they
were joined by his brother, Jan, and Jan's Czech wife, Miluška.
One of Kut's early visitors at Uxbridge was Stanislav Berton to
whom he had unintentionally given notice of his plan to leave
Czechoslovakia. As it happened, Berton himself left
Czechoslovakia in 1947 and Kut paid his university fees until 1948
when the Communists took over and Berton could apply to the
British Government for political asylum and financial support.

On returning to Britain, Kut – now 30 – was determined to
resume a flying career. Within three months, he was over at the
Hunting Flying Club at Luton to make half-a-dozen take-offs and
landings in a Percival Proctor trainer in order to quality for a B
licence. It was certified by J. Arnold and numbered 7888. Then, in
November 1946, Kut managed to join British European Airways

(BEA) two months after its change from the European Division of the British Overseas Airways Corporation (BOAC). First came ground instruction and examination at Aldermaston. Characteristically, he worked hard, typically seven hours' lectures in the classroom and four hours' study in the evening, and in a letter to Ruby he revealed that his score in one examination was 88% which was top of the class. Then came flying training on a combination of Doves, Dakotas and Vikings, an exercise to which he took naturally after all his experience of bomber and transport aircraft in the RAF.

After this induction process, Kut became 'operational' and spent his first five years at BEA as a First Officer on the twin-engined Vickers Vikings. One of his colleagues at this time was Captain Eric Pritchard, another member of the 'class of '46':

> I was called to see Charlie Riley, our Flight Captain on the Vikings. He said: 'Look, I think that you ought to wear your war ribbons on your uniform.' As I left the office, Karel went in and Riley obviously made the same suggestion to him. Outside the office, Karel said to me: 'Do we really have to do that?' The trouble was that, when he put them on, they went right up his left shoulder somewhere!

Among the many routes Kut flew on Vikings was the one to Prague where the airport of Ruzyně was shared by a transport unit of the Czech Air Force and the Czech civilian airline CSA. Here he saw his friend Marcel Ludikar who was with the Czech Air Force serving as a captain. Ludikar was delighted to renew the acquaintance: 'Any ex-RAF member was a friend. We were worse than freemasons.' In September 1947, Kut and Ruby even managed to spend a short holiday in Prague. However, the Communist coup of 1948 finished such contacts. From then on, Kut never returned to Czechoslovakia and for his part in 1948 Ludikar fled to Britain where he rejoined the RAF and served until his recent retirement.

Early in his BEA career, Kut was assigned to the vital De-Icing Trials on Vikings – his most exciting and his riskiest period of civilian flying.

Hardly had the new BEA started operations in late 1946 than, during that very severe winter, it came close to losing two of its brand new fleet of Viking aircraft, developed from the famous wartime Wellington bomber. What happened was that ice formed on the horn balances of the elevators under certain meteorological conditions causing over-balancing of the elevators which, in turn, made the aircraft 'porpoise' up and down out of control in flight. All Viking aircraft were grounded in order to establish the cause, which was still not known at that time, and to modify the aircraft accordingly.

Then a full scientific study was made into the handling characteristics of the aircraft under icing conditions to determine the optimum method of using the aircraft's fluid de-icing system. The Ministry of Supply commissioned BEA to conduct a series of flights to investigate these problems, the flights being conducted initially as Icing Trials in the winter of 1946–47, then later as De-Icing Trials during the winters of 1947–48 and 1949–50. A Viking aircraft of the King's Flight was made available and, so as to enable it to fly without hindrance anywhere in Europe, its RAF markings were removed and the civil registration G-AIJE granted. Captain Derek Mason, an ex-wartime bomber pilot, was allowed a completely free hand as regards the operation of the aircraft and selection of his crew.

These days Mason is out in the Sudan advising the Government on flight operations matters on assignment with the International Civil Aviation Organisation (ICAO). He explains:

> Karel Kuttelwascher was a natural choice as co-pilot because of his temperament and enthusiasm for the work which was not without very real risks. In BEA he had immediately gained the respect of all of us because, although his reputation preceeded him, yet he was never boastful of his many accomplishments; indeed, he hardly ever discussed his role during the war.

In between flights, the Viking was based at Aldermaston. The flights took Kut and Mason away for periods varying between one and two weeks at a time and the aircraft was based in a variety of locations including Copenhagen, Oslo, Trondheim, Hamburg, Iceland (flying north of the Arctic Circle), and amazingly Nice (where there was great success in locating icing conditions over the Massif Central). Mason recounts:

> During a flight over southern England on 10 May 1948, we were cruising in cloud at about 6,000 feet patiently searching for

ice-bearing clouds with the auto-pilot engaged. All was peaceful
and I was gently sipping a cup of tea when, out of the corner of
my eye and through the dense cloud, I caught sight of a
Constellation aircraft on a converging course. It was all over in a
fraction of a second because the visibility was only a matter of
yards and, fortunately, the 'Connie' passed just overhead so close
that the roar of its engines could be heard above the noise of our
own. My reaction, apparently, and without spilling even a drop
of tea was to say 'Christ!' Subsequently recounting this story on
the ground to our mixed crew of scientists and observers from a
variety of interested organisations who flew with us on all
occasions, Kut in his quaint English accent told the assembled
company: 'I heard the Captain say "Christ" so I look for Christ,
and what do I see – Constellation!'

On another flight, when we were based in Hamburg for flights
in the Heligoland Bight area, we built up such an amount of ice
on the wings and tail that not only did the elevators overbalance
but the rudder also. This meant that the aircraft was porpoising
and screwing all at the same time and I could not prevent the
movement of the controls. I was faced with something of a
problem since the freezing level extended down to the surface, so
there was no way in which we could melt the ice off the horn
balances of the elevators and rudder. Therefore a landing had to
be attempted with the aircraft wallowing and screwing its way
down the approach path. My work was cut out in simply trying
to fly the beast and, as always, Kut was terrific in that he relieved
me of all tasks such as communicating with the ground, tuning in
radio aids, carrying out cockpit checks and the like. Flying and
landing that aeroplane was a distinctly 'team effort'.

There is obviously no doubt in the mind of Mason – who knew the
Czech better than any one else in civilian aviation – about Kut's
flying abilities:

I was the only person on board with a decent camera and so I
took it upon myself to take 'official' photographs of ice formation
for reproduction into the official report on the Trials. On such
occasions, when the aircraft was loaded with ice and
approaching a stalled condition, my confidence in Kut was such
that I would go with my camera to the rear of the aircraft to take
photographs. I can assure you that I would not have left my seat

First Officer Karel Kuttelwascher, Captain Derek Mason and Radio Officer John Crisp receiving a meteorological briefing before taking off for de-icing trials.

Vickers Viking G-AIJE used for BEA's de-icing trials after landing at Northolt (Karel Kuttelwascher is standing at the foot of the steps.)

First Officer Karel Kuttelwascher at the controls of a BEA Vickers Viking a few years after the war.

The author Roger Darlington with his wife Vee, the elder daughter of Karel Kuttelwascher, looking at a painting made in 1942 of Kut's Hawker Hurricane IIC JX:E and other personal records.

under such conditions with a normal co-pilot left to mind things during my absence – such was our trust and faith in each other's abilities and experience. He was an absolute tower of strength to me throughout the two winters spent searching for icing conditions and, when it was all over, we frequently flew together on normal line flights.

Meanwhile Kut and Ruby's marriage was not a success and the arguments increased. On one occasion, matters became so serious that the police had to be summoned and embarrassingly the incident made the newspapers. Eventually they separated and Ruby took the three children. In 1951 Kut and Ruby were divorced with Kut being awarded custody of the nine-year old Huw and Ruby receiving custody of the seven-year old twins, Vera and Mari.

The same year that he divorced, Kut was promoted to Captain at BEA. Then, from the Viking aircraft, he went on to the Elizabethan fleet of Airspeed Ambassadors. One of the Ambassadors he flew was G-ALZO 'Christopher Marlowe' and interestingly, of the perhaps a couple of hundred individual aircraft flown by Kut in his extremely varied career, G-ALZO is the one known still to exist. In October 1971, it retired from service and Dan-Air now preserve it at the airline's maintenance base at Lasham, Hampshire. Finally, in 1958, Kut moved to the turboprop-powered Vickers Viscount which constituted BEA's No 4 Flight. This brought the total number of aircraft types flown by him to about 60, such were his ubiquitous flying skills.

Earlier in 1955, Kut had started a greengrocery business in Paddington which was run by his brother Jan and sister-in-law Miluška. The little time that Kut had over, after flying aircraft and managing a business, he spent in the garden of his modern continental-style house in Uxbridge. As he told a BEA colleague: 'If you fly, you must have quiet and relaxation – and where better could I get this than among my plants?'

Flying and business certainly kept Kut busy. Yet that was probably not the reason why he never attended any of the No 1 Squadron annual reunions held after the war. He did not want to look back; he lived for the future; but in his case that was to be all too short.

The last time the author's wife saw her father was just under a year before his death when – aged almost fourteen – she spent a week or so with him at his Uxbridge home at the beginning of

September 1958. Vee – as she is usually known – recalls:

That Saturday he took me to the Farnborough Air Display and patiently identified each of the aircraft for me. I had never been to an air display before – or to once since until I met you. Then a few days after the display he bought me a smart sailor dress and my first-ever pair of high heeled shoes which were red – I felt so grand. It's strange the childhood memories one has of parents. For some reason, one of my most powerful recollections of my father is black socks. They were part of his BEA uniform and to this day I am fascinated by black socks!

Then, in the summer of 1959, Kut decided to take a holiday in the china clay country of Cornwall. Eventually he chose the isolated Retillick Farm in a delightful little place called Roche, just outside St Austell, and early in August he drove down there with his sister-in-law, Miluška, and her two young children, Jan and Mimi. The owners of the Retillick Farm and Kut's hosts in his final weeks of life were members of the Driscoll family. Ivy Driscoll explains:

It was the first time I had taken visitors and we had no mod. cons. but we took to one another right away. Karl – as we called him – said that he felt free and really at home. They went out during the day and came back for an evening meal before going out to play in the fields with the children or take the dogs for walks. One day, they stayed home and built a raft for a pond which we had in the lane. At the end of the week, they asked to stay another week.

Her daughter Jane Gunningham (as she now is) – then only a child – continues the story: 'One evening we all had supper together and went out to play football. Karl became short of wind and out of breath. Us children were teasing him.' Kut had just eaten a rather fatty meal and thought that he had indigestion but, after making himself sick, he found that the pain spread up into his chest and became more severe.

He had to spend the next day in bed and at first a doctor was not called. Kut had had gallstones for sometime, but had refused to have an operation in case it interfered with his flying, so Miluška thought his trouble down in Cornwall was simply a recurrence of this gallstone complaint and gave him some of the large round tablets that he had with him. But this time the pain did not subside and after a couple of days a local doctor had to be called. The doctor immediately recognised the severity of the situation and had the patient inside the Royal Cornwall Hospital in Truro in a matter of twenty minutes.

Kut was admitted to the RCH on 13 August. The immediate diagnosis was coronary thrombosis confirmed by electro-cardiograph. However, the consultant physician handling the case, Dr J.D. Hardy, was confident that Kut would recover. Later he wrote to the Regional Medical Officer at BEA: 'Clinically we had not been unduly worried about him, but nevertheless we put into action full treatment precautions . . .[He] was making a normal recovery with anti-coagulant therapy.' At 10 pm on the night of 17 August, Kut was given another quantity of the drugs that he had been receiving several times for each of the past five days. Less than two hours later, at ten minutes to midnight, he was found dead and bathed in perspiration. Clearly he had had a second heart attack and it was believed that his death was practically instantaneous. The man who flew alone at night had died alone at night. Next day a post-mortem was conducted. It revealed extensive coronary thrombosis, practically the whole of the outer wall of the left ventricle being infarcted, and his heart was about one and half times the normal size.

Kut had still been aged only 42. In fact, he himself had told his family that he would die young: perhaps he alone was aware of the toll taken by the incredible stress of those night intruder operations of seventeen years previously. For some reason, all previous writers about Kut have stated that he died in 1960 instead of 1959. The historical records of No 1 Squadron at RAF Wittering include this inaccuracy and it may have been that other authors took this mistake from the squadron records or each other. Ivy Driscoll insists: 'I do know that he enjoyed himself very much in that last week of his life and I feel proud that I had such a brave man staying with us. We were very upset when he died.'

The news of Kut's death was flashed onto television screens throughout the country. One of Ruby's relatives saw it and telephoned her to pass on the announcement. Next day the *Daily Express* reported the death in a feature titled '"Old Kut" loses his last fight.'. He had a Catholic funeral attended by his three teenage children, Huw, Vera and Mari. Among the others present was his BEA colleague, Captain James Thain, the pilot at the controls of the ill-fated Ambassador G-ALZU which crashed at Munich on 6 February 1958 while transporting the famous 'Busby Babes' of Manchester United football club. Kut's grave – covered in green chipping – is in Uxbridge cemetery.

A BEA appreciation of his service published at the time of his death noted:

> During his 13 years, at one time or another he flew on every route operated by BEA and became well known to many thousands of passengers he carried. His cheerfulness, air of authority and dependability and his incredible row of decorations gave great confidence to all the passengers with whom he came into contact.

The BEA magazine reported:

> Kut, with his easy, friendly personality and romantic background, will long be missed by his friends. Even on first acquaintance he seemed a wonderful person. May we hope that one day a BEA aircraft may fly over Europe bearing the honoured name of Karel Miloslav Kuttelwascher.

*

Kut the man was a complex, private character with more than a hint of contradiction: he managed to combine coolness in the air with a certain irascibility on the ground, an often-attested public modesty with a strong personal ambition, and generosity to friends with meanness to some members of the family. To many British comrades especially, he was such a laconic individual that he seemed to use words almost as sparingly as he fired bullets. Certainly there was nothing particularly chivalrous about his conduct in the sky: he hated the Nazis with a consuming passion which perhaps can only come from seeing the rape of one's country and he was absolutely committed to shooting down as many as possible of the Luftwaffe.

Kut was an uncompromising character who was totally dedicated to his calling and craft. Above all, he was a complete professional who took his flying extremely seriously and loved nothing better than to be in the air. His austere, almost stoical, lifestyle most of the time excluded drinking, smoking, gambling and even – at least the night before an operation – parties. He was in no sense a rebel, yet he excelled when he was away from the pack: he was a loner rather than a leader and this was a major contributory factor in his success as a night intruder. More than a dozen British and Czech medals attest to his valour and his record all but speaks for itself.

Just how great a fighter ace was Kut?

There can be no absolute certainty about the victories credited to Kut or indeed to any other fighter pilot. In the Czech's particular case, there is the problem that most of his claims occurred while flying alone at night over enemy territory, so there were no colleagues to witness the action, no ciné-gun camera film to examine, and no opportunity to search for wreckage. On the other hand, most claims from fighter pilots derived from dog fights well away from the enemy's base and often one could not be sure which pilot actually hit a particular enemy aircraft or whether the latter managed to struggle back to base. By contrast, Kut's intruder victories were achieved in circumstances where there could be no doubt whose shells had penetrated the German bomber and – especially when he saw ground explosions lighting up the night – no difficulty about being sure that a Luftwaffe machine had been destroyed.

All successful combat pilots had their personal scores and Kut was no exception. Although wartime press reports credited Kut with various numbers of kills – American newspapers in 1943 consistently attributed 29 victories to him – his own claim was more modest. Kut himself – a meticulous keeper of records – reckoned that in fact he had shot down a total of 25 aircraft. The seven missing from the postwar 'official' lists consist of six allegedly destroyed while he was with the French Air Force, two or three of which claims receive some support from RAF and Czech records, and another night victory with the RAF which certainly was included in at least two Fighter Command Headquarters lists issued early in 1943. But of course this kind of exercise is meaningless because on this basis most of the other aces would have rather higher scores too.

One can only work on the basis of the widely published and generally accepted scores and rankings. In their 1966 book *Aces High* Christopher Shores and Clive Williams credit Flight Lieutenant Karel Kuttelwascher with 18 kills and rank him joint 53rd in the numerical list of fighter aces of the British and Commonwealth Forces in World War II. The precise rank is not important. It is sufficient to state that, on any basis, Karel Kuttelwascher was among the greatest of the RAF's fighter aces.

Of course, Kut's speciality was scoring at night. In the 1983 book *Air Aces* by Christopher Shores, Kut's night score of 15 ranks him sixth in the RAF's top-scoring night fighter pilots.

The highest night fighter score of the war in the RAF was achieved by Bransome Burbridge with 21. Ironically he was a conscientious objector for the first six months of the war. However, except for one aircraft, he had no success until 1944. Another great night fighter was John Cunningham who brought down 19 at night and earned the nickname 'Cat's Eyes'. He remained the top scoring night ace until overtaken by Burbridge in 1945, but – shortly after the conclusion of No 1 Squadron's night intruder operations – at the start of 1943 Kut and Cunningham were joint top night fighters with 15 kills each. The other top-scoring night fighters were John 'Bob' Braham – the most highly decorated fighter pilot of the war in the Commonwealth Air Forces – who destroyed 19 at night (out of a total of 29), the Irishman Desmond Hughes who was credited with 16½ kills at night, and Alan Owen who clocked up 16 victories, all at night.

Nevertheless, simple arithmetic does not tell the full story. While in no sense wishing to take away from the exceptional skill and bravery of these men, it should be noted that each achieved most or all of his victories in twin-engined aircraft: Braham in the Bristol Beaufighter, Burbridge in the de Havilland Mosquito, and Cunningham, Hughes and Owen in both the Beaufighter and Mosquito. So they had the aid of a radar navigator and increasingly sophisticated technical equipment. By contrast, Kut was on his own in a single-engined Hurricane with no technical aids whatsoever, since at first radar-equipped aircraft could not be spared for intruder operations. This made his night-time successes almost unique. Indeed some have argued that the only night fighter pilot who can be rated in the same class as Kut was Richard Stevens who was a totally different personality from the cool and calculating Czech.

Stevens was 32, the maximum age for pilot training, when he joined the RAF at the outbreak of war, but he had been a commercial pilot before the war and had 400 hours night-flying experience on the newspaper run between London and Paris. He was posted to 151 Squadron which, like No 1 Squadron, was flying Hurricanes with no radar. In one of the early night blitzes on

Manchester, his wife and children were killed and from then on he flew without any regard for his own life. Indeed, the rumour was that, whenever he contacted enemy bombers, he screamed like a man demented. Between January and October 1941, he achieved 14 night victories over England, becoming the RAF's top scoring night fighter at that time. At this point he was posted as a flight commander to 253 Squadron where the lack of enemy bombers led him in December to experiment with intruder operations over Holland of precisely the kind that were to be so successful for Kut a few months later. On his second sortie, he failed to return.

So Kut was someone very special among night fighter pilots and the finest exponent of the specific art of night intrusion. Also he was the highest scoring Czechoslovak in the RAF, his 18 victories with the British just beating the 17 scored by his compatriot Josef František whose record has been described earlier. Therefore the number and nature of Kut's kills really put him in a class of his own: the most successful night intruder and the highest scoring Czech in the RAF.

It is virtually impossible to imagine the kind of night intruder operation flown so successfully by Kut being carried out today. Regrettably this is not because air warfare is an experience of the past, but because developments in radar and missile technology make it inconceivable that these days an aircraft could roam above an enemy's airbase undetected, locate an enemy bomber simply through visual contact, and destroy it by approaching close enough to fire a burst of cannon shells. In the most unlikely event that such an operation could still be conducted somewhere in the world, the aircraft would certainly not be an RAF one and, even if it somehow were, there is absolutely no way that the pilot could be Czech. The 'Night Hawk' was a one and only and Kut's like will never be seen again.

Karel Kuttelwascher's Victories with the RAF

Date	Aircraft	Status	Place
2 February 1941	Messerschmitt Bf 109	Probable	Boulogne
8 April 1941	Messerschmitt Bf 109	Destroyed	Near Cap Gris Nez
21 May 1941	Messerschmitt Bf 109	Destroyed	Between Calais and Dunkirk
27 June 1941	Messerschmitt Bf 109	Destroyed	Le Touquet
1/2 April 1942	Junkers Ju 88	Destroyed	Melun
1/2 April 1942	Junkers Ju 88	Damaged	Melun
16/17 April 1942	Dornier Do 217	Destroyed	St André
26/27 April 1942	Dornier Do 217	Destroyed	Rouen-Boos
26/27 April 1942	Junkers Ju 88	Damaged	Rouen-Boos
30 April/ 1 May 1942	Dornier Do 217	Destroyed	Rennes
30 April/ 1 May 1942	Heinkel He 111	Destroyed	Dinard–coast
4/5 May 1942	Heinkel He 111	Destroyed	St André
4/5 May 1942	Heinkel He 111	Destroyed	St André
4/5 May 1942	Heinkel He 111	Destroyed	St André
2/3 June 1942	Dornier Do 217	Destroyed	Off Dunkirk
3/4 June 1942	Heinkel He 111	Destroyed	St André
3/4 June 1942	Dornier Do 217	Damaged	St André
3/4 June 1942	Dornier Do 217	Destroyed	St André
21/22 June 1942	Junkers Ju 88	Destroyed	St André
21/22 June 1942	Junkers Ju 88	Damaged	St André
28/29 June 1942	Dornier Do 217	Destroyed	Near Trévières
1/2 July 1942	Dornier Do 217	Destroyed	Near Dinard
1/2 July 1942	Dornier Do 217	Damaged	Near Dinard
1/2 July 1942	Dornier Do 217	Destroyed	Near Dinard

Totals: 18 destroyed
1 probable
5 damaged

No 1 Squadron's Night Intruder Victories

Date	Aircraft	Status	Pilot
1/2 April 1942	Junkers Ju 88	Destroyed	Kuttelwascher
1/2 April 1942	Junkers Ju 88	Damaged	Kuttelwascher
16/17 April 1942	Dornier Do 217	Destroyed	Kuttelwascher
26/27 April 1942	Dornier Do 217	Destroyed	MacLachlan
26/27 April 1942	Dornier Do 217	Damaged	MacLachlan
26/27 April 1942	Dornier Do 217	Destroyed	Kuttelwascher
26/27 April 1942	Junkers Ju 88	Damaged	Kuttelwascher
30 April/ 1 May 1942	Dornier Do 217	Destroyed	Kuttelwascher
30 April/ 1 May 1942	Heinkel He 111	Destroyed	Kuttelwascher
3/4 May 1942	Dornier Do 217	Destroyed	MacLachlan
3/4 May 1942	Heinkel He 111	Destroyed	MacLachlan
4/5 May 1942	Heinkel He 111	Destroyed	Kuttelwascher
4/5 May 1942	Heinkel He 111	Destroyed	Kuttelwascher
4/5 May 1942	Heinkel He 111	Destroyed	Kuttelwascher
30/31 May 1942	Junkers Ju 88	Damaged	Scott (W/O)
31 May/1 June 1942	Unidentified	Destroyed	Pearson
1/2 June 1942	Junkers Ju 88	Damaged	Connolly
1/2 June 1942	Dornier Do 217	Destroyed	English
2/3 June 1942	Dornier Do 217	Destroyed	Kuttelwascher
3/4 June 1942	Dornier Do 217	Destroyed	MacLachlan
3/4 June 1942	Dornier Do 217	Damaged	MacLachlan
3/4 June 1942	Dornier Do 217	Destroyed	MacLachlan
3/4 June 1942	Dornier Do 217	Damaged	MacLachlan
3/4 June 1942	Heinkel He 111	Destroyed	Kuttelwascher
3/4 June 1942	Dornier Do 217	Damaged	Kuttelwascher
3/4 June 1942	Dornier Do 217	Destroyed	Kuttelwascher
21/22 June 1942	Unidentified	Damaged	Pearson
21/22 June 1942	Junkers Ju 88	Destroyed	Kuttelwascher
21/22 June 1942	Junkers Ju 88	Damaged	Kuttelwascher
28/29 June 1942	Dornier Do 217	Destroyed	Kuttelwascher
1/2 July 1942	Dornier Do 217	Damaged	Campbell
1/2 July 1942	Dornier Do 217	Damaged	Pearson

Date	Aircraft	Status	Pilot
1/2 July 1942	Dornier Do 217	Destroyed	Kuttelwascher
1/2 July 1942	Dornier Do 217	Damaged	Kuttelwascher
1/2 July 1942	Dornier Do 217	Destroyed	Kuttelwascher

Totals: 22 destroyed
13 damaged

Karel Kuttelwascher's Comrades Killed

(A) *At No 1 Squadron*

Date	Name	Cause
8 October 1940	Sgt S. Warren	Accident
3 November 1940	S/L D.A. Pemberton	Accident
5 February 1941	F/O R.G. Lewis (Canadian)	Circus operation
19 March 1941	P/O Tony Kershaw	Convoy escort
22 April 1941	Sgt G.M. Stocken	Accident
11 May 1941	P/O František Běhal (Czech)	Night bombers
21 May 1941	F/O J.C. Robinson	Circus operation
17 June 1941	Sgt Albín Nassveter (Czech)	Dog fight
21 June 1941	P/O N. Maranz (American)	Circus operation
29 June 1941	P/O Bohumil Horák (Czech)	Accident
16 July 1941	F/Lt Antonín Velebnovský (Czech)	Night accident
27 August 1941	Sgt E. Bloor	Night accident
21 October 1941	Sgt R.H. Oakley	Accident – on detachment
11 February 1942	Sgt E.G. Parsons (Canadian)	Night accident
12 February 1942	F/Sgt E.F.G. Blair (S African)	Channel Dash
16 February 1942	P/O Eustace Sweeting	Accident
10 April 1942	Sgt Jan Vlk (Czech)	Accident
24 April 1942	Sgt Vlastimil Macháček (Czech)	Intruder operation
3 June 1942	F/Sgt G.C. English (Canadian)	Accident
4 June 1942	W/O Josef Dygrýn (Czech)	Intruder operation
26 June 1942	W/O Gerry Scott (Canadian)	Intruder operation

(B) *At No 23 Squadron*

Date	Name	Cause
28/29 July 1942	F/Sgt K. Hawkins	Intruder operation
28/29 July 1942	Sgt N. Gregory	Intruder operation
8/9 September 1942	Sgt G.R. Wright (American)	Intruder operation
8/9 September 1942	Sgt A.M.F. Cook	Intruder operation
8/9 September 1942	F/O I.N. Stein	Intruder operation
8/9 September 1942	Sgt H.G. Challicombe	Intruder operation
8/9 September 1942	F/Lt N.A. Buchanan	Intruder operation

(C) *Others Mentioned In The Text*

Date	Name	Cause
16 January 1943	F/O Bedřich Krátkoruký (Czech)	Collision during escort operation
6 March 1943	F/O Josef Příhoda (Czech)	Ramrod operation
28 April 1943	F/O Otto Pavlů (Czech)	Roadstead operation
14 May 1943	F/O Jarda Novák (Czech)	Roadstead operation
18 July 1943	S/L James MacLachlan	Ranger operation

Sources and Acknowledgements

My thanks are due to the following who have kindly given me permission to quote from material within their copyright control: the British Broadcasting Corporation's Written Archives Centre (wartime radio broadcasts), Editions France-Empire (*The Flying Sailor* by André Jubelin), Her Majesty's Stationery Office (*Over To You*), Hutchinson Publishing Group Limited (*The Saturday Book 3*), and Michael Shaw (*Twice Vertical* by himself).

The prime source for the accounts in this book of Royal Air Force operations has been the Public Record Office. As far as No 1 Squadron is concerned, the relevant Operations Record Books are classified under AIR 27/1, 2 and 3 and the relevant combat reports are classified under AIR 50/1. As far as No 23 Squadron is concerned, the relevant Operations Record Book is classified under AIR 27/287. As far as No 32 Maintenance Unit is concerned, the relevant records are classified under AIR 27/995. A variety of other files were consulted to a lesser extent.

Other organisations from which useful information has been obtained include Air Historical Branch, British Airways, British Broadcasting Corporation, French Embassy, Imperial War Museum, Ministry of Defence, Royal Air Force, Royal Air Force Museum, Royal Cornwall Hospital, Royal Greenwich Observatory and Service Historique de l'Armée de l'Air.

Individuals who have been helpful in supplying information include: Zdeněk Bachůrek, Jim Beedle, Trevor Bell, Chaz Bowyer, Colin Brown, R.E. Canterbury, R. Wallace Clarke, Alan Davie, John Foreman, Ron Gillman, Ken Hayr, John Holloway, Joe Hudrick, Zdeněk Hurt, Mike Janecek, Victor Kent, Milan Kocourek, Barry Kudláček, Frank Loucký, K. Náprstek, František Peřina, Mark Petrů, Milena Pippalová, Jan Posner, Karel Pospíchal, John Rennison, Michael Shaw, Adrian Stewart, J. Thuring, Manuel J. van Eyck, John Vasco, Ronald Wilson, and Ken Wakefield.

I am particularly grateful to the following individuals who are quoted in the text: David Annand, George Atkins, Lionel Baggs, Godfrey Ball, Stanislav Berton, Ben Bolt, Frank Churchett, Dick Corser, Leo Craven, Vee Darlington, Ivy Driscoll, Tim Elkington, Leslie Elvidge, Stan Greenwood, Jane Gunningham, Pat Hancock, Prosser Hanks, Josef Jaške, Peggy Jeffreys, Miroslav Jiroudek, Alfred Jones, Josef Josten, Miroslav Kutlvašr, Harry Lea, Antonín Liška, Freddie Lister, Marcel Ludikar, Derek Mason, Peter Matthews, Wilf Merry, Jocelyn Millard, Peter Pennant-Rea, Eric Pritchard, Henry Prokop, Huw Roberts, Sydney Sharp, Morris Smith, Larry Světlík, Ken Thomas, Jack Torrance, Sidney Turner, and the late Frank Wooley.

For translation work, my thanks go to Marcel Ludikar and Milan Kocourek in respect of Czech material and to Norman Beadle and Silvia Holden in respect of French material. For miscellaneous services, I must thank Dot Ducker, Pam Monk and John MacCarrick.

Special thanks go to my son Richard for his understanding and patience in allowing me to spend so many hours working in my study. Above all, my love and gratitude go to my wife Vee – Kut's daughter – who was the inspiration behind this book, a constant source of encouragement, and the person who typed every one of hundreds of letters and every page of several drafts.

Bibliography

Kuttelwascher Bibliography

Besides wartime press reports, the following books and articles – listed chronologically – are the main publications specifically mentioning Karel Kuttelwascher:

'Kuttelwascher, Czech Night-Fighter Ace', an interview with Bob Bowman, in *London Calling*, 23 July 1942.

'War Artists Exhibition' by P.J.B. in *Flight*, 29 October 1942.

'Academy Pictures' in *Aeronautics*, January 1943.

Over To You, broadcasts by the RAF prepared for the Air Ministry by the Ministry of Information, His Majesty's Stationery Office, 1943.

To Annie In America by Josef Josten, Lincolns-Prager Publishers Ltd, 1943.

The Czechoslovak Air Force, by Air Vice-Marshal Karel Janoušek, S. Sidders & Son Ltd, 1943.

'Intruder Ops' by Flight Lieutenant K.M. Kuttelwascher in *The Saturday Book 3*, Hutchinson, 1943.

Speaking To My Country by Jan Masaryk, Lincolns-Prager (Publications) Ltd, 1944.

'Czechoslovakia' in *The Aeroplane*, 18 May 1945.

'Československé zahraniční letectvo za druhé světové války' ('The Czechoslovak Air Force Abroad In The Second World War') by Kpt let K.M. Kutlvašr in *Havlíčkobrodsko v národním odboji 1914–1918, 1938–1945* ('The Area of Havlíčkův Brod In The National Resistance of 1914–1918 And 1938–1945'), Svoboda, 1946. (Note: This publication is in Czech.)

'Prvním kotlářem byl Čech' (First Trainbuster Was Czech') by Vojtěch Konopa in *Naše vojsko* ('Our Army'), 2 February 1946. (Note: This publication is in Czech.)

The Flying Sailor by Rear-Admiral André Jubelin (translated from the French by James Cleugh), Hurst & Blackett, 1953.

In All Things First: A Short History Of No 1 Squadron, Royal Air Force by J.L. Dixon, the Orpington Press Ltd, 1954.

'Brief BEAographies: No. 63 – Capt. K. Kuttelwascher' in *British European Airways Magazine No 83*, September 1955.

'Captain Karel Kuttelwascher' in *British European Airways Magazine No 126*, September 1959.

'K. Kuttelwascher mrtev!' ('K. Kuttelwascher Dead') in *Čechoslovák*, 28 September 1959. (Note: This publication is in Czech.)

The Narrow Margin by Derek Wood & Derek Dempster, Hutchinson & Co., 1961.

The Fighter Aces Of The RAF 1939–1945 by E.C.R. Baker, William Kimber & Co. Ltd, 1962.

The Hawker Hurricane by Francis K. Mason, Macdonald, 1962.

The Fighter Aces Of The World by Thomas S.M. Clarke, Mistral Publications Inc., 1963

Na Západní frontě ('On The Western Front') by Toman Brod & Eduard Čejka, Naše vojsko, svaz protifašistických bojovníků, 1965. (Note: This publication was only printed in Czech.)

'Profile Aircraft No. 24: The Hawker Hurricane IIC' by Francis K. Mason, Profile Publications Ltd.; reprinted in *Aircraft In Profile Volume 1 Part Two* edited by Charles W. Cain, Profile Publications Ltd., 1965; and reprinted with errata in booklet form, Profile Books Ltd., May 1981.

Aces High: The Fighter Aces of The British And Commonwealth Air Forces Of World War II by Christopher Shores & Clive Williams, Neville Spearman, 1966.

Battle Over Britain by Francis K. Mason, McWhirter Twins Ltd., 1969.

Famous Fighter Squadrons Of The RAF by James J. Halley, Hylton Lacy, 1971.

Twice Vertical: The History Of No 1 Squadron, Royal Air Force by Michael Shaw, Macdonald, 1971. (Note: At the time of writing, this book is being updated.)

Hurricane At War by Chaz Bowyer, Ian Allan, 1974.

'Fighters From Central Europe' by J.D.R. Rawlings in *Air Pictorial*, April 1975.

Fighter Aces by Christopher Shores, Hamlyn, 1975.

RAF Fighter Units, Europe, 1942–45 by Bryan Philpott, Osprey Publishing Ltd., 1978.

'La Bataille D'Angleterre Tomme III' ('The Battle of Britain Volume III'), *Icare No. 99*, Syndicat National Des Pilotes De Ligne, Winter 1981–1982. (Note: This publication is in French.)

The Battle Of Britain Then And Now edited by Winston G. Ramsey, Battle of Britain Prints International Ltd., first edition 10 July 1980, revised edition 15 September 1982.

Poslední pocta ('The Last Honour') by Jožka Pejskar, Konfrontation AG/SA v Curychu, 1982. (Note: This publication is in Czech.)

Hurricane: The War Exploits Of The Fighter Aircraft by Adrian Stewart, William Kimber & Co. Ltd., 1982.

'Karel Kuttelwascher – A Forgotten Hero' by Roger Darlington in *Post Office Engineering Union Journal*, October 1982.

Air Aces by Christopher Shores, Bison Book Corp, 1983.

'The RAF's Greatest Night Intruder Pilot' by Roger Darlington in *Gateway* (the magazine of RAF Brize Norton), April 1983.

'Karel Kuttelwascher – Night Reaper' by Roger Darlington in *Fly Past*, July 1983.

'Nights To Remember' by Roger Darlington in *Chichester Observer*, 8 September 1983.

'Noční sekáč' ('Night Reaper') by Roger Darlington in *Kanadské Listy* ('Canadian News'), 15 September 1983. (Note: This publication is in Czech.)

'Vánoční vzpomínka na Karla Kuttelwaschera' ('Christmas Memory of Karel Kuttelwascher') by Vee Darlington in *Vzlet* ('Take-off') No. 4, December 1983. (Note: This publication is in Czech.)

Guide To Tangmere Military Aviation Museum, English Life Publications Ltd, 1984.

Fighter Pilots Of The RAF 1939–1945 by Chaz Bowyer, William Kimber, 1984.

General Bibliography

Besides those works which specifically mention Karel Kuttelwascher, a number of other books have proved useful for background information.

The situation of pre-war Czechoslovakia is described in:

Europe And The Czechs by S. Grant Duff, Penguin Books Ltd, 1938.

Accounts of No 1 Squadron's contribution to the Battle of France are contained in:

Fighter Pilot by Wing Commander Paul Richey, B.T. Batsford Ltd, 1941; revised edition, Hutchinson & Co. (Publishers) Ltd., 1955; new edition with additional photographs, Jane's Publishing Company, 1980.

Squadrons Up! by Noel Monks, Victor Gollancz Ltd., 1940.
Much more complete accounts of the Channel Dash can be found in:
Channel Dash by Terence Robertson, Evans Brothers Ltd, 1958.
Fiasco by John Deane Potter, William Heinemann Ltd, 1970.
More information on Czech airmen in wartime can be found in:
Wings In Exile edited by Bohuš Beneš (translated by Robert Auty
    and Arthur R. Weir), 'The Czechoslovak' Independent Weekly,
    1942.
Red Sky At Night by Josef Čapka, Anthony Blond, 1958.
Vzpomínky na padlé kamarády ('Remembrance Of Fallen Friends') by
    Frantisek Fatjl, Mladá fronta, edice Třináct, 1980. (Note: This
    publication – an account of Czechs in France, Britain and the
    USSR – is in Czech.)
The Sky Is Our Ocean by Bart M. Rijnhout and John P. Rennison, Wyt
    Uitgevers, 1980. (Note: This publication – the history of the Czech
    bomber squadron 311 – was only printed in Dutch and – by the
    underground press – in Czech.)
Jak se plaší smrt ('How To Drive Away Death') by Antonín Liška, Naše
    vojsko, 1983. (Note: This publication – an account of life with the
    Czech fighter squadron 312 told in novel form to avoid censorship –
    is in Czech.)
Details of the Luftwaffe's 'Baedeker' raids can be found in:
The Defence Of The United Kingdom by Basil Collier, Her Majesty's
    Stationery Office, 1957.
More general books on night flying in the last war include:
Night Fighter by C.F. Rawnsley & Robert Wright, William Collins
    Sons & Co. Ltd., 1957.
Night Fighters: A Development & Combat History by Bill Gunston, Patrick
    Stephens Ltd., 1976.
Night Intruder by Jeremy Howard-Williams, David & Charles, 1976.

Index